C000137784

Caught in the web:
a tale of Tudor times

Faith Cook

EP BOOKS (Evangelical Press)

1st Floor Venture House, 6 Silver Court, Watchmead, Welwyn Garden City, UK, AL7 1TS

www.epbooks.org
admin@epbooks.org

EP Books are distributed in the USA by:
JPL Distribution, 3741 Linden Avenue Southeast, Grand Rapids, MI 49548

www.jplbooks.com
orders@jplbooks.com

© Faith Cook 2006

First published 2006
This edition 2017

British Library Cataloguing in Publication Data available

ISBN 978-1-78397-215-9

To my four daughters-in law:
Jane, Gillian, Rachel and Sue

Contents

Glossary of historical or archaic terms

forasmuch as: because, since

gibbet: a gallows

kirtle: a woman's gown or outer petticoat

maslin bread: bread made from mixed grain, especially rye and wheat

Master of Horse: the highest-ranking official in a Tudor household, a post which often carried wide-ranging responsibilities

pottage: soup or stew

(gold) sovereign: a former British gold coin worth one pound sterling

wattle and daub: a material traditionally used in building walls, consisting of a network of interwoven sticks and twigs covered with mud or clay

To the reader
—an explanation...

Much has been written and said about the Tudor period of English history. Many people are familiar with something of the story of Henry VIII and his six wives. But the Tudor years were also years of great suffering. Queen Mary I, who reigned from 1553-1558, is known historically as 'Bloody Queen Mary', for she was responsible for the cruel martyrdom of at least 283 faithful Christians, fifty-six of them women. There may well have been many more whose sufferings were not recorded.

Caught in the Web is an attempt to recapture and commemorate the circumstances, trials and endurance of those days. The account is based first of all on the life of young Lady Jane Grey, nine-day Queen of England, herself both a victim and a martyr; then on the frightening cruelties which followed her death during the reign of Mary Tudor. To bring the record to life I have chosen to use a narrative form in which a number of the characters are fictitious, even though the setting of their lives and experiences is not. As a reader, you may well ask, 'How then can I distinguish fact from fiction? How can I know which people in this book are historical figures and which are not?'

Of the major characters, Hal Tylney, Lady Jane Grey's page, is largely fictional; so too are Sarah Bridges and Ebenezer Squires. Lady Jane did in fact have a page boy whose presence on important occasions of her life is mentioned in several early records. But I have chosen to give him a name and character, and through his story to introduce readers to the lives of many authentic men and women of the times. Among the lesser characters, Elizabeth Tylney, Hal's mother, is a historical figure; so too are Adrian Stokes, stable lad at Bradgate Park, and Lady Jane's other attendants, Mistress Ellen and Mistress Jacobs.

All information about the principal historical figures who appear in these pages is factual, and any important words attributed to them can be traced to their actual writings or recorded sayings. Lady Jane Grey, her family and tutors are included in this number; so too are the martyrs, Lady Anne Askew, John Bradford, Nicholas Ridley, Hugh Latimer and Thomas Cranmer. Queen Katherine Parr, Lord Admiral Thomas Seymour and Bishop Edmund Bonner are each represented accurately. All political facts and situations have been carefully researched and presented as they actually occurred, together with the social customs of the period.

One aim of this book is to recapture these stirring events and sufferings of the past, especially for those whose memories of school history lessons may have prejudiced them against reading accounts of former days. But these pages are not written solely as a memorial and reminder of the heroism of a bygone age. In our own generation there has also been widespread persecution and martyrdom of Christians—in China, Africa, Indonesia and many other places. Some have even predicted that such events could again take place in the West. So, as we trace God's dealings in the lives and experiences of these Christian men and women of Tudor times, may we find in their noble example an encouragement and challenge for ourselves today.

Faith Cook

1
The wild boar

'I must away,' said Matt Tylney tersely, pulling himself as gently as he could out of his wife Elizabeth's arms. 'God will care for you, my dear one, and for our son. Only do not fear for me.' Deaf to Elizabeth's tearful pleadings, Matt disappeared into the gathering darkness of that September evening. It was a night that would change Elizabeth Tylney's life for ever, and one that she and her six-year-old son, Henry, always known as Hal for short, could never forget.

It had been the same each night for many weeks now. As darkness fell, Matt would take down his bow and arrows from the peg on the wall. Setting off from his village home in Newtown Linford, he would vanish into the night with a group of other men. Hal did not know where his father went each night, only to return early in the morning as dawn began to break, and to sleep most of the day. He had not always done this, and the boy was well aware that his mother Elizabeth was troubled about Matt's strange activities.

Now in her mid-twenties, Elizabeth had been only seventeen when she married Matt seven years earlier. Life had seemed peaceful and predictable as the young couple set up home together. Matt was earning an honest if meagre wage caring for the livestock belonging to the monks at Ulverscroft Priory, which lay several miles from their village home. Every morning he would call for his neighbour Hugh Lambert, who also worked at Ulverscroft, and together they would set off for the priory. Skilled as a shepherd, Matt knew almost instinctively if any of the flock was showing signs of sickness. He had become experienced at dealing with difficult births at lambing time and was expert at shearing the sheep and grading the wool for sale.

Matt was also responsible for keeping the boundary fences of the priory lands in good repair in order to protect the livestock from the ever-present menace of prowling and hungry wolves that roamed the Benscliffe Wood, lying immediately to the south of the priory. Although his wages only amounted to £4 a year, low even for those times, with the vegetables he could grow on the smallholding around his cottage home, he and Elizabeth had been contented enough.

Then came a blow as unexpected as it was final. Early in 1539, as winter days gave place to spring, officials arrived in Leicestershire from far-off London. Before long they were calling at the Ulverscroft Priory and the monks knew well enough why they had come. With orders from none other than Henry VIII himself, all-powerful King of England, and his Privy Council, they demanded that Ulverscroft, like every other priory and monastery in the area, should be closed down immediately.

The lands, livestock, furnishings, libraries, silver plate and religious relics—in fact everything that belonged to the priory—were to be compulsorily sold to the Crown. Dismayed and furious, Matt Tylney and his neighbour Hugh Lambert knew at once that they would be without work. Although the monks would also lose their secure way of life, many would be able to find alternative employment in various skills, but it was far different for labourers such as Matt and Hugh. Matt had been well aware of a number of odd, even evil, practices that had been taking place in the priory in the name of religion, but was willing enough to ignore such things for the sake of his job. With little understanding of the politics and burning issues of the day that lay behind the widespread closure of all monasteries in the country, Matt felt bewildered and cheated. Now he must return to his home in Newtown Linford and break the news to Elizabeth that he had no work.

'What troubles you?' Elizabeth had asked as she saw Matt's angry and distressed face when he returned to his home that evening.

'I have no work,' Matt responded abruptly, burying his face in his hands. 'It is a monstrous evil and I cannot tell what to do.'

'Have they come even to Ulverscroft then?' cried Elizabeth in dismay, for all in the area had heard of the dramatic closure of nearby monasteries. 'Then we must starve if you can find no work!' Just at that moment Hal had entered the cottage. Glancing swiftly from his father to his mother, he knew immediately that something was seriously wrong and ran out again as quickly as he had come.

With hundreds of others in the area also seeking fresh work, Matt Tylney tried ceaselessly to find some other way to support his family. How could he let Elizabeth and Hal suffer the shame of poverty and forfeit the roof over their heads? Perhaps they would become inmates of a poorhouse, for he knew that he could no longer pay the rent due to the Marquess of Dorset, on whose land his small wattle-and-daub cottage stood. Day after day Matt tramped out to distant farms to offer his skills, but without any success. And when Elizabeth told him that she was expecting another child, he became desperate for work.

Hugh Lambert too was struggling to find some way of earning a living and one morning Hal was surprised to see their neighbour arrive at the cottage door.

'Be your pa in, my boy?' asked Hugh kindly, bending his head as he entered the low doorway. Hal had always liked his neighbour and had often played with his son, Will. Good-natured and friendly, Hugh had a family of three to provide for, including two-year-old twins, Lucy and Betsy. Like Matt, he too was almost in despair of ever finding work again.

Elizabeth happened to be outside tending the vegetable plot when Hugh called and in a few moments the two men were deep in earnest, whispered conversation. Hal meanwhile sat quietly in the corner of the room, and the men seemed scarcely to notice him. He could not hear much of what was passing between them, but noticed that his father looked troubled even though he was nodding in agreement. Hal could only pick up the odd snatch of words—phrases such as 'meet at nightfall,' 'None will see' and 'What if we're caught?' What was his father planning to do? The boy did not know.

In fact, Matt and Hugh were deciding to join a gang of poachers. It was a dangerous and desperate enterprise: both men were well aware of the risks they were taking. The dense woodland that surrounded their village home—Blakeshay Wood, Benscliffe Wood and Swithland Wood, all part of the great Charnwood Forest—belonged to the Marquess of Dorset, Sir Henry Grey of Bradgate Manor. If the steward of the manor, who had charge of the property, or any of the gamekeepers should catch the poachers, no mercy would be shown and, as likely as not, they would be hung on the local gibbet for their crime.

'Matt, I beg you, I urge you, do not so!' sobbed Elizabeth. 'It cannot be long before the steward's men must catch you; then what must befall us?' But despite Elizabeth's pleas, Matt felt it was a risk he must take.

'Better that than starve,' he told her firmly. Each night as darkness fell, Matt, Hugh and other members of the gang ventured stealthily into the woods, making their way as quietly as they could through the undergrowth. Armed with his bow and arrows, Matt would look for wild boar, deer, badgers, or even hares and rabbits, which he could shoot and sell for meat. Always one man would be on guard to keep watch for any who might spy on them or report their activities to the steward of Bradgate. At an agreed signal the men would disappear into the thick undergrowth if the look-out man spotted any danger.

On occasions the poachers would dig a sizeable pit in some clearing among the trees. Overlaying it with thin twigs and a final layer of fallen leaves and undergrowth, they hoped that some animal might stumble into their trap. So well disguised was the pit that even the poachers would not find it again unless they drove a large stake into the ground to mark its whereabouts. One pit completed, the men dug another, and another, only finishing their night's work as dawn began to lighten the eastern sky.

The following night Matt and his fellow poachers would return to inspect the pits, and to share out their catch. Some pits remained intact, but before long they would discover one into which some wild boar or deer had fallen. An arrow or the swift thrust of a spear would put the creature out of its misery. Then, slinging his share of the booty across his shoulders, Matt would make his way home. The proceeds from the sale of meat or fur would be sufficient to keep Elizabeth, Hal and himself for some weeks.

And on this dark moonless night late in September 1539, Matt set out yet again, despite Elizabeth's frightened protests. Before long the poachers discovered to their satisfaction that a large sow had fallen into one of their pits. But no sooner had they killed the animal than, without any warning, its mate, a ferocious boar, bristling with rage at the pitiful squeals of the trapped sow, burst out of the undergrowth and charged at the gang. The men scattered in panic. The boar turned and charged again. This time its sharp tusks caught Matt on the thigh, tossed him high in the air like a plaything, and as suddenly dropped him again. Then it crashed back into the undergrowth. Severely wounded, Matt fell to the ground with a groan, bleeding profusely. Hugh rushed forward, stripped off his own shirt and tried to staunch the flow of blood. But nothing that anyone could do seemed to help. All that remained was to carry the injured man home as gently as possible and tell Elizabeth what had happened.

That night Hal had been unable to sleep, tossing and turning on his rush mat in the corner of the room. It seemed harder than usual. But mostly he sensed that his mother was anxious and he was not sure why. The small lamp in the corner of the room with its tallow wick spluttered and glowed, casting weird shadows round the room, which seemed to mingle with his troubled thoughts. Then he caught the sound of distant footsteps. Elizabeth had heard them too and had already jumped up from her mat and was standing at the door. But when Hugh Lambert stooped to enter the cottage carrying Hal's father in his arms, the boy burst into frightened tears. Laying his burden down carefully near the dying embers of the charcoal fire, Hugh told Elizabeth what had happened. Hal could see well enough that his father was badly hurt. Perhaps his papa would die; then what would they do?

'Hal, my son,' said Matt feebly to his child, 'look after your mother for me and don't grow up to be a bad man like I've been.' These were the last words he spoke. Hours later Matt died in Elizabeth's arms.

Now the family was indeed destitute. The cost of burying Matt in the burial ground of the nearby parish church of All Saints ate up all of Elizabeth's small savings. Worse than this, the sorrow and shock of Matt's death brought on the premature birth of her child and not many days later she buried her infant next to its father. Hugh Lambert and his wife Joan grieved with her; so did the other neighbours, but such circumstances were commonplace among them, and there was little enough anyone could do to help Elizabeth. Perhaps the widow and her child would now have to go to the poorhouse in Leicester.

2
A bold plan

The shadow of these sad events formed one of Hal's earliest childhood memories. Previously he had been a bright, adventurous child; now he appeared older than his years, often making serious remarks that sounded strange coming from a lad of his age. The responsibility Matt had laid on the boy's young shoulders of caring for his mother seemed to weigh heavily on him.

As Elizabeth gradually regained her strength, she began to turn over in her mind any options now open to her. Glancing despairingly around the single room of her cottage home, she wondered how long she would be able to stay there. At any time the steward of nearby Bradgate Manor would come knocking at her door, demanding the rent. She knew she could not pay. If she borrowed money from a neighbour it would only postpone her troubles for a few more weeks. Her own mother, living not far away in Rothley, was in no position to help. She too had been widowed in recent years and still had a large family dependent upon her.

Elizabeth's skill in the kitchen had given her a reputation in the village: the pottage she made and the maslin bread—staple food of the poor—were freely acknowledged to be excellent. Gradually a bold plan began to form in Elizabeth's mind. What would happen if she dared to approach the steward of Bradgate and offer her services as a cook, or even a kitchen maid, for the marquess and his wife, Lady Frances? Certainly, she could lose nothing by the attempt, and if she were accepted she would at least have a roof over her head and the hope of providing for her son Hal.

Few villagers had a good word for the Grey family. The first Marquess of Dorset, Sir Thomas Grey, grandfather of the present marquess, had forcibly uprooted many of their parents from their previous homes and rehoused them in Newtown Linford. Whatever reason he may have given for his action, they all knew well enough that it was because their small thatched huts spoiled his view and were in the way of the impressive approach road to Bradgate House, the palatial new home he was building.

Undoubtedly, the villagers reasoned, Sir Henry Grey would certainly be the same sort of man as his grandfather. In addition, rumours of the character of his ambitious wife, Lady Frances, niece of King Henry VIII himself, had circulated around the village. Some of the older women, however, felt sorry for Lady Frances, for she was only sixteen when she married Sir Henry and even before her twentieth birthday she had lost two infants in death. Her third child, according to local gossips, an auburn-haired girl known as Lady Jane, was now two years of age, but she was far from strong. Many assumed that she would not survive. And probably the baby Lady Frances was now expecting would also die, or so they whispered darkly among themselves.

Tales of the luxury of the Bradgate kitchens, and the fabulous entertainment offered to many of the rich and noble in the land, had also filtered through to the villagers of Newtown Linford, making the Grey family envied and disliked. The tables at Bradgate House groaned under the weight of expensive dishes served daily to well-fed guests. Perhaps her plan was a foolish one, thought Elizabeth, and in any case it would certainly be better not to share it with her neighbour Joan Lambert, or with anyone else, at least not at present.

So one October day, almost a month after Matt's death, Elizabeth decided that she must act without further delay. Nervously she smoothed down her homespun kirtle, threw on her outer gown and knotted her headscarf carefully over her long dark hair. Taking Hal by the hand, Elizabeth slipped out of her cottage and was soon hurrying down the path that joined the main driveway leading to Bradgate House. As they made their way between the rows of young oak trees that lined the impressive approaches to the mansion, troubling thoughts raced through Elizabeth's mind. The marquess and his wife feasted on venison and pheasant, together with trout from the River Lin, which flowed not far from the house. Perhaps she was foolish to imagine that she could work in their kitchens. Only her personal need drove her on.

At last she reached the steward's lodge, a sturdy, brick-built home beside the outer gate of Bradgate House itself. Even here Elizabeth almost lost her courage and would have turned back. But she had been seen. A moment later the heavy door creaked open and the steward's maid appeared.

'May I ask your business, madam?' enquired the young woman.

'Tell her to come in,' called a loud voice from within. Ushered into a room more luxurious than she had ever seen before, it took Elizabeth a few moments to regain her poise.

'What brings you here, my good woman?' barked the portly steward. Hal gazed around wide-eyed and not until his mother had been asked yet again what she wanted did she pluck up courage to speak.

'I'll be wondering if there might be a place for another woman in the kitchens at the manor house,' she faltered, 'or even in the scullery, sir,' she added lamely. The steward looked the young woman up and down, as if weighing her up.

'This your boy?' he asked at last, jerking his thumb in Hal's direction.

'Yes, sir,' replied Elizabeth, 'and his father, he's dead. It was a dreadful accident, sir, as took him, and I have no way left to pay my rent.' Elizabeth had blushed crimson and Hal glanced anxiously at his mother.

'Can you cook well?' snapped the steward, still fixing his eyes intently on Elizabeth.

'Why yes, sir,' replied the young woman. 'At least so my neighbours say,' she added quickly for fear of sounding boastful.

'It seems you've come here on the right day,' the steward was saying. 'There is indeed a vacancy which you may take up next week.' A surge of untold relief swept over Elizabeth and a deep sense of gratitude to a God about whom she knew little enough, but to whom the monks prayed many times each day—or so Matt had told her. Perhaps he cared even for widows and their children, she thought to herself.

Not many days later, trundling all their possessions along in a small wooden handcart, the pair made their way up the long drive once again. The bracken on the hills that rose on either side of the path had turned to bronze and the trees shone red and gold in the late October sunshine. The river along the valley bubbled and foamed among the boulders, here and there dropping downwards in a small waterfall. Now and then trout leapt from the water and fell back with a splash. Dapple-coated deer bounded freely among the rocky outcrops. Elizabeth began to feel faintly hopeful for the first time since Matt's death and squeezed Hal's hand reassuringly. Then from the distant woods came the cry of huntsmen in full chase of some boar or fox. Elizabeth shuddered at the sound but pressed on.

From time to time a wealthy dignitary would canter past them on horseback, the glimmering jewels on his horse's reins and saddle sparkling in the autumn sunlight. Each nobleman wore a richly embroidered cloak flung around his shoulders. It would seem that an important event was about to take place in the Bradgate household, for every rider appeared to be carrying a gift. Perhaps, thought Elizabeth with a pang as she remembered the infant she had so recently lost, that child that Lady Frances had been expecting had been safely born and these were guests arriving for the christening celebrations. She had guessed rightly. Ten days earlier Lady Frances Grey's second daughter, Katherine, had been born: a sister for two-year-old Lady Jane, a title the child carried as great-niece of the king. The christening ceremony was due to take place shortly and these members of the nobility had been invited to attend.

At last Elizabeth and Hal reached the magnificent house where Henry and Frances Grey held court, its towers, pinnacles and tall chimneys piercing the skyline. Elizabeth gulped nervously as she reported her arrival to the porter and timidly asked her way to the servants' quarters. 'Your room is at the top of the central tower,' replied the porter as he led the pair around to the side of the house.

Up countless rough-hewn steps he led them, round and round the massive tower block. On each landing Hal peered curiously through the tall narrow window let into the thick walls. Every time he looked the ground seemed further and further away and still more steps rose above them. At last they reached the large attic room at the top of the tower—a room which Elizabeth and Hal would share with several other members of the kitchen staff.

Dark and musty it may have been, but Hal could never have imagined that anyone could live in such a wonderful place. Coals glowed in the iron grate, while the dim light flowing from the narrow windows showed a pile of straw mattresses in one corner—a luxury compared with the rush mat he usually slept on. Several small stools were scattered around and a sturdy oak table stood in the middle of the room. Oak chests were placed here and there around the attic walls; and in one of these they would store all their possessions, so the porter informed them.

Hal ran to the window and gazed out once more. He usually had plenty to say, but now he was speechless with amazement as he looked down over the rolling hills and trees, with the river shining along the valley like a silver ribbon. This grand setting would be the backdrop of his life for many years to come, and memories of the thatched hut where he had been born—the heavy mud walls, home to an army of creeping things such as lice and bedbugs, the old cooking range, the rush mats on which he lay at night—would be all shadowy memories of days long past. But never could he erase from his memory that last night of the life of the father whom he had admired and loved.

3
The collision

Early next morning Elizabeth reported to the kitchens dressed in her new black kirtle and clean white apron. Clearly extra help was needed to prepare for the christening feast. All the delicacies to be served must be to the highest standard, for a table loaded with luxurious dishes was regarded as a mark of prosperity and intended to show the grandeur and importance of the Grey family. Mistress Jacobs, head of the kitchen staff, merely nodded briefly at the newcomer and said, 'You can be turning that spit, and mind you don't let the meat burn.'

Elizabeth looked nervously at the great roasting spit above the kitchen fire. On it was suspended a whole side of pork, possibly from some wild boar caught in the woods the previous day. The fireplace itself was fifteen feet wide[1]—larger than Elizabeth could have imagined possible. Venison, turkeys, sides of pork and joints of beef were all waiting to be cooked in turn. Never had she seen such a quantity of meat in one place before.

Knowing she must not fail on her first day, Elizabeth turned the spit for hour after hour until her arms ached and her head seemed to

---

[1]   A little more than 4.5 metres

be spinning around as well. Now and then she glanced across at Mistress Jacobs, for she was anxious to prove her worth and win her approval. Mistress Jacobs appeared too busy preparing dishes of trout and other savouries for the feast to notice Elizabeth. Without knowing it, the newcomer had already gained the respect of others in the kitchens for continuing to rotate the spit long after most would have given up in exhaustion.

Nor was six-year-old Hal allowed to remain idle. Given a basket almost as big as he was, the boy was sent into the parkland to collect kindling wood to stock up the supply used to light the household fires. A high wind the previous night had brought many smaller branches crashing to the ground and before long Hal dragged his basketful of wood back to the kitchen. Flushed and tired, Elizabeth smiled quickly at her boy as he stood in the doorway, but Mistress Jacobs did little more than take and empty Hal's basket and return it to him, sending him off to refill it.

Hal was not the only child in the servants' quarters at Bradgate Manor. Ben Jacobs, eight-year-old son of Mistress Jacobs, eyed the newcomer with a mixture of curiosity and resentment. Hal thought it would be best to avoid Ben if he could. But Annie McNeil was different. A quiet girl of seven, she was the daughter of Mistress Ellen McNeil, a practical and kind-hearted Scottish woman who acted as nurse for two-year-old Lady Jane Grey. Annie had been little more than a baby when her father had died six years earlier and her mother had been engaged to serve the marquess and his wife. As Henry and Frances Grey spent much of their time up at the royal court in London, or else out hunting in the Charnwood Forest, a woman was needed to care for any children the couple might have. Even though the lives of the first two Grey infants had been brief, Mistress Ellen, as she was known, had found her job secure, for Lady Frances was soon pregnant again and in due course Lady Jane was born.

Annie could not remember anything apart from her life at Bradgate. She listened wide-eyed as Hal told her tales of life outside the park. Strange tales they were, tales of hunger, of hardship, of women and children sent to the poorhouse because they could no longer pay their rent, and of men who crept into the woods at night searching for wild animals to trap and kill. Annie and Hal became instant friends and whenever she could Annie helped Hal with the tasks he was expected to carry out.

Gradually the guests who had attended the christening celebrations for the new baby made their way homeward. Elizabeth was relieved as the pressure in the kitchens eased and before long she found herself transferred to the bakery. Here her baking skills were soon noticed. Even Lady Frances had been heard to remark on the improved texture of the white bread that reached her table.

Hal, whose usual job was to help Ben's father, Richard Jacobs, in the gardens, had only seen two-year-old Lady Jane Grey once. A petite, auburn-haired child, Jane was walking in the park with Mistress Ellen. The boy peered curiously at the small figure from behind a tree, but knew he was not allowed to come near her. Jane was the same age as Prince Edward, King Henry VIII's son, whose birth had brought celebrations up and down the land. Hal understood that the prince and Jane were cousins and he could hardly imagine what it must be like to be a cousin of the boy who would some day be king of all England. Jane might even marry the prince, or so people whispered to each other. Hal found himself bursting out laughing at the very thought of such a tiny child as Jane becoming Queen of England.

Ben Jacobs seemed to dislike Hal from the start and was ready to mock him if he ever made a mistake. Hal did not understand that the older boy was jealous—because it seemed to Ben that Hal had all the easy jobs to do, and was never in trouble. Worse than this, from Ben's point of view, was the fact that his own mother appeared to favour the younger boy, offering him small sweetmeats from the kitchen as rewards for jobs well done.

Hal avoided Ben whenever he could. But one day, after he had collected a full basket of sweet-smelling herbs from the kitchen garden to be scattered on the newly-scrubbed bakery floor, Mistress Jacobs pressed a delicious lump of candied aniseed into Hal's hand. The boy's eyes shone with delight. Never before had he had such a treat. As he set off to look for a hidden corner where he could enjoy his reward in peace, he suddenly saw that Ben was following him.

'What's that you've got?' demanded the older boy.

27

'It's mine,' retorted Hal defensively.

'Give it me right now,' demanded Ben.

'You can't have it,' shouted Hal, beginning to run. In no time Ben was hot on his heels. In a blind panic Hal dashed into the servants' hall with Ben in pursuit. Now Ben was gaining on him, but where could he go? Without a second thought, Hal charged on through the Servants' Hall into the Great Hall that lay beyond. This was forbidden territory to the servants unless they were waiting at the tables, and Hal had never been there before. Here the marquess and his wife entertained their important guests, and here the family had their meals at tables on a raised dais at one end of the hall.

Tears were now streaming down Hal's cheeks. He could scarcely see where he was going; nor did he realize that Ben was no longer following him, for the older boy knew full well that if he entered the Great Hall he would receive a beating from his father. Quite suddenly, Hal crashed into something large and soft. He had run straight into a woman's arms, knocking that person against the wall. A moment later he felt an iron grip on one shoulder. Looking up through his tears, he thought that Ben had caught up with him at last. Instead he found himself looking right into the hard, angry eyes of a woman whom he instantly recognized to be Lady Frances herself.

'Oh! I'm sorry, ma'am,' Hal blurted out in confusion. 'Ben was after me.' The face did not soften. Instead Lady Frances grabbed the boy by both shoulders, shaking him so fiercely that he lost his balance and fell to the ground. 'You dare come charging into this hall like a wild boar! I'll have you taught a lesson you will never forget,' she shouted.

'Jacobs, take this boy and thrash him for me,' she called out as Ben's father poked his head into the hall to see what all the commotion was about. It was a thrashing that Hal would remember for many long days. Again and again the birch rod crashed down on his tender back. But all the time, in spite of the pain, Hal made sure he kept his candied aniseed well hidden. Nothing would persuade him to part with that.

'Now get out,' shouted Jacobs, 'and never you dare go into the Great Hall again!' Hal ran blindly out into the park. His back was sore and bleeding, but the thought uppermost in his mind was of his mother. Perhaps Elizabeth would lose her place among the Bradgate servants. Then what would they do? Hal could not face such disgrace. He must hide, but where could he hide? Then he remembered the cellars under the Great Hall. No one would ever find him there. Stumbling down the steps, he lifted the latch and pushed the heavy door. It gave slowly under the pressure and in a few moments Hal found himself standing at the top of a further flight of steps.

Down he went as the outer door clicked shut behind him. Everything here was cool and dim, and for a while Hal could see nothing. Then as his eyes grew accustomed to the dark he could make out the great barrels of wine stacked one on top of another and, beyond them, several enormous butts full of beer—both strong and light beer, the normal drink for the servants. Finding a dark corner, the boy at last slumped down and buried his face in his hands. Hot tears ran down his cheeks. His back hurt so badly from the beating he had received that he scarcely knew where to put himself. How could he ever face anyone again? No, he would stay there in the cellar for ever, he determined, even if he died down there. And at least he could eat his sweetmeat in comfort. As he slowly licked the aniseed's sticky sweetness, he began to feel a small shred of comfort stealing over him. Curling up in a ball, Hal closed his eyes—eyes that ached with crying—laid his head on his arms and was soon fast asleep.

How long he slept, he never knew. Waking suddenly, Hal blinked in the darkness. Was it the middle of the night? Was it morning? All was silent around him. Where was he, anyway? Hal was cold and stiff and very hungry; then it all came back to him in a flash, and particularly as he tried to rise to his feet and felt the pain from the beating Ben's father had given him. Just as he stood up Hal thought he could hear footsteps. Then the great oak door of the cellar creaked open and a shaft of light fell across the stone floor. Someone was coming down the steps. Hal was so frightened he scarcely knew what to do. Would he be beaten again? Flattening himself against the wall of the cellar, he stood absolutely still. Then to his astonishment he thought he could hear voices. Two people must be coming. The footsteps sounded light—not like a man's heavy tread.

Elizabeth had spent a wakeful night, wondering whatever could have happened to Hal. She had heard from Mistress Jacobs of Hal's collision with Lady Frances and of the well-deserved beating he had received. But where had the boy gone? She had searched all around the grounds. If Hal had run into the woods he could have been torn to pieces by wolves... Perhaps a wild boar could have gored him... Her imagination ran to all the possible disasters that could have overtaken the child. He was all she had following the loss of her husband and her baby's death. After scouring every place she could think of, Elizabeth had been forced to give up for the night. She could do no more.

Then a thought struck her. Perhaps if she could go into the chapel where the christening had been held and kneel down and pray, maybe God would care for her boy. Again she remembered what Matt used to tell her of how the monks prayed in their cells at night. Maybe if she knelt down in the chapel and tried to pray it might make a difference. But even as she did so, her mind was still haunted by frightening thoughts of what might have happened to Hal.

To make it worse, Elizabeth could not begin to understand why her son should have run into the Great Hall in the first place. Something must have made him do it. Ben had kept very quiet when he was questioned about the incident. When Mistress Ellen had suggested the following morning that they could look in the cellars, Elizabeth was doubtful about the idea. Hal would have been too afraid of the dark to venture down there. But, anxious enough to try anything that would lead her to the lost child, she agreed to look. Carefully now, she and Mistress Ellen peered here and there in the gloomy darkness, but could see nothing.

Then, quite suddenly, Hal sneezed. He had not meant to, but the sneeze came so quickly that he was unable to stop it. With a cry Elizabeth ran towards the sound, and a moment later Hal was in his mother's arms. Gratefully she led him back up the stone steps and then up flight after flight of stairs to their quarters at the top of the servants' tower. Each step was painful, for Hal was badly bruised. Carefully his mother bathed his sore back and, after she had given him a little pottage to eat, Hal curled up on his mattress and was soon fast asleep once more.

Ben Jacobs was obviously ashamed of his part in the incident, and began to respect Hal in a new way, especially when the younger boy told no one apart from his mother what had really happened. Lady Frances, who had heard of Hal's disappearance, decided that the boy and his mother had been punished enough over the incident and that she would allow Elizabeth to keep her job after all, reversing her initial resolve to dismiss the woman.

4
A strange friendship

More than two years had passed since Hal and his mother had first come to Bradgate House, and Hal was now nearly nine years old. Dark-haired like Elizabeth and with the same clear grey eyes, the boy was well liked among the servants at Bradgate. Sometimes Lady Frances eyed him curiously from a distance and she had even sent down instructions that he should be taught to ride one of the ponies from the Bradgate stables. Remembering his first encounter with her, Hal had tried to keep a safe distance from Lady Jane's fiery-tempered mother.

Spring had come early to Bradgate that year. Soft greens clothed the hillside and early flowers brought colour and life to the formal gardens where Hal worked for much of his time. Ben had been much kinder to him since the incident of the collision with Lady Frances, but recently the older boy was being trained to care for the many hunting dogs which the marquess and his wife kept for their favourite sport. Dogkennell Meadow, as it was known, lay at some distance from the house so that the family and their guests would not be disturbed by the yelps and barking of the dogs. Ben now slept and had his meals in the lodge not far from the kennels.

But two things had happened early in 1542 that horrified Hal. The first was terrible news that had just reached Leicestershire from London. Catherine Howard, King Henry VIII's new queen, whom he had called his 'rose without a thorn,' had been executed on Tower Green in the Tower of London. Hal shivered at the mere thought. What could the beautiful young queen, only twenty years of age, have done to deserve such a dreadful punishment?

'Terrified, she were, kept cryin'. An' 1 don't blame 'er, 1 don't,' announced Meg Saunders dramatically. Meg was one of the scullery maids who seemed to enjoy being the first with any bad news. 'But what a ghastly way to die!' thought Hal as he tried to push the news to the back of his mind. Yet each night as he closed his eyes he seemed to see a panic-stricken young woman kneeling on a scaffold waiting for that fearsome axe to fall. There was a lot of whispering going on in the Servants' Hall and Hal suspected that people knew more about why Catherine was executed than anyone was prepared to tell him or speak of openly.

Then some other news reached Hal, of an event much closer to hand, that horrified and distressed him even more. Again, it was Meg Saunders, who had also lived in Newtown Linford before coming to Bradgate, who was first with the news. She had heard it from her mother, who still lived in the village, and was just telling another maid when Hal walked in the door after finishing work in the gardens for the day.

'They hung 'im up, they did, right in the centre of the village,' she was saying.

'Who did they hang up?' asked Hal in alarm.

'Why, poor Hugh Lambert. Caught poaching, he was; 'ad a great stag right across 'is shoulders, that he did,' concluded the girl confidently.

Hal turned pale and hurried outside. How could they hang a kind man like Hugh Lambert? How dreadful to kill someone who was only trying to keep his family alive? What would happen to Hugh's family now? What about his friend Will and the twins, Lucy and Betsy? The news lay like a lead weight on Hal's mind. There had been some sort of a trial, but it had only lasted a few moments, so Meg had added. 'Condemned to hang before Eastertide,' had been the verdict.

'Condemned... Condemned... Condemned.' The word kept throbbing through Hal's brain like the beat of some loud drum. And Catherine Howard was condemned too—condemned to die on the scaffold. Always a serious boy, Hal had often thought of his father's last words to him: 'Don't grow up to be a bad man like I've been.' His father had not seemed bad in Hal's eyes. He had found it hard to imagine that Catherine could be so bad, and he was quite sure poor Hugh Lambert was not a bad man. Perhaps his father would have been hung too if that accident had not happened. It made Hal feel sick even to think about it. And how could he stop growing up to be bad as well? What if he should do some terrible thing one day and then be hung for it? The thoughts circled endlessly in the boy's mind. He must find some quiet place where he could sit and think; he must get as far away from everybody as possible for a while. This was always Hal's instinct when he was in trouble. Far into the darkness he sat on a stump of a tree deep in the woods, struggling with his questions. At last the sound of the howling of wolves not far away roused the boy from his thoughts. Slowly, and with a heavy heart, he made his way back to his tower room. Elizabeth glanced anxiously at her son. She too had heard the news of their former neighbour and by the look on Hal's face she realized that he must know as well.

Quite recently a new chaplain had arrived at Bradgate House. As well as taking services for the family in the chapel, Master John Aylmer had come as a tutor to Lady Jane, who had turned four years of age the previous October. If Jane were to join the royal court in London when she was older she would need to start her lessons very early. The new chaplain was only twenty years of age—the same age as Catherine Howard had been when she died, thought Hal. One of the first things that Master Aylmer had done was to insist that all the servants should also attend a daily service to be held after he had finished conducting morning prayers for the family. He would read to them from a large book that rested on the lectern at the front of the chapel, a book he called the Great Bible. Hal had never seen such a big book before—no wonder they called it a 'great' Bible. Although Hal did not understand the words that he heard the chaplain read, he was sure they must be important.

One morning as Hal was standing at the back of the chapel, crushed into a corner by all the other members of the domestic staff, he heard Master Aylmer reading some words that he thought were very wonderful. Hal repeated them over and over again in his mind so that he would not forget them: 'God sent not his Son into the world to condemn the world, but that the world through him might be saved. He that believeth on him shall not be condemned...' Not condemned? There was that word again. Poor Hugh Lambert had been condemned. That book Master Aylmer was reading from said that those who believe in God's Son are not condemned. A small ray of hope lightened Hal's spirit. Perhaps there might be mercy even for him.

When everyone else had left the chapel, Hal crept to the front and looked at the book chained to the lectern from which Master Aylmer had been reading. He ran his fingers reverently over the strange black marks on the page. He knew they were letters and words, but he had not been taught his alphabet. If only he could read, then he could come into the chapel and read this book for himself. Glancing nervously at the door in case anyone should catch him touching the book, Hal turned to the front of it. He gazed with astonishment at the title page.

There he saw a picture of one whom he supposed to be Henry VIII on his throne, giving a book to those around him. They in turn appeared to be giving the book to others. Maybe the king wrote this book, thought Hal. But then he dismissed the idea. That must be wrong, for Master Aylmer had said it was God's book. Hal turned sadly away. No one would ever trouble to teach a poor servant boy to read, but at least he could try to learn by heart some of these words that he heard each morning. Perhaps Master Aylmer would be able to tell him the answers to his questions if only he could speak to him.

One day as he was working in the gardens Hal saw Master Aylmer walking slowly along. He thought at first that the chaplain was on his own. Perhaps this was his chance to speak to him. Then Hal noticed a strange thing. The chaplain was carrying little Jane Grey in his arms. Hal wondered whatever he could be doing until Elizabeth explained that Master Aylmer was actually teaching the child her first lessons. Jane was small for her age; to Hal she looked more like a doll than a little girl, dressed just like her mother with a hood set with jewels over her auburn hair, a long skirt and embroidered bodice with frills at the wrists. Hal felt sorry for her. How could she run and play in all those clothes?

Not long after this Hal was chopping up logs for the fire. Even though he was tall and strong for his age, he found it exhausting work, and every few moments he had to stop for a rest and to wipe the sweat out of his eyes with his sleeve. Spring was well advanced now. The oak trees were all in leaf and the new soft green fronds of bracken were uncurling on the banks of the river. Birds chirped cheerfully all around. The depression that had been resting on Hal's spirit was gradually lifting and he began to whistle to himself as he paused in his work. But suddenly Hal thought he heard a different sort of sound. He stopped to listen but all was quiet. Perhaps he was just imagining it. So he picked up his axe once more and soon the chips of wood began flying in all directions. Then he stopped working again for a further rest. And, yes, there was the sound again. He had not imagined it. What could it be? It sounded like a child crying, but that was impossible. He was about to start his work once more, but then decided he would go and investigate.

As he moved in the direction from which the sound seemed to come, the crying grew louder. Peering in among the bushes, Hal was amazed to catch sight of a small child sitting on a fallen branch of a tree, sobbing bitterly. As he moved a little closer, he recognized the child. To his astonishment he realized it was Lady Jane.

Hal had never been so close to the girl before, and even now he thought he had better leave her alone in case he found himself in trouble. He stood irresolute: a kind-hearted boy, Hal could hardly bear to abandon Lady Jane in distress. But Jane heard the crackling sound in the bushes as Hal approached and looked up quickly. Her expression reminded Hal of a startled deer. 'What's the matter?' he asked kindly, drawing a little closer. Jane looked as if she were about to run away, but then changed her mind.

'Who are you?' she asked timidly.

'I'm Hal Tylney, and my mother works in the bakery,' said Hal quickly.

Jane gazed at the boy through her tears and then suddenly blurted out, 'My ma's just beaten me again and I am so unhappy.'

'Why?' gasped Hal. He could hardly imagine so small a child deserving a beating.

'Nothing I do can please mama,' Jane continued in a rush. 'Whether I speak, keep silent, sit, stand or walk, eat, drink, be merry or sad, sew, play, dance, or anything else, I must do it as perfectly as God made the world, or else I am cruelly threatened and beaten.'

Hal gazed in amazement at Jane's freckled, tear-stained face and serious brown eyes. She hardly sounded like a four-year-old at all. Never could he have imagined that Lady Frances would treat her own child in such a way. He had good cause to remember the beating he had received when he was only six. But what could he say to Lady Jane? In the end he sat down on the branch with her, one arm round her shoulder, and waited quietly until she was calm. At last with a final sniff Jane rose to go, for already Hal could hear Mistress Ellen calling her name. 'I wish I had a brother like you,' she said over her shoulder as she left, 'then I would not be beaten so much. But both my brothers died before I was born.'

Hal remained frozen to the spot. He dared not emerge from the bushes until he was certain that Lady Jane had gone, or else they could both be in trouble. Thoughtfully he went back to chopping up the logs. He had always imagined that life for someone in Jane's position must be a very happy one. Now he knew it was not. And this was the beginning of a strange friendship between the high-born girl, cousin of the heir to the throne of England, and the poor servant boy at Bradgate House. Whenever she saw Hal at work in the house or gardens, Jane would wave enthusiastically. Hal waved back, always hoping that no one would tell Lady Frances that one of the servant boys had been waving to her daughter.

5
A brave act

Hal stood spellbound. Never before had he been allowed to watch the annual jousting tournament held in the tiltyard next to Bradgate House. But he had recently turned eleven years of age and was at last considered old enough to join the spectators who stood around the yard waiting expectantly for proceedings to begin. Hal had been anticipating this day for weeks and now, feeling strange in his new breeches and stiff embroidered shirt, he stood breathless with excitement, eyes fixed on the jousting pavilions from where the two principal jousters and their attendants would emerge.

The sun beat down from a cloudless sky. Birds of prey seemed to hang motionless in the blue high above them. Hal could not have imagined a better day for the tournament. Not far from where he was standing, all the important guests were seated on benches draped with tapestries and with a canopy overhead shielding them from the hot sun. Lady Frances was there, dressed in a magnificent silk gown in Tudor green, her hard face looking almost attractive as she too waited eagerly for the tournament to begin, her task being to present the ornate silver trophy to the winner. Not far from her sat her two daughters, Lady Jane, now almost six years old, and her younger sister

Katherine, not yet three. The Duchess of Suffolk, Catherine Brandon, whom Jane's grandfather Sir Charles had married after the death of her grandmother, Princess Mary Rose, had come to the tournament. So had their two sons, Henry and Charles—and no wonder, for was not their father, Sir Charles, to be the principal jouster? The boys were really Jane's uncles but Henry was only nine and his brother eight. As Hal measured himself up in his mind against these high-born boys, he was pleased to note that he was considerably taller than Henry.

Jane smiled quickly across at Hal as soon as she saw him, but it was her younger sister Katherine who was obviously the centre of attention. Already a beautiful little girl with dainty features and auburn hair just like Jane's, the child was clearly far too young to understand much of what was going on. Mistress Ellen was finding it nearly impossible to keep her sitting still on the bench. Only Sir Henry Grey was missing from the family group and Hal knew well that it was because he would be competing in the joust against Sir Charles Brandon, his father-in-law. Reputed to be the best jouster in the land, Brandon had rarely been knocked from his horse in a tournament except when competing against King Henry.

'Sir Charles will win,' muttered Ben Jacobs, who was standing by Hal. 'Better than the king, he is, but he always has to let the king win —wouldn't do to beat him, you know.' Hal was not so sure. Sir Charles was already sixty years of age and his reactions might not be as quick as once they were, particularly when faced with his agile twenty-six-year-old son-in-law, Sir Henry.

Suddenly the excited hubbub stilled. Hal glanced across the yard. There was Adrian Stokes, the new stable boy, leading one of the horses out into the yard. Hal felt a pang of jealousy, for Adrian was only twelve—just a year older than he was—and had not long come to Bradgate. Tall and good-looking, he seemed already to be a favourite with Lady Frances. From the opposite side of the yard came an older stable hand leading another horse. Decked with brilliant saddle cloths of scarlet and silver over their protective armour, the horses tossed their proud heads, the bells on their manes tinkling merrily and their jewelled reins gleaming in the sunlight. Now their riders emerged from the pavilions where they had been waiting, scarcely recognizable beneath their splendid suits of armour and gorgeously plumed helmets. Soon they were mounting their horses. Hal decided he could tell the two apart, both from their figures—the one portly, the other slim—and from the effortless way that one man sprang into the saddle in spite of the heavy armour.

At last the bugle sounded for the tournament to begin. Losing no time, the riders cantered towards each other, their blunted lances outstretched. The clash of steel on steel rang out as the jousters lunged at each other from each side of the narrow dividing fence. Forward they charged, again and again; now one seemed to be gaining an advantage, now the other. Who would be the first to fall? It was impossible to tell. Sir Charles, heavier and more experienced, seemed the better fighter, but Sir Henry's reactions were quicker, his movements deft and nimble. Now nothing could be heard except the angry snorting of the horses, the loud thud of their hooves as they pounded towards each other and the repeated clang of weapons as each man tried to unseat the other. Faster and faster grew the pace: the horses had barely turned before they were charging again. Every eye was fixed on the fight. Hal could hardly breathe with suppressed tension.

Then quite suddenly there was a movement from a spot not far from where Hal was standing, followed by a delightful peal of childish laughter. Little Katherine Grey had managed at last to escape from her nurse's arms. Without the slightest awareness of any danger, the child rushed gleefully towards the charging horses. A great gasp went up from the spectators—in another second the small girl would be trampled to death under the hooves of her own father's horse. Like an arrow from a bow, Hal shot forward without a moment's thought for his own safety. He managed to grab Katherine by the arm and drag her towards him with only inches to spare before the heavy animal would have crushed her. Spinning round, the boy pushed the child out of the way, but as he did so he crashed headlong himself across the grass. As he fell his right leg took a sharp blow from the horse's back leg as it thundered past. Mistress Ellen, the tears streaming down her face, rushed forward and grabbed Katherine, who was now screaming with indignation at being trapped once more.

'Take her away,' yelled Lady Frances, white with fear at the calamity that had so nearly struck her favourite daughter. Suddenly aware of the crisis, Sir Henry had reined in his horse sharply and was cantering across to the family group. For a few moments no one seemed to notice that Hal was still lying on the grass where he had fallen, writhing in pain. Then Elizabeth ran forward. One glance at the shape of Hal's leg told her that her son had suffered a severe fracture.

'Oh, my poor, poor boy!' cried his mother, as one or two of the men came forward and stooped to lift Hal as gently as they could, carrying him to the side of the yard. Hal was trying to be brave but the pain was so intense that he cried out before he could help it.

'He's a brave boy,' said Sir Henry sincerely, taking off his helmet and bending over Hal. 'You saved my little girl's life, and I thank you right heartily.' Hal turned his eyes on Sir Henry. It was the first time he had ever seen him close at hand, and he was surprised to notice the unhappy look on Sir Henry's face. In spite of his pain, Hal managed a faint smile. Then he lost consciousness altogether.

Hours later Hal regained consciousness only to find himself lying on his straw mattress at the top of the tower. How had he got there? He did not know. His mother was sitting beside him, anxiety written all over her face. Would Hal ever walk again? Although the question remained unspoken, she couldn't help worrying.

'Who won?' murmured Hal.

'No one,' Elizabeth replied. 'They decided to stop the joust.'

'But why?' persisted Hal. Before Elizabeth had a chance to answer she heard footsteps approaching. Soon two men whom Hal had never seen before, and who both looked very clever, entered the room. Sir Henry had insisted that Hal should have the best physicians in Leicester to set his broken leg because such injuries so often led to permanent lameness.

The next few moments were ones that Hal would try to forget in the days ahead. One man held him down while the other twisted and wrenched the injured leg, forcing the bone back into line. Elizabeth held his hand as Hal squeezed his eyes tight shut and clenched his teeth so that he would not cry out, for the pain was excruciating. With two splints firmly strapped to either side of the broken leg, the physicians gave Elizabeth instructions that Hal must not be moved for at least six weeks while the bone healed, and then disappeared as suddenly as they had come.

Hal slept much of the time during the next few days, but the pain in his leg frequently kept him awake at night. During the long wakeful hours as he lay on his lumpy mattress, he often found himself asking questions—questions for which he had no answers. Again and again his thoughts went back to matters of life and death. His father had died in front of his eyes when he was only six. Annie McNeil's father had died too. Then there was poor Hugh Lambert, hung for poaching, and Catherine Howard who was executed... What lay beyond this life? What would have happened to him if he had been killed by that horse instead of just breaking his leg?

Sometimes Hal remembered snatches of words that Master Aylmer had read from that beautiful book in the chapel. There was one bit about Jesus as a shepherd. Hal liked that because his father had been a shepherd as well. As far as he could remember, Jesus had said something about giving his sheep eternal life so that they would never perish. That sounded strange, and yet it was very wonderful too. One story Hal remembered clearly was about a man who had been lame for thirty-eight years. One week seemed bad enough to Hal—he could not begin to imagine what thirty-eight years must have been like. But Jesus had said to the lame man. 'Rise, take up your bed and walk.' Even the clever physicians from Leicester could not do things like that.

Sometimes Annie came to sit with Hal. She would tell him stories of all the things that were going on in the kitchens and beyond, such as how Meg Saunders had broken one of Lady Frances' best porcelain dishes. 'Poor Meg, you should have seen how scared she was, but Lady Frances just laughed. She has lots more dishes even better than that one,' Annie continued. Then Ben Jacobs had been bitten by one of the dogs when he went too close to her puppies... Adrian Stokes was having riding lessons on Lady Frances' own mare... But most of all Hal enjoyed hearing stories about Lady Jane which Annie heard from her mother, Mistress Ellen.

43

'Lady Jane is very clever,' said Annie solemnly. 'She can read that book that Master Aylmer reads from in the chapel, and mama told me she is learning a language called Greek and can write in Latin. She can play the lute too, I heard her once and it was very beautiful. But she cries a lot as well and I think her mama is not very kind to her.'

Sometimes Annie told him about what was happening out in the park, of how the bracken was turning from green to gold; of how a pack of wolves had been spotted not far from Dale Spinney; of how a fox had entered the pheasantry, killing many of the birds; and how the rutting season was beginning and the stags were fighting... But when she looked down at Hal she saw that he was fast asleep.

The days were still warm even though it was almost October. The tower room where Hal was confined grew oppressively hot at times. Light from the narrow windows was poor and often Hal became fretful and bad-tempered as he lay day after day with one leg propped up on a bolster. No matter how hard she tried with the best dishes the kitchen staff would allow, Elizabeth found that Hal had hardly any appetite. With little to occupy his mind Hal began to observe small things that he had never noticed before. Right up in the corner of his tower room he watched a large spider beginning to spin her web. Amazed, he watched as she hung her intricate shining threads between two of the roof beams. Then she retired to the top of the web to wait for any unfortunate fly to become entangled in her trap.

Before long a noisy bluebottle buzzed into the room through one of the narrow windows. Hal wondered whether it would be caught in the web. Round and round the room it zoomed, always appearing to avoid the web and the spider that lurked expectantly in its corner. Then quite suddenly it flew straight into the web. Despite its struggles, its attempts were useless as first its wings and then its legs became enmeshed in the fine filaments of the web. Its efforts to escape alerted the spider and Hal watched in fascination as the owner of the web hurried to the spot and before long began to consume the fly. Always a thoughtful boy, Hal began to wonder whether that was a picture of life. 'Is this world a giant web in which unfortunate people are trapped?' he pondered. 'Are some people spiders and others flies?'

As Hal was reflecting on these unanswerable questions something happened which made him forget about spiders and flies altogether:

he caught the sound of footsteps he didn't recognize approaching his tower room up the winding stairway. It sounded as if two people were coming, though one tread was much lighter than the other. To Hal's astonishment Mistress Ellen entered the room and close behind her was Lady Jane herself. Hal could hardly believe his eyes.

'Mama says I can come and read to you if you like,' said Jane shyly.

'You puir bairn,' chipped in Mistress Ellen, 'we all be right sorry for you downstairs, and my lady here can read that grand as will soon git thee better.' And with a swish of her long linen kirtle, Mistress Ellen turned and disappeared back to her rooms.

'I shall read thee a merry tale of Boccaccio,'[1] announced Jane, perching herself on a nearby stool. Opening a strange-looking book, with colourful letters at the beginning of many pages, Jane began to read. Hal was enthralled. Now he was far away from the dingy tower room and following the adventures of Boccaccio's hero in a distant country called Italy where skies were always blue and the sea sparkled in the sunshine. Hal thought books were only written to teach people things, but this was an exciting story—almost as good as watching a joust.

And so it was that each day Lady Jane made her way up to the servants' tower room to read to Hal. She seemed so happy when she was reading that he found it hard to believe Annie's words that Lady Jane cried a lot. 'How did you learn to read like that?' asked Hal one day. He hardly expected the answer he received:

Master Aylmer teaches me so gently, so pleasantly ... that I think all the time nothing that I am with him. And when I am called from him, I fall on weeping because whatever I do else but learning is full of grief, trouble, fear and wholly misliking to me.[2]

Hal gazed at the small figure in astonishment. That explained many things. It seemed that she was only really happy when she was having

---

[1]   Giovanni Boccaccio, an Italian poet and writer (1313-1375), was famous for the introduction of the short story, particularly in his best-known work, *The Decameron*.

[2]   Recorded by Roger Ascham in *The Scholemaster*, 1711 edition, p.35.

her lessons with Master Aylmer. But why should she cry so much? He must find out.

For a few moments Hal said nothing. But then he blurted out, 'Does your mama really beat you, like you once told me?' Jane merely nodded, her eyes filling with tears. Each day after that the two children had serious conversations when Jane had finished reading the story. She would turn seven that month and Hal was now eleven, but the difference in their ages hardly seemed to matter. Jane was so serious, so thoughtful. Perhaps she would understand about some of the questions that were troubling him.

'My papa died from a dreadful accident,' he ventured one day when Jane closed the book. Even Jane must not know what really happened. 'Just before he died he told me not to grow up bad like he had been. But my papa was not bad, my lady, he was a kind papa to me. If he was bad, then I suppose I will grow up bad too.' It had all come out in a rush, and Hal waited nervously to see what Jane would say.

'Master Aylmer says we're all bad,' answered Jane thoughtfully, 'but he says we can be made good through Jesus. I don't really understand it, but it is written in the New Testament that he taught me to read. One day I will ask him to tell me more; then I can tell you.'

'I wish I could read,' was Hal's only response.

Not long after this Hal had yet another visitor. 'My Lady Jane tells me you would like to learn to read,' said a kindly voice. Hal had been half asleep at the time and it took him a few moments to realize that it was Master Aylmer himself speaking.

'Oh, sir! Would you teach me?' asked Hal in astonishment.

'Why, yes! We can start now, if you are ready.'

Without a moment's delay Master Aylmer produced something that he had been hiding behind his back: a horn book to teach Hal his letters. Now fully awake, Hal proved a ready learner, and after only two days he could recognize most of his letters. Before a week had passed he could spell out the words of the Lord's Prayer written below the alphabet on his horn book. Master Aylmer left the 'book' with him

46

and now the hours passed quickly as he strained his eyes in the half-light to read the words.

One day, to Hal's delight, Master Aylmer brought a small copy of part of the very book that he read from at morning prayers. 'It's called the New Testament,' the chaplain told him. Hal fingered it reverently, and then asked shyly, 'Who wrote this book?'

'It's God's book,' replied Aylmer promptly, 'and it shows us the way to heaven.'

'But how did you get it?' was Hal's next question.

'It was written in Greek almost 1,500 years ago when God told some men whom he had chosen the things that he wanted us to know. Some day I will tell you about a brave man who translated this book from Greek into English so that boys just like you could read it in their own language. His name was Master William Tyndale and his enemies wished to destroy him because they did not want the common people to read this book for themselves or to find out the way to God on their own.'

'What happened to him then?' asked Hal, now very interested.

'Someone who pretended to be his friend betrayed him, and Master Tyndale died a terrible death. But it was too late to stop people reading the book because copies had been smuggled across the sea into England from Germany, where Tyndale was hiding. People were secretly buying it all over the country.'

'How did he die?' Hal's voice revealed his concern.

'They put him in a cold, damp prison in a place called Vilvorde, near Brussels,' replied Aylmer, 'and then they took him out, strangled him and then burnt his body, tied to a stake.'

Hal shuddered. 'That's dreadful,' he murmured. He did not think he wanted to hear any more. That was worse than the way Hugh Lambert had died, and yet somehow the book he held in his hand seemed even more wonderful because a courageous man had died trying to give it to the people of England to read.

'Then are we allowed to read it now?' Hal wanted to know.

'Why yes! Just before Master Tyndale died he prayed, "Lord, open the King of England's eyes," and God heard his prayer because now the king says people can read the New Testament if they wish.'

'Does the king know that this book is Master Tyndale's translation?' Hal asked.

'I cannot say for certain but methinks he does not, because a friend of mine called Master Coverdale helped to finish parts that Master Tyndale could not do after they threw him in prison. And this book does not bear Master Tyndale's name.' Hal was about to ask more questions but Master Aylmer suddenly rose to go, saying he was already late for Lady Jane's lesson, and she would be waiting for him to come.

The next three weeks seemed to fly past as Master Aylmer came every day to teach Hal. Soon the boy was able to figure out some of the stories he had heard in the chapel. Perhaps it was worth breaking his leg after all, he thought to himself. Two things had happened that might never have happened otherwise: he had been able to talk to Lady Jane at last, and now he could read.

Soon after this the clever physician from Leicester returned. He undid the strapping round the splints on Hal's leg. Hal was ashamed of how dirty it had become but when he looked down at his leg, he was astonished and dismayed to see how thin and white it looked. 'Will I ever be able to walk again?' he asked anxiously.

'Why, that you will,' boomed the physician. 'Straight as if you never broke it. And another good job done, I'll say,' he added half to himself with a measure of satisfaction. 'A little bit each day, and you'll be fine again.' And with that he was gone.

6
The gold sovereign

Hal's back ached. He had been planting out row after row of young cabbages in the kitchen gardens and still had more to do. Suddenly a strident but familiar voice rang across the gardens: 'Hal, Hal, where are you?' Mistress Jacobs herself had rushed from the kitchens, her flushed face and urgent tone suggesting to Hal that he was wanted immediately. 'Haste you, boy!' cried the flustered woman as soon as she saw him. 'My lady wants you now, and no delaying!'

Never had Hal been summoned by Lady Frances before, and the boy wondered wildly what she could want him for. Had he done something wrong? Since his unfortunate first encounter with Lady Jane's mother, Hal had avoided meeting her whenever possible. After he had saved little Katherine from certain death at the joust two years earlier, Lady Frances had clearly regarded him more favourably but, even so, Hal was wary of her, knowing that her temper could flare out of control in an instant. 'You'll be a-finding of her in the Winter Parlour,' added Mistress Jacobs over her shoulder as she disappeared back into the kitchens.

Hurriedly Hal washed and tidied himself as much as possible before presenting himself nervously at the door of the Winter Parlour, where Lady Frances was sitting working at some embroidery. 'You need not look so frightened, boy,' she remarked as Hal entered, but even so, her gaze seemed hard and critical as she looked him up and down. 'Stand up straight, can't you, and listen carefully to what I tell you.' Hal straightened up and forced a smile and a nod at the imperious young woman who seemed to keep all who worked at Bradgate House in a state of uneasy tension.

'How old are you?' snapped Lady Frances.

'Thirteen years, ma'am, come the summer,' Hal replied.

'My daughter, the Lady Jane, is now nine years old,' stated her mother, 'and it is high time she learned some court manners and etiquette suitable to her station as cousin to the prince. All this book learning—Greek, Latin, Spanish, French...' Lady Frances seemed to be talking to herself more than to Hal, but suddenly she fixed her eyes sharply on Hal again and continued, 'I have made arrangements for her to take up a place at court as one of the maids of honour for Her Highness the Queen.' Hal listened in amazement, and thought sadly of Jane, still so young and now having to leave her home in order to live at the royal court. Perhaps he would never see her again. He could scarcely begin to imagine what life must be like in such a place as Hampton Court Palace, where he had heard that Queen Katherine Parr had her apartments. 'But then what has all this to do with me anyway?' he thought suddenly.

Lady Frances was still speaking in her dry, rasping voice: 'Why it should be, I know not, but my daughter has asked that you should be allowed to accompany her to London as her page boy. In my mind you are quite unfitted for such a position—only the son of a poor village girl ... no family background.' Hal flushed with inward anger at such a cruel stab at his mother, but bit his lip and said nothing. 'Now if she had asked for Adrian Stokes to take up such a position,' continued the voice, 'I would have no difficulty. A handsome boy is Adrian, better looking than you—why, just look at the way you be standing again!—and from a respectable family too.' Hal straightened up and looked steadily at the speaker. 'I thank you, ma'am, for the honour, but may I not ask that Adrian should go instead of me?'

'Weepin' and beggin' she were when I said it should be Adrian, so what could I do? No, you are to go, and mind you do not disgrace the house of Grey in the royal courts. At least you can read and write, which is more than poor Adrian has had time to learn, so I desire you to send me reports of my daughter, and see to it that she attends to all the social life of the palace. But Adrian will also go to Hampton Court with you. He shall have the care of the horses, accompanying my daughter and her ladies to London together with Master James Abell, my journeyman, who knows the dangers of the way. You will travel with Master Richard Jacobs ahead of the company, driving the baggage carts, with all that is needed for the comfort of my daughter in London and with gifts for His Majesty the King and for Her Highness Queen Katherine of the house of Parr. Now you may go.'

Stunned, Hal turned to go, but just as he reached the door Lady Frances had one more thing to say: 'I have decided also that your mother, Mistress Tylney, shall join Mistress Ellen McNeil as one of my daughter's lady attendants.' So his mother would go too. Hal was glad of that, but could scarcely take in all this news at once and spent most of the rest of the day wandering from place to place, his mind a whirlpool of hopes, excitement and fears.

Preparations for the journey to London filled the next few days. Hal must have new clothes made. He would still wear his normal clothes for all his work in the kitchens and any menial tasks Jane required, but must have formal wear for court appearances, whenever he accompanied her on some state duty, carrying anything she needed for the occasion. With a fine embroidered linen shirt, a stiffly starched ruff around his neck, handsome new breeches to his knees, silk stockings and decorated velvet shoes, Hal felt more like crying than laughing. How could he wear such garments? Yet even he had to admit as he pressed his soft silk cap trimmed with gold thread over his unruly dark hair that he had never looked so grand in his life before. Thankfully he took his new clothes off again and laid them out for his mother to pack.

Three days later all was ready, and the two carts were loaded with all the baggage not needed on the journey and that could not be carried in the horses' saddle packs. Hal and Master Jacobs were to set off ahead of the main party in order that they might reach London in good time to ensure that all was in readiness for Lady Jane's arrival. She had visited Hampton Court before, although always in the company of her parents, but for Hal it was the first time he had travelled beyond the borders of the Marquess of Dorset's Leicestershire estates.

Many were the rumours that Hal had heard of the dangers of the way. The journey might well take two or more weeks, depending on the condition of the roads. Robbers could be lurking behind every bush or clump of trees, and inns were few and far apart. Not for them the luxury of entertainment at some nobleman's home along the way, such as the main party would enjoy. Uncertain as it all seemed, Hal loved adventure and once he had got over the initial shock of his new appointment, he felt a surge of suppressed excitement at the thought of leaving the secluded woods and hills of Bradgate Park for a visit to the great city.

On a bright May morning in 1546 Hal and Master Richard Jacobs set off on their long trek to London. The oaks in the park were clothed in fresh green; the hawthorn bushes were all in flower; young deer staggered on wobbly legs after their mothers; birds sang from every tree. Hal was in high spirits, for even though he was nervous of the journey, he was full of anticipation of the new experiences awaiting him. Dressed in his poorest clothes, so that no wayside gang of robbers would imagine that his cart was laden with costly gifts, Hal waved his farewells to the members of the kitchen staff who had come to see them off. Master Jacobs was less happy than Hal at the prospect of the journey ahead. Making out his will in case he never returned, he said an emotional farewell to Mistress Jacobs and to his son Ben, now fifteen years of age and soon to marry Annie McNeil, Hal's first friend at Bradgate.

But Hal had a further reason for his happiness. In the pocket of his outer jacket he was carrying a very special gift. Just hours before he was due to leave, Master Aylmer had summoned him. 'Because you have made excellent progress with your reading, I wish to give you this copy of the New Testament,' he had told the astonished boy. Much of it is the work of Master Tyndale himself, although it does not bear his name. Take care to read it often, for it is God's Word to guide you in the path of life. It is of more worth than all the treasures you carry to the court, for in it is written the way to heaven.' Hal gasped, the tears welling up in his eyes. Never could he have imagined possessing a copy of this wonderful book as his very own. Merely nodding dumbly, he was quite unable to express his gratitude, but he could see that Master Aylmer understood his feelings.

At last the carts rumbled away along the tree-lined driveway leading from Bradgate House and off down the lane, heading south towards Leicester. Hal fully expected robbers to spring out from behind every tree, but the track was deserted apart from the occasional herdsman driving his cattle to some market. Even though Master Jacobs was armed with a sword for his protection, he had decided that it was safer to avoid Watling Street, the usual route to London, which led through Tamworth, for along that road thieves would regularly lie in wait for unwary tradesmen, assaulting and robbing them. Instead they would travel the Fosse Way as far as the outskirts of Warwick and then make their way east along country lanes to Towcester, joining Watling Street at Stony Stratford, and then on through Dunstable to London. The Fosse Way was in a worse state of repair than Watling Street and the journey would take longer, but with so valuable a load to protect such a diversion might be wiser. They must therefore try to reach Littlethorpe before nightfall, for Jacobs knew of a well-reputed tavern in the village where they could spend the night.

Hour after hour they trundled on, stopping only for a mug of ale and a round of bread and cheese on the way. At last Littlethorpe was in sight. Dogs barked an uncertain welcome but Hal, who was aching in every joint from his long ride, was only too glad see the sign of Ye Olde Bull's Head swinging from a pole in the distance. After a coarse meal of salted beef, bread and ale, Hal and Master Jacobs were shown to the loft, where the floor was strewn with rushes and covered over with several mats. Hard as it was, and despite the fact that Hal could see fleas hopping across the floor, the boy soon fell into a deep sleep.

As soon as it was light, Master Jacobs paid for their accommodation with a silver coin from a small wallet sewn to his belt. 'Go and harness up the horses,' he ordered Hal, who was still half asleep. And off they set once more, jogging along, hour after hour.

As day followed day it was the same: sometimes they became lost and had to retrace their steps; sometimes the wheels of the carts stuck fast in the deep ruts along the way. Sometimes sheeting rain turned the tracks into mire; at others the path was blocked by a dead horse still lying where it fell. And always they must keep a watchful eye for any sign of robbers hiding in the bushes. Each night they would find an inn or alehouse where they could sleep and rest the horses.

As soon as Hal heard Master Jacobs' rhythmic snoring, he would take out his treasured New Testament and in the half-light strain to read the words. At first he flicked through the pages looking for familiar stories or parts that Master Aylmer had read to him. Then he decided to try to read it all through from the beginning. The first book was called 'The Gospell of S. Mathew' and Hal slowly figured out the words of the sections of each chapter, one by one.[1] Much of it he could not understand, but here and there sentences seemed to light up as he read them. Sometimes he was troubled by what he read, and particularly when he found some words that said, 'Narrow is the way that leads to life and few there be that find it.'[2] Master Aylmer had said that this book told of the way to heaven, but Hal began to feel certain that he would not be among the few that found that way. Lady Jane would find it, he felt sure, but he had told too many lies and so often felt angry inside against many of the things that had happened to him.

At last, after almost two weeks of travelling, Master Jacobs and Hal reached Dunstable. Ever since they had arrived at Stony Stratford the road had been busy with travellers—some off to the nearest fair, some carrying important messages, some taking goods to London. The Cock and Hen in Dunstable was already crowded when Hal and Master Jacobs arrived, but apparently there was room for everyone. After finishing his bowl of hot fish pottage, Hal's companion, who seemed more tired than usual, turned in to sleep, leaving Hal to come up later.

---

[1]   There were no verse divisions in the 1526 Tyndale Version of the New Testament.

[2]   Matthew 7:14

A babble of loud voices and raucous laughter attracted Hal's attention, and soon he was engrossed in watching two men playing backgammon while others stood around roaring their approval or dismay as first one seemed to be winning, then another. Stakes were high and money was constantly changing hands. Never had Hal seen so many valuable coins in his life before. Players swapped over as others took their turn and still Hal watched in fascination. One player, a small black-bearded man with thick eyebrows and tiny eyes, who cackled with laughter every time he won, was gambling with ever-higher stakes. Quite suddenly Hal noticed that a small coin had slipped from the player's hand and had rolled onto the floor. No one had seen or heard it fall. No one appeared to notice the loss. And Hal wanted that money. He wanted it more than anything else in the world at that moment. He could spend it in London and buy himself some luxuries that he had never possessed before.

Gradually the players drifted away, tired after their journey or else impoverished after their evening of gambling. And still Hal watched and waited. At last when no one was looking, as quick as a flash he dived under the table and picked up the small coin—a gold sovereign piece. Clutching it as tightly as he had once clutched his aniseed sweetmeat when Ben Jacobs was chasing him for it, Hal climbed the ladder to the loft and lay down to sleep. But that night he did not feel like reading Master Tyndale's New Testament even had there been enough light to do so. Nor could he sleep. That money was not his and he knew it. Tossing back and forth on his straw mat, Hal tried to quieten his conscience. 'Why shouldn't I have it?' he argued. 'No one has missed it. It will only go into the innkeeper's pocket otherwise.' But it was no good. He could not sleep. At last he decided that he must return the money to the man with a black beard in the morning. Then he rolled over and was soon fast asleep.

But when he joined the crowd of men preparing for their journey, Hal could not see the owner of the sovereign anywhere. He looked all around, but there was no sign of him. Clearly he must have set off at dawn and could be far down the road by now. Determining to return the money if he ever saw the man again, Hal slipped the coin into his shoe and harnessed the horses to the carts as he waited for Master Jacobs to settle the accounts with the innkeeper.

Passing at last through St Albans and on to Barnet, Hal and Master Jacobs made their slow way towards London city. Up Colney Hatch Lane they climbed and then, at the top of the hill, to Hal's amazement he could see the whole city spread out before him. There was the River Thames shimmering in the distance like a silver snake, and never had Hal seen so many church spires puncturing the skyline. It was a Sunday morning and the bells were deafening, as each rang out its invitation to worship. But Hal and Master Jacobs dared not leave their carts to enter a church, nor were they dressed for such an occasion, and so they turned their horses south-west towards the village of Acton, stopping at the village inn for the night.

Leaving the village early the next morning, they soon reached the north bank of the Thames. Hal gazed in amazement at the many vessels making their busy way up and down the river, and still the travellers pressed on, following the line of the river. Now they were passing magnificent mansions, homes of the nobility of England, and Hal began feeling strangely out of keeping with his surroundings. As Syon House, with a commanding view across the Thames, came into sight Hal wondered which nobleman lived in so grand a home.

At last, after almost three weeks on the road, the travellers approached the village of Kingston, not far from their journey's end. But nothing he had seen on the way prepared Hal for his first glimpse of Hampton Court Palace. As he gazed at the impressive towers and massive archways, a surge of homesickness swept over the boy and for a fleeting moment he found himself longing for the small wattle-and-daub cottage in Newtown Linford where he had been born.

7
Like a fly in a web

Explaining their business to the guards who watched the great outer gates of Hampton Court Palace, Master Richard Jacobs and Hal Tylney drove their carts across the moat and through the vast archway leading to the inner gatehouse. Past the ornate Chapel Royal they rumbled until at last they reached the Fish Court where the servants' quarters lay. Here, as they were shown into the narrow alleyways and dimly lit rooms of the service area, Hal began to feel a little more at ease. As Master Jacobs stabled the horses and began to unload the carts, the boy was conducted up to one of the many turreted rooms, carrying his few personal possessions. He was informed that he would be sharing the accommodation with another youth, the stable hand from Bradgate Park. Hal had little difficulty in guessing that it would be Adrian Stokes, the young lad favoured by Lady Frances. Unsure of how he would cope with such an arrangement, Hal was glad he had arrived first and would be able to find his bearings in these strange new surroundings before Adrian and the main party arrived.

Overwhelmed as he was by the grandeur of his new circumstances, Hal was not slow to sense a strange heaviness in the atmosphere—a feeling of oppression, even sadness, that seemed to pervade the whole palace. Had something dreadful happened? Or was some frightening event about to take place? It reminded him of the way he had felt on the night his father had died all those years ago. No one seemed to want to talk to him, nor did Hal dare ask if anything was wrong.

Only three days later the main party from Leicestershire cantered through the main gates and were shown into a suite of rooms far different from those which Hal and Adrian would occupy. Lady Jane looked exhausted after her long journey and Mistress Ellen soon had the child in bed. Hal's mother, Elizabeth, would sleep not far away, so that they could attend to any of Jane's immediate needs, and before long Adrian joined Hal in the servants' quarters.

The two youths eyed each other warily as they began to prepare for the night. Adrian was taller than Hal, fair-haired and with attractive blue eyes. His winning smile had always quickly gained him friends wherever he went, although beneath a pleasant surface he hid a spirit that could often be spiteful. He had never liked Hal, and he resented the fact that the younger boy had been chosen as Lady Jane's page in preference to himself, whereas his own task was to care for the horses. Born into a family of successful Leicester wool merchants, he regarded Hal with a measure of disdain as being a mere village lad. Hal, on the other hand, with dark hair and wiry in build, was more reflective, even secretive by nature, and found it difficult to make easy conversation.

So after asking Adrian about his journey from Bradgate, Hal could not think of much else to say and the two fell silent. But as Hal was removing his shoes ready for the night there was the sudden tinkle of a coin falling on the hard floor. The small gold sovereign hidden in Hal's shoe rolled away and settled in a crack in the wooden floorboards. Hal dived to retrieve it, but not before Adrian had caught sight of it.

'Where did you get that from?' he demanded.

'Someone gave it to me at the Cock and Hen in Dunstable,' lied Hal.

'Someone gave it to you?' echoed Adrian, with an incredulous sneer in his voice. 'Someone gave it to you? And you think I'll be believing that? I'll wager you stole that from My Lady Frances. You wait until I tell My Lady Jane what you did!' Hal was now crimson with anger and ready to raise his fists and give Adrian Stokes a blow on the face that he would not easily forget. But he thought better of it, and merely muttered, 'Think what you like.' And, flinging himself on his mattress, he rolled over facing the wall. How he wished he had never touched that money! How he wished he could find the small man with a black beard and return it to him! What would happen to him if Lady Frances heard about it? He was sure Jane would not believe Adrian's accusation, but her mother thought so highly of Adrian that she could well do so if the story reached her ears. Troubled thoughts raced through Hal's mind as he tossed backwards and forwards on his mattress.

Suddenly his attention was arrested by a small buzzing sound high up in the rafters. It reminded him of something. At first he could not think what it was; then he suddenly remembered: it was that fly that had been caught in a spider's web which he had watched all those years ago after he had broken his leg. Perhaps he was like that fly now, he thought gloomily. Perhaps he would be sent back to Leicestershire in disgrace—or something worse... Then he remembered some words that he had only recently read in the New Testament that Master Aylmer had given him. He had reached the ninth chapter of the first book, and had come to the place where Jesus spoke to a sick man. He had said, 'Son, be of good cheer, thy sins are forgiven thee.' Yes, Hal thought, he too had sinned in taking the money, he knew that, but he had been most sorry about it and had wanted to give it back. So perhaps Jesus would forgive his sins as well. With a measure of comfort from this thought, Hal was soon fast asleep.

The next day Master Jacobs gave Hal careful instructions concerning the duties he was required to perform as Lady Jane's page. Each morning he would clean out the fires in the apartments that had been set aside for the use of the party from Leicestershire. Then he must lay them again in readiness for the evening because even in summer the great rooms of Hampton Court felt draughty and cold. He must clean any boots needed for hunting in the park, and above all else must always escort the Lady Jane at any important engagement she might have to attend.

Hal was grateful to have his mother nearby, especially when he heard that Jane was soon to be presented to Queen Katherine. Elizabeth Tylney came across to Hal's tower room to check that her son was correctly dressed to accompany Jane on the occasion. With all his finery in place, his dark hair neatly tucked under his silk cap, he set off for the royal apartments, but not before he had noticed the look of envy mingled with malice on Adrian Stokes' face as he passed him on the stairway.

Lady Jane's small face lit up when she saw Hal although for a moment she did not recognize him in his formal court clothes. Only nine years of age, the girl had also felt lost among all the grandeur of the court, but the sight of Hal gave her a measure of confidence, even though she could hardly stop laughing at his changed appearance. Nor did she realize that her page boy was even more apprehensive than she was. As they were ushered into the royal presence Hal gave a suitable bow, but the queen had eyes only for Jane. Her face wreathed with smiles when she saw her and she gave the child a warm embrace.

Jane's earlier visits had already endeared her to King Henry VIII's sixth wife, Katherine Parr, who had acted as a mother to the two motherless royal children, Prince Edward and the Lady Elizabeth. Hal stood to attention at an appropriate distance but had opportunity to study the queen. Dressed in ornate royal robes and decked with exquisite jewellery, she nevertheless had a kindly, serious face. But Hal could not help noticing the look of deep anxiety, even of sadness, written on her features. Once again he found himself wondering whether there was some imminent disaster hovering over the royal court.

That evening, as Hal was sitting with his mother after Lady Jane was in bed, Elizabeth told him some of the court gossip that she had picked up during the day—gossip which explained why everyone was so troubled. According to the reports Elizabeth had heard, one of the queen's ladies-in-waiting, Lady Anne Askew, had recently been arrested and was now being held in Newgate—a dreadful prison from which most only emerged to face a horrible death. She had in fact been arrested the previous year, but had eventually been released without any formal charge. This second arrest looked far more ominous.

'But why?' gasped Hal, 'What has she done?'

'She is accused of sins against the church,' replied his mother solemnly, 'and particularly of believing certain things which she has read in the New Testament—that book that Master Aylmer reads from in chapel. Our Bishop Bonner of London and Bishop Gardiner of Winchester have charged her with holding to things that are false.' Hal turned pale. He had been reading that same New Testament as well, and so had Lady Jane. Would they both be arrested too? He remembered the story Master Aylmer had told him of the dreadful death that Master Tyndale suffered for translating it into English.

'But why do the bishops hate and hurt people who read that book?' persisted Hal. 'Isn't it God's book, and shouldn't we believe it?'

'My son, I cannot tell,' Elizabeth replied slowly, 'but My Lady Anne was heard to say, "I would sooner read five lines in the Bible than hear five masses in the church," and I understand that such words are thought to be a serious offence. It seems that it is all to do with what the church teaches about the mass—and those things that have been accepted in our land for many hundreds of years, but which some people now think are quite wrong.'

By this time Hal was even more confused. 'If only Master Aylmer were here,' he thought, 'he would explain such things to me.' But worse was to come. 'And I hear our queen might also be thrown into the Tower,' confided his mother in a hushed tone. 'My Lady Anne and My Lady Catherine Brandon and many others of the royal household have been meeting with the queen to read God's book. Good Father Latimer used to come to preach to them. At first our lord, King Henry, allowed it but now, alas, by his will Master Latimer too is in prison. If the Lady Anne breaks down under the terrible trial that awaits her, and reveals the names of those who meet with the queen, who can tell what might happen?' Hal began to tremble. He thought he could tell.

Had not Queen Anne Boleyn and Queen Catherine Howard already died at the hand of the public executioner? A similar fate could await Queen Katherine Parr and her ladies-in-waiting. And what would happen to him and to the Lady Jane? Little did his mother realize that hidden under his mattress was a copy of that same New Testament. What if Adrian Stokes saw it? Hal knew well that a law had been passed allowing the churches to possess the book, but what about the ordinary people? To believe its truths and hold views contrary to the teaching of the church appeared to be a terrible offence. Perhaps it would be better if he stopped reading it—and yet its words seemed to reach out to his deepest longings. How could he stop reading it?

The next day such troubling thoughts were banished from Hal's mind when Master Jacobs informed him that Lady Jane was to meet her cousin Prince Edward at noon, and he must attend as well. To see the boy who would one day be King of England was something Hal could never have dreamed possible in his wildest fancies. What was he like? Hal found his heart thumping with excitement at the thought.

The prince's apartments lay in a distant part of the palace and before long Hal was following Lady Jane and her royal guides through a maze of corridors and stairs. He had heard that Prince Edward was very clever and, even though he was only nine years old, he could already write letters in Latin to his stepmother Queen Katherine and to his father Henry VIII. Like Jane he was learning Greek and Spanish as well, but in Hal's mind he could not possibly be as clever as Lady Jane!

A slim, fair-haired boy, the prince greeted Jane warmly, but only after she had curtseyed three times and kissed his hand. She then seated herself on a cushion at his feet and before long the two children began to laugh and chat and play games together, much like any other nine-year-olds. Hal meanwhile stood stiffly to attention at the far side of the courtroom until his back ached and his head began to swim. But just as he thought he could stand it no longer, he noticed that the prince and Lady Jane had lowered their voices. Hal could only catch snatches of their conversation, but it was enough to tell him that they were discussing Lady Anne Askew's forthcoming trial.

'I fear she may burn,' whispered the prince. 'When I am king, none shall burn for believing God's book.'

'I too believe God's book,' returned Jane in a low voice. 'Then are not all of us in danger? Hal could hear little more, but now he understood why all in the palace went in fear, not only for the Lady Anne, but for the queen herself and for Lady Catherine Brandon, Lady Herbert, Lady Lane and all who gathered together with the queen to read God's words.

At last Lady Jane kissed the prince's hand once again and walked backwards out of his presence, followed by Hal. She was due to join the hunt in the park that afternoon, and Hal would not need to attend on her. But Adrian Stokes would be at the hunt. Hal feared that he might take the opportunity to suggest to Lady Jane that he had stolen that gold sovereign from her mother.

8
Trial by fire

Two months had passed since Hal had first come to Hampton Court
—months of tension and fear as the fate of Lady Anne Askew hung in
the balance. Few at court had time or inclination to speak of much
else. Rumours flew from one to another in the servants' quarters.
Some said that Lady Anne was being tortured to force her to name
the other ladies with whom she studied the Bible. Some said that
Lord Chancellor Wriothesley himself had tightened the rack to which
Anne had been tied until all her bones were pulled out of joint.
Others said it was Sir Richard Rich, Chancellor of the Court, who
tortured her, and yet others that both joined to force her to betray her
friends. 'I fear,' said Elizabeth to Hal as they sat together one evening,
'her spirit will break, and then who knows what may happen?'

'Have you heard,' Adrian asked Hal one night early in July as they
were preparing for the night, 'that there has been a new Act of
Parliament?' There was a certain twist to his words that made Hal
wary. He did not answer, and so Adrian continued, 'I hear by royal
pronouncement that a law has been passed that from today none
shall receive, take or keep in his possession any copy of the New
Testament made by Master Tyndale, by Master Coverdale or any

other writings of such men.' Hal jumped involuntarily, and Adrian noticed it, and continued in the same monotone, but with a hint of glee: 'All such books must be delivered to the bailiff to be publicly burned.'

'I know not what you mean,' said Hal desperately. 'Why should you tell me of such a pronouncement?'

'Did not Master Aylmer instruct you from that book?' persisted Adrian. 'I'll warrant you know more than you say. If our Bishop of London, Master Bonner, had his way,' he added menacingly as if he were enjoying Hal's anxiety, 'all heretics that read such books would burn with them.' Hal felt a cold chill of fear run down his spine, and resolved that he would not read any further in his book—at least not while he was at Hampton Court.

Queen Katherine was now spending much time with the king. A sick man, he rarely left his royal apartments at the Palace of Whitehall not far outside the old city walls. In order to be near him the queen and her attendants had also moved from Hampton Court to Whitehall.[1] This meant that Lady Jane, and those who had come with her from Leicestershire, must move there as well. It was another splendid palace built on the banks of the River Thames, and Hal was delighted to find that the attic room which he and Adrian would share looked out across the river. Never had he seen anything like it in his life before. All day long the boats criss-crossed far below his window: stately galleys passed by with twenty or more men, stripped to the waist, pulling at the oars, each galley decorated with colourful flags fluttering in the breeze; busy little boats hurried up and down the watery highway, for this was the easiest means of transport. And beyond, on the far bank of the river, lay open fields and trees which reminded Hal of his home. Sometimes he almost forgot his duties as he watched all that was going on.

A vast sprawling palace, Whitehall was the centre of government and members of the king's Privy Council would arrive for audiences with him. Each day Queen Katherine made her way across the

---

[1]   This palace, originally York Place, had belonged to Cardinal Wolsey, but was taken from him by Henry VIII. It was situated between the present-day St James's Park and the River Thames, and was destroyed by fire in 1698. All that remains of it today is some parts of the Banqueting House.

courtyard to the king's apartments and would sit there with Henry. Often she would dress his painful ulcerated leg, chat to him of all that was going on and always try to cheer him and comfort him. Lady Jane, who sometimes accompanied the queen, had told Hal that they spoke together much about religion, for the queen was deeply concerned in case King Henry should die without a knowledge of the faith that saves the soul.

Hal shuddered when he heard that. 'Will not our queen be in great danger by speaking so to His Majesty?' he asked Lady Jane on one occasion. But Hal knew well that even though she was so young Jane shared those same strong convictions and was becoming fearless in defending her faith. She had even joined the group of ladies who studied Master Tyndale's New Testament in secret. For himself, Hal had kept his copy carefully hidden, knowing that if Adrian Stokes saw it, he might well try to bring further trouble on him. He was glad that Lady Jane had instantly dismissed Adrian's unlikely accusation against her page that he had stolen money from her mother. She hardly bothered to ask Hal how he had obtained that gold sovereign. Although Hal was thankful for this, he felt sure that his rival would certainly seek some other opportunity to bring disgrace on him— perhaps hoping to be promoted to take Hal's place as Lady Jane's page.

On a number of occasions Hal saw the robed figure of Bishop Stephen Gardiner lingering around the precincts of the palace. His hard eyes seemed to be darting here and there, his strong mouth set in a determined line, his expression cruel. What was he doing? Hal knew he had been one of those involved in Anne Askew's trial and torture. Perhaps he was now watching the queen too. Perhaps he was trying to pick up any comments Katherine might have let slip which he might use to condemn her to her husband Henry VIII. Surely, thought Hal, the king would not allow his own wife, the loving stepmother of his children and his patient companion during his days of illness and pain, to be taken to the Tower. But who could tell?

Only a week later, on 16 July 1546, an event took place that Hal could never forget. It was a warm, still day and Adrian Stokes was clearly in a hurry as he changed out of his working clothes. Hal wondered where he could be going. 'Have you an appointment with My Lady Jane this afternoon?' he ventured at last. Adrian turned sharply and answered with something between a sneer and a snub: 'Have you not heard? Why all the world knows that tonight they burn My Lady Anne at Smithfield, and Master Lassell as well, and two more heretics, to boot—just as they have been burning Bibles all week. Master Jacobs and I go to watch. But we must be there early, or we shall not find a place to view the scene. Do you not wish to come? Sure I am that all London will be there to see the sight.' And with that Adrian rushed down the steps to join Master Jacobs at the stables.

Shocked and troubled, Hal made his way slowly across to Lady Jane's apartments. As he passed through the open courtyard, he could hear the excited shouts and cries from the crowd outside the gates as all pressed in one direction. A public execution was a sight few wished to miss. The desire to cheer the sufferers on, or to heap abuse upon them, formed a popular diversion among the people. But Hal's mind flashed back to poor Hugh Lambert strung up on a gibbet in his own village for poaching to keep his family alive. He felt no desire to see a young woman cruelly burnt to death for believing those very words that he too had been reading in secret. Perhaps the king would send her a last-minute pardon, he thought desperately. But in his heart he knew that such a pardon would probably come at the price of denying her faith—a thing he was sure Lady Anne would not do.

All afternoon Hal thought about Lady Anne and of the agony of the death she must undergo that night. Night-time had been chosen for the dreadful deed, for the execution of a young woman of noble birth could cause uproar among the citizens of London. Hal only saw Jane once and noticed her face swollen with crying. Had Lady Anne betrayed the queen and her ladies in the end? Would she decide to save her life by agreeing at last that the church's long-held teachings on the mass were indeed correct, and that the bread and wine did actually turn into the body and blood of Christ after the priest had blessed them? And why was it so important anyway? Surely it was not worth dying for such a thing, thought Hal. Better by far to deny it for the present and return to it when times changed for the better. Everyone at court knew that Henry could not live for much longer.

As darkness fell Hal finished his duties and returned to his tower room. Adrian would not be back until late so he ventured to slip his small New Testament out from under the mattress. He had not dared read it for some time, but now turned to the page he had last reached. And the first words that met his eyes answered all his questions about Lady Anne, for Jesus was saying to the people, 'Fear ye not them which kill the body, and be not able to kill the soul. But rather fear him which is able to destroy both soul and body in hell.'[2] Now he felt sure that Lady Anne would not deny her faith to save her life. But he also knew that he himself would be too weak and too scared to endure such terrible pain.

Hal could not sleep and at last the sound of approaching footsteps alerted him to the fact that Adrian was back. With lightning speed he thrust his book back under the mattress and waited apprehensively. Adrian burst into the room full of excitement. 'What you have missed tonight!' he exclaimed. 'They had to carry My Lady Anne from Newgate Prison to the stake at Smithfield on a chair, for all her bones were out of joint with the torments of the rack. She looked almost dead already. She was chained around the waist to the stake or else she could not have stood. Never have I seen so great a crowd gathered together and My Lord Chancellor Wriothesley...'

'Did the king offer her a pardon?' interrupted Hal.

'Why yes, just before they lit the fires, My Lord Chancellor sent someone across to offer her a royal pardon if she would recant her faith.'

'And did she?' asked Hal although he was sure he knew the answer.

'Why no, fool that she was!' replied the other. 'She said, "I am not come hither to deny my Lord and Master." Then they lit the fires. How bright they shone against the night sky!'

'She was no fool, Master Adrian. Did not Christ say, "Fear not them that kill the body; but fear him who can destroy body and soul in hell"?' retorted Hal almost before he could stop himself. Adrian whirled round.

'I do believe you are a heretic as well, Hal Tylney. You take care or it will be you that is a-burning next.' His voice had taken on an ugly

2   Matthew 10:28

undertone, and Hal said no more. Perhaps he had said too much already.

He had indeed. Not many days after the Master Jacobs eyeing him curiously. Hal tried to avoid being alone with him, but one morning as he was busy cleaning out the fire in one of the palace kitchens he was aware of someone close behind him. Turning quickly he saw Master Jacobs standing in the doorway. 'How is it, Hal Tylney, that you are able to quote words from Master Tyndale's New Testament?' he asked pointedly.

'Why, sir, Master Aylmer taught them to me after I broke my leg,' replied Hal quickly as he stood up to face the older man. The look Jacobs gave the boy showed clearly that he did not believe him. Since that first beating he had given Hal as a six-year-old, Hal had nursed a simmering dislike for him. Clearly Master Jacobs was no friend of his.

'I warn you now, young man,' continued Jacobs, 'heretics get burnt in this place. I saw four perish in the flames last week, one but a simple tailor from Colchester—a slow and terrible way to die,' he added with something between a threat and a sneer in his voice. 'And do you not know,' he persisted, 'that only last month Master Worsley, a page boy like yourself, was burnt without mercy for holding views our church does not allow?' Hal did not reply, but his ashen face told Jacobs that he knew more than he was willing to admit.

9
Hal's discovery

The following few weeks were quiet at the Palace of Whitehall. The shock of Lady Anne's death had affected everyone deeply, from the queen herself down to the youngest servant maid in the kitchens. Who could tell what might happen next? The whole court seemed apprehensive that fresh disaster might strike at any moment. Prince Edward had left for one of his country residences and Lady Jane too spent time at Greenwich Palace, where she joined the classes in the royal schoolroom.

This was a new experience for Jane and she had much to tell Hal when she returned: about the prince's tutor, Sir John Cheke, or about Barnaby Fitzpatrick, the Irish boy who made her laugh as she had never laughed before. She had met Edward Seymour, another of the prince's cousins, a few years her senior but kind and understanding. The Lady Elizabeth, Prince Edward's clever thirteen-year-old half-sister, sometimes joined them too.

Hal found he had much time to himself during those days. Sometimes he sat by the window watching the river traffic pass up and down and listening to the shouts and curses of the boatmen, especially if there was a near collision. He would often wander around the palace exploring some of the winding corridors, or the gardens, and sometimes even venturing secretly near the royal apartments, hoping to glimpse the queen or Lady Catherine Brandon, whom he had seen in Bradgate Park when she attended the joust two years ago. Pompous figures came and went—ambassadors from different countries, members of the Privy Council and even important churchmen like the Archbishop of Canterbury, Thomas Cranmer, would come to visit the queen, or to pay their respects to the sick King Henry. Honest and with a kindly look about him, Cranmer seemed to Hal to be one of the few trustworthy men surrounding the king. On occasions the Lord Chancellor, Thomas Wriothesley, would sweep past Hal on some pressing errand. Hal disliked him intensely, remembering that it was he who had himself tortured Lady Anne in an attempt to make her betray the queen. Could he be spying on the queen? Hal was sure there was more trouble in store.

Everything was quiet at the palace one evening in late August. Duties were complete for the day; the shadows of night were beginning to gather. Hal was wandering across the open palace courtyard, exploring areas where he was not officially supposed to be. Suddenly he became aware of footsteps. Quickly hiding behind a large pillar, he watched to see who could be coming. In fact it sounded as if two people were approaching. Then the menacing figure of Bishop Gardiner came into view, his long clerical robes flowing out behind him and a strange look of triumph on his face. Beside him walked the Lord Chancellor, his handsome robes of office splendid in the half-light of evening. He too looked unusually self-satisfied. Hal held his breath as the two men passed close to the spot where he was standing; they were deep in conversation, but the page could not catch what they were saying.

Just after they had passed him, however, Hal noticed to his surprise that a small piece of paper fluttered from under the Lord Chancellor's cloak, a sudden gust of wind taking it up and blowing it into a corner. 'What can that be?' the boy wondered. Certainly neither man noticed that the paper had been dropped. When he was sure that the two had gone, Hal darted out from behind the pillar and grabbed the piece of paper. There was just light enough to read by, and the first thing that he noticed was that at the bottom of the paper in shaky writing were the words '*Henricus rex*'—'Henry, the king'. The king himself must have signed this piece of paper! Looking more closely, Hal could begin to make out the words and, as he read, all the colour drained from his cheeks. This was a warrant for the arrest of Queen Katherine, accusing her of heresy, and signed by the king. Hal's hand was trembling. Whatever must he do?

Hurrying back towards the servants' quarters, he suddenly saw Lady Catherine Brandon approaching. She had been out walking her small dog, whom she had named Gardiner—much to the annoyance of Bishop Gardiner, who knew well that it was a joke at his expense. Hal had always liked Lady Catherine. Even though she had been married to Lady Jane's grandfather, Sir Charles Brandon, she was actually younger than Jane's own mother and her two boys were both about Hal's age.

Without a word Hal thrust the piece of paper into Lady Catherine's hand. One look at the boy's white face was enough to alert her to the seriousness of its message.

'Where ... where did you find this?' she gasped.

'My Lord Wriothesley dropped it as he crossed the courtyard,' Hal replied breathlessly.

Without pausing even to thank Hal, Lady Catherine gathered up her long skirts and began to run as fast as she was able towards the queen's apartments. There seemed nothing more that Hal could do and so he wandered slowly back to the room he shared with Adrian. Footsteps kept passing backwards and forwards around the palace long into the night. Hal thought he could hear the sound of loud sobbing coming from the direction of the queen's apartments. That frightened him. He did not know what was happening, but wondered if the queen was being taken off to the Tower.

Nor could Hal get to sleep. But as he lay tossing on his mattress, listening to Adrian's rhythmic breathing and the quiet splashing of water against the palace steps, he began thinking about Lady Anne once more. Jane had told him that not long before she died Anne had prayed for her enemies, asking God to forgive them for their wicked deed against her. He was sure that he could never have prayed such a prayer. Then he remembered another part of her prayer. Although he was not sure of her exact words, he thought it was something like: 'Fight thou, Lord, in my stead, for on thee I cast my care...' If God would only fight for the queen now, maybe she would be saved from her enemies who wanted to destroy her. Perhaps if he said those same words to God, even though he had often been very bad himself, God would hear him. Burying his face in his bolster, Hal whispered, 'Fight thou, Lord, in her stead,' and then added, for himself as much as for the queen, 'for on thee I cast my care.' Comforted, Hal was soon fast asleep.

The following day Lady Jane told Hal more of the strange events that had taken place. Apparently the queen had spoken a little too freely to the king about the state of his soul in the sight of God, and Bishop Gardiner and Thomas Wriothesley, who were visiting Henry at the time, could see how annoyed the king looked. Here at last was their opportunity. As soon as the queen had left they seized the moment to paint a picture of her as a heretic, refusing to obey the king's laws about reading the Bible and disobeying other religious laws passed by Parliament. Even worse, she had presumed to preach a sermon to the king himself! Irritated and in pain, the king was indeed offended with Katherine and when these two crafty men presented him with an indictment against the queen all ready for him to sign, together with a warrant for her arrest, he was easily persuaded. As soon as the ink was dry on the paper, the two schemers left Whitehall and were about to organize armed men to seize the queen—until Wriothesley discovered that he could not find that vital piece of paper bearing the king's signature.

'What's going to happen, then?' asked Hal anxiously.

'I know not,' replied Lady Jane, 'but I hear that Her Majesty wept sore when she read so grievous an indictment against her. Nay, nor would she be comforted by any, for now she knew that she too would die in as fearful a manner as did our Queen Anne Boleyn, or even My Lady Anne Askew. Hearing by a messenger of his queen's dire distress, our king first sent his physician to discover the cause of her trouble, and then ordered that he himself should be carried to her bedchamber. They tell that he has forgiven her for her wrong.'

'Then is she safe once more?' was Hal's next question.

'Who can tell?' replied Jane. 'With our king in so great pain, no one's life is secure.'

When Hal heard the remainder of this extraordinary saga from his mother, Elizabeth, several days later, he knew in his heart that God had indeed saved Queen Katherine from her enemies. He learnt that when the queen visited her husband the next evening, she cast herself on his mercy and begged once again for his forgiveness for her folly, pleading that her only motive in talking to him about religion was to turn his mind away from his acute suffering and to cheer and comfort him.

'And is it even so, sweet heart?' replied Henry as he kissed his wife tenderly. 'Then perfect friends are we now again, as ever at any time heretofore.'

The next day, as the queen sat in the sunshine with Henry in the gardens at Whitehall, both were alerted by the approach of tramping feet. Between the bushes they could glimpse shining axeheads attached to long poles gleaming among the trees. They were carried by forty soldiers, for Thomas Wriothesley, unaware that his plans had gone seriously wrong, had come to arrest the queen and conduct her to the Tower of London. Amazed to see her sitting beside the king and apparently chatting cheerfully to him, Wriothesley bent down to whisper something in Henry's ear. 'Fool, beast, arrant knave, begone!' roared the enraged monarch. Without a second's delay Wriothesley and his forty men withdrew, knowing full well that the next moment it could be the chancellor's turn to be conducted to the Tower. Katherine, who had not immediately understood the purpose of the Lord Chancellor's mission, kindly asked the king to forgive him, but Henry merely told her, 'Ah, poor soul! Thou little knowest how evil he deserveth... On my word, sweet heart, he hath been to thee a very knave.'

Hal rocked with laughter as he heard the story, and was even more pleased when he heard that both Wriothesley and Bishop Gardiner had now lost the king's favour, and therefore their own power to harm the queen or any of her ladies-in-waiting who believed and studied the Scriptures.

10
Bishop Bonner's bonfire

Adrian Stokes had been out all day accompanying Lady Jane and other members of the royal household on a hunt. Hal had watched from high up in his tower room as the hunt set out: hounds yelping, horses stamping impatiently, all waiting for the signal for the hunt to begin. Hal knew well that Jane would have much preferred to spend the time studying, but as her cousin Prince Edward was also to be there, together with Lady Catherine Brandon's boys, Henry and Charles, she had no choice in the matter.

With time on his hands after all his duties in the kitchens were completed, Hal wandered around the palace grounds. Shouts from the handsome new octagonal cockpit recently built by order of the king arrested his attention. Like any other boy, Hal enjoyed watching a fight, and because he was one of Lady Jane's personal attendants, he was allowed to enter the cockpit without paying the usual charge of one penny. Finding a seat as near to the action as he could, Hal watched as the unfortunate gamecocks, with spurs reinforced with extra pieces of bone, flew viciously at each other, clawing wildly. At last one limp bundle of feathers lying motionless on the ground, not far from where Hal was sitting, proclaimed the other bird the winner.

Leaving the cockpit, Hal discovered that a dinner of boiled beef and vegetables was waiting for him in the kitchens, cooked by his mother. Soon afterwards he decided to return to his attic room. Rays of late September sunshine streamed in through the narrow windows, bathing the usually dark corners with a warm glow, turning the fine threads of the cobwebs high up among the rafters to silver. Again Hal thought of the days he had spent studying the spiders while lying on his back after he had broken his leg three years earlier. With little else to do now, he began to watch the boats passing up and down the river, but after a while decided that this might be a good opportunity to read a little more of his New Testament while he was sure that Adrian was out.

The tension at the Palace of Whitehall had eased since Bishop Gardiner and Lord Chancellor Wriothesley had fallen from the king's favour, although Hal well knew that the queen still grieved over the cruel death of her lady-in-waiting, Anne Askew. In spite of this, the ruling against possessing any writings by men such as Master Tyndale, Master Coverdale or of any other Reformer remained in force. Hal had heard that the Bishop of London, Edmund Bonner, had organized a massive bonfire to be held at St Paul's Cross on 26 September in order to destroy all the Bibles and any other such writings that frightened citizens had handed in. Hal felt angry inside that the bishop should order the books to be burnt in that way. He thought of how Master Tyndale had become an exile from his homeland, and was eventually betrayed and killed because of his determination to give the people God's words in English so that they could all read them. Glad that no one had discovered that he himself owned a copy of William Tyndale's New Testament, Hal knew he must be extra careful. When young Prince Edward became king things would be different—of that he felt sure—but now the times were dangerous.

Turning away from the window, Hal crossed over to his mattress and reached under it to find his book. He could not feel it at first, which was strange, as he always left it in the same spot. Stretching out his arm as far as he could, he felt all around under the mattress, but still could not find his New Testament. Quickly the boy scrambled to his feet and rolled up his mattress in order to make a thorough search.

Then the colour drained from Hal's face. It was not there. His New Testament was nowhere to be found. Whatever could have happened to it? Perhaps, he thought desperately, he had put it somewhere else, although in his heart he knew he had not. Crossing over to the chest where he kept his personal possessions and clothes, he opened the lid and began peering inside. Just at that moment he heard footsteps coming up the stairs and so he shut the lid quickly. Adrian was back sooner than he had expected.

'Lost something?' enquired Adrian casually, as he entered the room, and flung himself down on his mattress. He had arrived just in time to see Hal shutting the lid of his chest. 'The hunt was fine,' he continued. 'Master Henry Brandon shot the stag—killed it straight away, quite the biggest I have ever seen; you should have seen the size of its antlers.'

In spite of Adrian's chatter, the look of concealed glee on his face told Hal everything. He realized in a flash that Adrian must have suspected that he possessed a New Testament and have searched for it while he was out of the room. What had Adrian done with it? Then another thought crossed his mind—one that he tried to push away at first. Could Adrian possibly have given his precious New Testament to Master Jacobs to be added to Bishop Bonner's bonfire? It seemed almost too painful to think about—how could he dare do such a thing? But Hal's most valued possession had gone, and yet he was afraid to say a word about it in case it led him into further trouble. A surge of hatred welled up in Hal's heart against Adrian Stokes: one day he would pay him back for so wretched a deed ... one day... And now he had lost his opportunity to read God's book for ever.

Hal made no reference at all to his missing New Testament—at least he could rob Adrian of the opportunity to gloat over him—but somehow the other boy had gained a secret power over Hal. At any moment he could betray him to the church and Hal knew well that he would be defenceless if it were discovered that he had hidden the book rather than obey the will of Parliament. At the same time fresh tensions were gripping the royal court. Everywhere Hal went he found small groups of Privy Councillors whispering darkly among themselves in corners. What could be the cause? Hal saw little of Lady Jane, since much of her time was now spent at Greenwich Palace, or even as far off as Enfield Palace, where she was studying. The queen did not need her, it seemed, for she spent most of her time at the bedside of the sick king. Hal soon guessed that the sense of impending crisis was because Henry VIII could not have much longer to live, and all the Privy Councillors were juggling for positions of power in the government which would take over until Edward was old enough to reign alone.

As Christmas approached rumours spread around the court that the king was now certainly dying. Few were allowed to see him; even the queen and his daughters, Mary and Elizabeth, were not permitted to visit his apartments, but were sent to Greenwich Palace. Here they stayed until early January 1547, by which time the king, who was feeling a little better, summoned the queen back to Whitehall. Hal was glad to accompany Lady Jane to Greenwich and to be free from Adrian's watchful eyes for a short while.

These were frightening days and nobody knew quite what would happen when the king died. For thirty-seven years he had held the lives of his subjects in his hands, sending anyone who happened to offend him to face the executioner's block. Sometimes Catholics faced torture and burning, sometimes Protestants, depending upon Henry's political circumstances or current religious inclinations. Even as recently as four weeks ago the young Earl of Surrey, Henry Howard, a man whom Hal had admired, had been arrested and sent to the Tower on a rumour that he might try to push his own claim to the throne after the death of the king. No one was surprised when the earl was sentenced to death on 21 January. Henry VIII was determined that Prince Edward alone would succeed to his kingdom, and so any possible rivals must be eliminated.

Among all the noblemen, churchmen and Privy Councillors who crowded to the court in those days, there were two whom Hal noticed in particular. Both fascinated him, but for different reasons. The first was Sir Thomas Seymour, Prince Edward's younger uncle. Tall and with a striking red beard, the young man was dashingly handsome and ambitious. His loud voice and boisterous laugh echoed around the palace, and no one could avoid noticing him whenever he was present. Hal was even more impressed by the reports that few, if any, could ever unseat him in the tournaments.

Athletic and rich, he was the sort of man any boy might admire. But Hal had noticed something else as well. Whenever the queen was passing between the king's apartments and her own, Sir Thomas was never far away. With low sweeping bows he paid his respects to Her Majesty and, judging by the way the colour rose in the queen's cheeks when she saw him, it was clear that he was trying to gain her attentions.

The second man whom Hal noticed was the archbishop, Thomas Cranmer. Serious and manly, the archbishop often looked troubled and Hal wondered why that was. Perhaps, like the queen, he was concerned about the soul of the dying king. Sometimes Hal wished he could speak to the archbishop. Often at night as he tossed about on his lumpy mattress questions would come into his mind— questions for which he had no answers—and now that he had lost his New Testament he feared he might never find the answers. The last words that his father had spoken would come back to Hal's mind: 'Don't grow up to be a bad man like I've been.' But how could he stop being bad? That was the question he still asked himself. And was there any way that bad people could go to heaven?

On Sundays Hal would listen to the court preachers together with the rest of the palace staff. The queen was usually there, and so was King Henry when he was well enough. Dressed in his best court clothes, Hal would sit very still not far from Lady Jane, but usually he did not understand what the preachers were saying, and before long his thoughts would be far away. But one Sunday early in January the archbishop was to be the preacher. Hal decided that he must try extra hard to understand what he was saying. Slowly Master Cranmer climbed up into the tall pulpit and opened the large Bible—one that looked exactly like the Bible that Master Aylmer read from back at Bradgate. His very first words gripped Hal's attention:

> Because all men are sinners and offenders against God
> and breakers of his law and commandments, therefore
> can no man by his acts, works and deeds (seem they
> never so good) be justified and made righteous before
> God.

Hal's heart sank. Was there no hope for him, then, however good he tried to be?

But before he had time to give in to the wave of despair that began to sweep over him, he heard the archbishop continuing:

> It is our duty ever to remember the great mercy of God, how that he sent his only Son our Saviour Christ into this world to fulfil the law for us by shedding his most precious blood, to make amends to his Father for our sins... No-one is justified by the works of the law, but freely by faith in Jesus Christ.[1]

The archbishop's sermon went on for a long time, and before long Hal's attention had drifted, and even Mistress Ellen looked as if she was about to go to sleep. But at least Hal had understood one thing: there was mercy for poor men and women, but it was not to be earned by doing good deeds. 'Freely by faith in Jesus Christ' were the exact words Master Cranmer had used and Hal repeated them over to himself several times, so he could think about them later.

As those short dark January days gradually wore to a close, all knew that the king could die at any time. His strength was gradually draining away and during that last week of January Queen Katherine was summoned once more to his bedside. 'It is God's will that we should part,' whispered the dying man and then, battling against tears, he motioned for her to go away, for he could say no more. It seemed that in spite of his uncertain tempers he had truly loved his last queen. Before long he was scarcely able to whisper. At last one of his physicians dared to tell the king that he must prepare to die, as nothing more could be done for him—something no one had been bold enough to tell him before. Then Henry indicated that he wished to see Archbishop Cranmer.

On receiving the summons, the archbishop hurried to Whitehall from his home in Croydon, but by the time he arrived Henry could no longer speak. As he saw his old friend standing in the doorway, the king merely stretched out his hands towards him. Solemnly the archbishop crossed the room and grasped the king's hand. 'Your

---

[1]   Thomas Cranmer, *Writings and Letters*, Cambridge, 1846, p.128.

Majesty, put your trust in Christ alone, and implore him for his mercy,' he urged. Seeing that the king was fast failing, he continued: 'Give me some token with your eyes or hand that you trust in the Lord.' The dying king pressed Cranmer's hand with as much strength as he was able, and only a few hours later this monarch who had himself sent so many to their deaths was summoned to face the Judge of all.

11
Meeting Master Squires

Never could Hal have imagined a more splendid occasion than the accession and coronation of the nine-year-old Prince Edward to be King of England, Ireland and France. For two days Londoners were agog with excitement: first came the royal procession through the city, and all who were able crowded the streets to watch the new king pass by on his progress from the Tower of London to the Palace of Whitehall. The boy was seated high up on a magnificent horse, its crimson saddlecloth contrasting with his shining silver gown, embroidered with gold and studded with rubies and diamonds. Even Edward's white velvet cap, gleaming with jewels, seemed to brighten up the grey February day. Impressively dressed nobles, the very men Hal had seen whispering in corners not long before the death of the old king, rode on each side of Edward. Ahead, leading the procession, was Sir Henry Grey himself, Lady Jane's own father, bearing the sword of state.

As the colourful pageant entered the City of London along Mark Lane, a volley of cannon fire boomed from the battlements of the Tower, while roars of 'Yea, yea! Long live King Edward!' sounded from every throat. A robed choir sang his praises from the corner of

Fenchurch Street, and other attractions were staged along the route to amuse the young monarch during the four-hour parade. Lady Jane, dressed in a velvet gown of Tudor green, her long auburn hair flowing down her back, had a place of honour in the procession, for she was now third in line to the throne according to the will of the dead king. Next to her rode her mother, Lady Frances, and her seven-year-old sister Katherine. Behind them walked Hal, wearing his new scarlet breeches and embroidered jacket. Surely this was a day he would never forget. Wherever they turned as the parade wound its way slowly through the streets of London to its destination at the Palace of Whitehall, resounding cheers and cries of 'God save the king!' greeted the boy from his loyal and enthusiastic citizens.

The coronation itself was to take place the following day in Westminster Abbey, a short walk from the palace. Privy Councillors, gentry with their ladies, churchmen and dignitaries from all over the country had gathered for the occasion, and Hal found himself crushed up against one of the abbey's massive stone pillars. Lady Jane was seated nearby on a hard wooden bench between her mother and sister. Not far away from them sat the two princesses, thirteen-year-old Elizabeth and her half-sister Mary, already thirty years of age, her face careworn and bitter.

Gloomy and cold, the old abbey smelt of incense, and Hal shivered as he glanced towards the boy seated on St Edward's Chair. Now robed in crimson with St Edward's Crown on his head, he seemed so young, no older than Lady Jane herself. But even so he was listening earnestly to Master Cranmer's words—words addressed to him alone, but echoing and re-echoing around the immense walls of the old abbey so that everyone could hear:

> You are to reward virtue, to revenge sin, to justify the innocent, to relieve the poor, to procure peace, to repress violence, and to do justice throughout your realms...

Hal wondered how a boy of nine could possibly do all those things, and yet he well knew that if Edward had been king Lady Anne Askew would never have been tortured and burned. Nor would his New Testament have been thrown on the Bishop of London's bonfire. Hal glanced across at the hard-faced bishop standing not far from him, his rotund form hidden under a magnificent clerical gown. Perhaps he would not be a bishop for much longer now that Edward was king, thought Hal hopefully.

The sermon seemed to go on for a long time, for the archbishop had much to say about the changes that he hoped would take place in the country now that Edward was king, but Hal was not really listening to him. 'What is going to happen to Lady Jane now that Katherine Parr is no longer queen?' he wondered. Perhaps they could all go back home to Bradgate Park. At least he would be safer there and away from Adrian Stokes' watchful eyes.

Back at the Palace of Whitehall once more with all the celebrations over, Hal soon learned that Lady Katherine, as he must now learn to call her, was moving to her own home, Chelsea Manor, a stately mansion given to her by Henry, which lay a short distance upriver from Whitehall. Everything was bustle and hurry as the former queen's household prepared for the move. Hal felt sorry for young King Edward, for Katherine had cared for him like a mother, and now it seemed that he might hardly see her at all. Apparently Lady Elizabeth was to join her stepmother at Chelsea.

Two days later, as Hal was busy cleaning out the fires in Lady Jane's apartment, he suddenly became aware of a large figure filling the doorway. Looking up sharply, he saw none other than Lady Frances standing there. As Hal hastily jumped to his feet, she addressed the boy: 'Master Hal, I will have you prepare to return to Leicestershire tomorrow morning,' she snapped. 'Master Jacobs is already packing the carts and you will assist him when you have finished your tasks here. My daughter tells me you have performed your court duties well,' she added in a kinder voice. A surge of relief swept over Hal, first because he was going home and also because it did not seem that Lady Frances had received any adverse reports about him from Adrian.

'I thank you, ma'am,' he said, bowing slightly.

'My daughters will spend some weeks at Suffolk Place with us, for Sir Henry has matters of importance to which he must attend,' she told Hal, and as an afterthought continued, 'Master Adrian will also

remain in London with us and with your mother and Mistress Ellen.'
Finishing his tasks quickly, Hal joined Master Jacobs, helping him
pack the carts. He was thankful to note that the older man seemed to
be in a good mood and was even whistling a merry tune. He too
appeared pleased at the prospect of returning to Bradgate and to his
family. 'We leave at first light,' he announced as the last cords were
tightened over the baggage, 'and I will have no delaying.'

Up as soon as the early grey streaks of dawn stole in through the
turret windows, Hal dressed hastily and crossed over to the kitchens
where his mother was already waiting with some hot porridge and
food prepared for the first day. Out through the palace gates the two
carts rumbled, Hal following close behind Master Jacobs. Because
there were no longer any costly gifts among the baggage, they decided
to travel north along Watling Street rather than the roads they had
taken before. But first they must pick their way along the Strand, and
both Hal and Jacobs had difficulty in avoiding the many gaping
potholes in the road, filled with stagnant water from the recent heavy
rains. Before long they passed the great gates to Seymour Place, home
of the red-bearded Lord Thomas Seymour whom Hal had seen
paying his attentions to the queen.

On into Fleet Street they trundled and across the Fleet Bridge. Hal
glanced down at the murky waters of the Fleet, choked as usual with
rubble and silt. Turning sharply left, they followed the road which ran
parallel to the great walls of the city, towering high above them, walls
that seemed to shout defiance at the very strongest of enemies.
Before long they had passed the heavy, grim-looking archway leading
to Newgate Prison. Hal felt an inner revulsion creeping over him as
he thought of Lady Anne Askew, who had been tortured so terribly in
that place. He wished with all his might that they could avoid
crossing Smithfield, where she and three others had perished in the
flames for no other offence than that of believing the things they read
in the Bible.

Hal hoped that they might rest a while in the village of Islington,
but Master Jacobs called over his shoulder, 'We must reach Muswell
Hill by midday and Barnet by nightfall, for the days are short. We dare
not enter Boreham Wood once darkness gathers.' But progress was
slow and the bitter wind whipped newly fallen snow in their faces.

Again and again their cartwheels stuck in the mud-filled ruts, and only by harnessing both horses to the one cart could they manage to pull them free. Certainly February was no time of the year to be on the roads. Hal was exhausted by the time the small inn at Barnet at last came into sight, and after the best rabbit stew the landlord could produce, both Hal and Master Jacobs were grateful for a night's rest.

Leaving Barnet early the next morning, they soon found themselves on the outskirts of Boreham Wood. The path through the wood was dark and muddy, but at least there was shelter from the biting winds and before long the travellers reached the old Roman road of Watling Street, which was in better repair than many of the roads they had travelled the previous day. By night on the second day they had reached St Albans once more and by the end of the third were back at the Cock and Hen in Dunstable. Sitting down beside a roaring log fire, Hal held out his frozen hands to warm. But there was something else on his mind as well. If only he could see the black-bearded man with the small eyes and the raucous laugh again, he might be able to return his gold sovereign which he had taken from under the table. Day after day Hal had worried lest Adrian should find some way of causing more trouble for him over that money. Now he scanned every face in the tavern anxiously but it seemed an empty hope.

Then he heard it—a loud, unmistakable cackle of laughter coming from the yard outside the tavern. Hal jumped in spite of himself and Master Jacobs, who was just finishing off his beef-and-onion stew, had noticed it. Huffing and puffing and shaking the rain off his thick black beard like a wet dog, the owner of the laugh entered the tavern. Quite clearly he was a regular customer, for the landlord roared his welcome: 'How fares it with you, good Master Squires?'

'As well as may be, for a rough night it is, Master Green,' replied the other, squeezing his ample body down beside Hal near the fire. 'And I will have some of that stew, if this young man has not eaten it all.'

Hal felt his heart thumping wildly as he plunged his hand deep into the pocket of his breeches to feel for the gold sovereign. If he did not take this opportunity he might never have another chance. So anxious was he to speak to Master Squires that he was unaware that Master Jacobs was watching him closely.

'And if it please you, sir,' began Hal. The stranger turned and gazed at the speaker, his small black eyes twinkling.

'What may you be wanting with me, my good young friend?' enquired Squires in a voice loud enough to be heard in every corner of the tavern. All eyes turned towards Hal and Master Squires. If Jacobs had not noticed anything before, he certainly had by now.

'If it please you, sir,' Hal repeated, 'this is your sovereign. I found it on the floor while you were playing backgammon when Master Jacobs over there and I were here last.' The words had come out with a rush, and now it was Master Squires' turn to look amazed. Then he began to guffaw with laughter.

'Now could you believe it? Could you ever believe it? A boy returns a sovereign piece to me from under the table. Could you believe it? Who's your master, boy?' Hal jerked his thumb towards Master Jacobs, who was now standing over Hal.

'Sir, in my reckoning Master Hal here stole that money,' interrupted Jacobs, 'I have good reason to know...' But Master Squires was not taking any notice of the accusation.

'Stole it? Stole it?' he thundered, 'Not he.' And turning to Hal he declared, 'By my troth, young man, you are as honest a fellow as ever I have seen. You are to keep that sovereign. Do ye hear? You are to keep it. And if you ever have any trouble,' he added, shooting a quick glance at Master Jacobs, 'just you say that Master Ebenezer Squires, Master of Horse for the late Sir Charles Brandon, Duke of Suffolk, and his good wife, the Princess Mary Rose, has given it to you.'

Hal was speechless with surprise. Master Jacobs' face had gone the colour of a beetroot. To think, Master Squires had actually held an honourable position in the duke's household. Certainly, he dared say no more. 'I thank you, sir,' was all Hal could manage to say, but in his heart he determined that he would save the sovereign in order to buy another New Testament like the one he had lost.

Before positioning himself at the backgammon table for an evening's gaming, Master Squires had informed all in the tavern that he was on his way to London to take up an appointment as Master of Horse to the honourable Sir William Cecil, secretary to the new Lord Protector of England, Edward Seymour, now named as Duke of Somerset. But as Hal was helping Master Jacobs to harness the horses the following morning, the black-bearded man suddenly approached them.

'And whither are you bound this day, my young friend?' he boomed.

'We journey to Leicestershire, sir,' replied Hal, 'for we are in the service of My Lady Frances of Bradgate House.'

'Ho! Ho! Ho!' roared Master Squires. 'And who would have thought that? Why I remember her ladyship as a small wench, and a fine one she was too! Ho! Ho! Ho! Now, young man,' he continued in a more serious voice, 'if ever you stand in need of help, just you ask for Master Ebenezer Squires,' and still chuckling to himself he set off to harness his own horse.

For two more weeks Hal and Master Jacobs were on the road. Travelling conditions were bad, and both were exhausted each night as they reached some wayside tavern. At no time did Master Jacobs refer to the incident at the Cock and Hen; nor did Hal think it was wise to raise the matter. Both were thankful when at last they turned down the long tree-lined avenue leading to Bradgate House.

12
The missing bracelet

Everyone at Bradgate House was under suspicion. A costly bracelet belonging to Lady Frances was missing. With inset rubies and diamonds and made of the finest gold, the bracelet had been carefully inscribed with her name. It was worth at least £50, a working man's wage for ten years or more. But the financial value was not Lady Frances' main concern. After all, she had more expensive jewellery than that. No, it was its associations. It was the fact that her own mother, the Princess Mary Rose, favourite sister of Henry VIII, had given it to Frances as a wedding present in 1533. The princess, the beauty of the London court, had died shortly afterwards, and Frances, who was still only sixteen at the time, had been heartbroken. This was a last gift from her mother—perhaps the only person Frances had ever really loved in her life—and now the precious bracelet was lost.

Without doubt some member of the household staff had stolen it; the most likely culprit would be someone with connections in the village of Newtown Linford. It could then be smuggled from Bradgate House and passed on to a relative or friend to be sold.

'Sooth, ma'am, I ain't touched it, I ain't,' declared Meg Saunders vehemently when she was questioned. 'Why, ma'am, could I do so terrible a thing?'

'Search all her belongings,' commanded Lady Frances dryly, her eyes swollen and red with crying. But there was no evidence that Meg Saunders had stolen the bracelet. Day after day the search continued, as all members of the household had their possessions examined for any sign of the missing bracelet. Then Adrian Stokes had a thought. Surely, Hal Tylney was the sort of boy who stole things. Hadn't he stolen that gold sovereign he had in his possession in London? So why not the bracelet? Adrian had not heard about the incident at the Cock and Hen in Dunstable, nor had Hal had any wish to tell him about it. Perhaps, decided Adrian, he ought to share his suspicions with Lady Frances. Even though Lady Jane had not taken him seriously when he had accused Hal of stealing while they were in London, Lady Frances surely would, and particularly at this moment. With free access to the family apartments, a privilege none other outside the family was granted, it was not long before Adrian had told Lady Frances of his fears regarding Hal.

'I understand you had a gold sovereign hidden in your shoe in London, Hal Tylney,' snapped Lady Frances. 'Where did you get it from?'

'Ma'am, I found it under the table at the tavern in Dunstable, and I put it in my shoe for safe keeping. It belonged to Master Ebenezer Squires and I wished to return it to him, but he had already left early the next morning. You may ask Master Jacobs, ma'am, and he will tell you. When I saw Master Squires once more as we returned from London I gave it back to him, but he refused it, telling me to keep it.'

'And what do you know of Master Squires, young man?' demanded Lady Frances, her eyes wide with astonishment.

'Ma'am, he told us he was Master of Horse to your father, the honourable Duke of Suffolk, ma'am. We met him twice at the Cock and Hen in Dunstable. He was travelling to London to take up a new appointment with Sir William Cecil.'

'You may go,' said Lady Frances sharply. 'So strange a story I never heard, and most surely I will be asking Master Jacobs for his account, and let me suggest that if I discover you to be lying, you will hang for your crime.' Troubled by the accusation and even angrier that Adrian should have chosen this moment to make it, Hal was yet hopeful that Master Jacobs would give a true account of the incident, and so resumed his work.

It was mid-April in 1547. Edward had been king for little more than two months, but already changes were beginning to take place. Master Aylmer, who had listened sympathetically to the story of how Hal had lost his New Testament, had told him that the laws against possessing the book had now been repealed. He had accepted the gold sovereign from Hal to keep it safe, assuring the boy that when he next travelled to London he would use it to buy him a replacement for his loss.

Lady Jane had returned to her studies with Master Aylmer, but she did not look happy. Hal guessed that she was missing Lady Katherine and all the freedom she had enjoyed in court life. More than this, there were rumours flying around about a marriage contract for Jane. It was an open secret that Sir Henry and Lady Frances were anxious that the girl should make a marriage that would give them, as her parents, a yet more significant position in the country. Perhaps this was the 'business' that had detained the family in London after the coronation. 'Aye, and I've heard she might even marry His Majesty King Edward,' boasted Meg. Hal said nothing, but in his heart he hoped that this might indeed happen, for he had seen how happy the cousins were together.

One bright spring morning two weeks after it had been discovered that the gold bracelet was missing, Hal was hard at work chopping up logs. Sitting down on a tree stump to rest his arms for a few moments, he suddenly heard a rustling noise in the hedgerow behind him. He turned sharply and saw a cheeky-looking robin not far away watching him with its bright beady eyes, head cocked on one side. Perhaps she has a nest nearby, thought the boy, and being curious, he stood up to investigate. Carefully he parted the twigs and peered around, as the robin protested loudly with a warning 'tic-tic' cry. Yes, there it was, compact and carefully woven together, complete with four white eggs, speckled with red. Hal marvelled at the sight.

Then he saw something else. Just below the nest, caught on a small twig, was what appeared to be a large ring, gleaming in the spring sunshine. Hal reached out and grasped the ring, but it was not a ring; he knew immediately that this must be the missing bracelet. Hal gasped with astonishment as he held the beautiful thing in his hand. He rubbed it on his jacket and saw the name 'Frances' inscribed in the gold. Clearly Lady Frances must have caught it on the branch as she was walking past. No one had stolen it at all. Hal sat down on a log with a thump. He was trembling all over. Whatever was he going to do? If he told Lady Frances that he had found her bracelet, she would never believe him. He would be accused of theft and doubtless would be hung like poor Hugh Lambert. Hal knew well that boys could be hung even for stealing apples. Anyone stealing such a bracelet could not hope to escape. But if he put it back on the branch, she might never have the joy of finding her bracelet again.

Then an idea occurred to Hal. At first he dismissed it, but gradually it seemed more and more attractive. Why, here at last was the opportunity he had been looking for to pay Adrian Stokes back for stealing his New Testament, and even more for suggesting to Lady Frances that he might be the thief. He would put the bracelet in the pocket of Adrian's doublet. Then the other boy would have the problem of explaining to Lady Frances just how and why it was there. And what better opportunity than that very afternoon, when a big hunt was to take place and the whole house would be deserted? It scarcely crossed his mind that Adrian too might be hung for theft. He was Lady Frances' favoured servant, and would escape lightly. As soon as the hunt was well underway, silent as a shadow, Hal crept into Adrian's apartment and slipped the bracelet into his doublet pocket. Unseen by any, he returned to his work and waited to see what would happen.

He had not long to wait. Terrified at the discovery, and at a loss to understand how it should be in his pocket, Adrian knew immediately that he was in deep trouble. With personal access to the family apartments he would have had a unique opportunity to steal the bracelet; how else could it have come to be in his possession? Someone must have put it in his pocket—but who? Even his protestations of innocence would sound hollow in the circumstances and his suggestion that Hal might be the thief would certainly turn against him now. Only one course of action seemed open to him, and he decided on it immediately. Slipping into the family parlour later that evening, Adrian placed the bracelet behind a large vase, hoping that when Lady Frances next went in she would think it had been there all the time. But just as he was leaving he heard footsteps approaching. Sir Henry entered the room and the look of guilt on the boy's face immediately aroused his suspicion. Sir Henry had never liked Adrian—in truth he resented his wife's affection for the lad—an affection she had made a little too obvious, and which was becoming a point of gossip among the staff.

'And what do you think you are doing here, young man?' enquired Sir Henry brusquely.

'Nought, my good lord, I ... I but searched for my lady,' stammered Adrian.

'Then go!' commanded Sir Henry.

When the bracelet was found in the morning, Sir Henry was quick to connect Adrian's secret visit with the discovery. Nothing that the stable lad could say would convince the marquess that Adrian was not the thief. 'You shall most surely hang for this,' he shouted angrily. 'Make your peace with God, for you hang at dawn tomorrow. I shall not have thieves in this place.' The sooner he could arrange for the execution, the better he would like it, for he feared that Lady Frances might intervene and beg for the boy's life.

Distraught with terror, Adrian fell to his knees, protesting his innocence. But it was useless. For Sir Henry the supposed crime presented an ideal opportunity to rid himself of a youth who had most obviously stolen his wife's affections. When Hal heard that Adrian was to hang for stealing the bracelet, he was appalled. Whatever had he done? He had only intended to give Adrian a severe fright. It would be better for him if he were hung instead. But what could he do now? Already the village gibbet was being erected, as Meg Saunders freely informed everyone.

That night Sir Henry could not sleep. In spite of his desire to rid himself of Adrian he was not an unjust man and at the back of his mind there was a nagging fear that the boy might indeed be innocent.

Lady Frances sobbed inconsolably and begged her husband to show pity, though she well knew that if it had been any other servant apart from Adrian she would not have hesitated to have the sentence carried out. At last he gave in. Rising from his bed, he strode over to the servants' quarters. Adrian was not in bed. He was cowering in the corner of the room, whimpering like a puppy, his face ashen. 'I have decided to show mercy, though I fain would see you strung up for so great a felony. You shall be beaten instead,' he announced. And with that he went back to his bed.

'Take the boy and thrash him soundly,' he commanded Jacobs in the morning.

Hal's relief when he heard that the sentence had been revoked was indescribable. Even the thought that Adrian was to be beaten, however—an experience that the favoured young man had not known before—gave him little satisfaction. His sin against Adrian weighed on his conscience. What if Adrian had been hung? He would have been responsible for his death. He would have been a murderer. How he wished he had never done it! It would have been many times better to leave the bracelet where he had found it, rather than to act as he had. But he saw no way now of putting things right with Adrian. To confess his offence would be to invite the most fearsome punishment. Nor would anyone believe that he was innocent of theft.

Hardly had things returned to normal at Bradgate House before a surprising visitor arrived. Hal was hard at work in the gardens one day early in May when he heard the drum of horses' hooves resounding on the path. Looking up quickly, he only had time to glimpse a tall, athletic-looking man with a long red beard pounding past him on a sweaty black steed. Hal knew the identity of the visitor in an instant: none other than Sir Thomas Seymour, now Lord Admiral of England. But why was he visiting Sir Henry Grey? Hal guessed, and guessed correctly, that it was something to do with Lady Jane. That night the place was buzzing with gossip as pieces of information about the important visitor filtered down among the household servants.

'Married her, he did, and so soon after his death. It weren't decent, that's what I say,' Meg Saunders was declaring roundly as Hal entered the scullery.

'Who has married who?' demanded Hal.

'Sooth, boy, ain't you heard? Why, My Lord Admiral has wed My Lady Katherine Parr—and our king not cold in his coffin ten weeks.' Hal said nothing. He was not surprised that Lady Katherine had married Thomas Seymour, for he had seen the attentions the admiral was paying to her even before Henry had died. But he was surprised that it had been so soon. That did not explain, however, why the admiral had come to Bradgate.

The next day, as Hal was at work in the gardens planting out young vegetables, he became aware of voices nearby. A tall hedge hid the speakers from view but one voice he recognized instantly was that of Sir Henry Grey, and he had little difficulty in guessing that the other was the Lord Admiral. 'Grant that she may but live with me, and I will hope to gain the marriage contract you desire,' one man was saying. Obviously they must be discussing Lady Jane's marriage plans. The girl would turn ten that year and it was time, in view of the customs of the time among the nobility, for some settlement to be made.

'My Lady Frances wishes to see you,' called one of the kitchen maids as Hal was cleaning out the fires the next morning. Smartening himself up as best he could, Hal presented himself at the door of the family parlour. Lady Frances gazed at him coldly. Recently turned fourteen, Hal had grown tall in the last year. He had matured during his time in London, and although he would never have Adrian's charming manner or looks, she had to admit reluctantly that Hal had served her well. Even so, she had never particularly liked him, and still found it hard to believe that her favourite had actually stolen her bracelet. But in the absence of any other explanation she had little option. Now Hal's serious grey eyes met her stony gaze.

'You asked to see me, ma'am?' he began.

'Yes, yes I did,' she replied. 'You must prepare to return to London in three days' time. You will travel with My Lord Admiral and my daughter, together with my daughter's attendants.'

'Whither are we bound, ma'am,' ventured Hal in surprise, 'and will Master Adrian accompany us?'

99

'What concern is that of yours?' snapped the impatient woman. 'But no, I need Master Adrian here, for I am training him up as my Master of Horse. The Lady Jane is to become ward of Sir Thomas and Lady Katherine. She wishes your services as her page once more and, having little other use for you, I have consented to her request. Your mother and Mistress Ellen will also go. And, yes, you will go to Chelsea Manor immediately but sometimes My Lady Katherine resides in her country home at Hanworth House.'

Frantic days of preparation followed. Hal only saw Jane on one occasion, but the fleeting smile she gave him assured him that she herself was pleased at the thought of returning to the care of Lady Katherine. She would share lessons with the Lady Elizabeth, who was living with her stepmother, and perhaps even see her cousin the young King Edward, although that was less likely as he was heavily protected wherever he went. The journey promised to be much easier. Not for the Lord Admiral any smoky, flea-ridden wayside taverns, but the best hospitality that could be provided by members of the aristocracy whose stately homes lay near the roads they would use. Once again Hal would drive the cart carrying all the baggage, but this time he would accompany the main party instead of going on ahead. Nor would he need Master Jacobs to help him, for at fourteen he was considered to be almost an adult.

The journey was leisurely, often with breaks of two or three days in any one place, but at last, towards the end of May, the party arrived at Chelsea Manor, not far from the Palace of Whitehall and once more overlooking the River Thames. Trade vessels and galley ships hurried backwards and forwards and boatmen plied the river carrying passengers to their varied destinations. Hal was delighted to discover he had a room to himself. Master Aylmer had returned his gold sovereign, instructing him as to where he could buy a replacement New Testament. 'At last,' thought Hal, 'I will be able to read God's book with no one to spy on me.'

Lady Katherine, now looking much more relaxed and happy, welcomed Jane warmly, throwing her arms around the girl, and even the Lady Elizabeth looked pleased to have her young cousin back once more. Tall, with long auburn hair similar in colour to Jane's, Elizabeth only threw a passing glance at Hal, who had accompanied

Jane to the schoolroom where they would share their lessons under Master William Grindal as their main tutor.

Hal soon found his bearings in his new surroundings, and even discovered that Lady Katherine remembered him from his time at Hampton Court. She had also heard that it was Lady Jane's page who had discovered the warrant for her arrest carelessly dropped by the former Lord Chancellor, Wriothesley, a discovery that had saved her life. Hal for his part learned with surprise that Lady Katherine herself had written a book, and might soon have it published—a thing which astonished Hal. 'It's called *The Lamentations of a Sinner*,' Jane had told him. That sounded a strange title to Hal. He wondered how such a good woman could possibly be a sinner. He could well understand that he was a sinner, and particularly after what he had done to Adrian Stokes, but surely not Lady Katherine? Perhaps one day he would buy that book.

In the meantime he was anxious to see if he could purchase a New Testament. A small shop in Chancery Lane sold them, Master Aylmer had told him. He must walk along the Strand, past Seymour Place and, just before entering Fleet Street, must make a sharp left turn into Chancery Lane. The shop was about halfway along the lane. Following the instructions carefully, Hal set out two days later. The small shop was open, and it was in the charge of a large, cheerful-looking man. Hal was delighted to find that the book he wanted so badly was available. 'But it will cost you twelve shillings and three pence, young sir,' said the bookkeeper doubtfully. His look of astonishment when Hal produced his gold sovereign added to the boy's satisfaction. At last Hal could read about the way to heaven, and even more about how his sins could be forgiven, without anyone to prevent him from doing so.

13
Can the Lord Admiral be trusted?

The Lord Admiral's presence seemed to fill Chelsea Manor. His hearty laugh resounded through the gardens and corridors. His tall athletic figure, gorgeous jewelled cloaks, flashy red beard and clever swordsmanship made him a natural focal point for the whole household. Lady Katherine adored him, and always accompanied him with obvious pride and delight. Lady Jane too laughed merrily at his jokes and enjoyed his witty conversation. But Hal Tylney was not quite so sure about the handsome, persuasive Thomas Seymour. He could not forget the attentions the Lord Admiral had paid to Katherine even before Henry VIII had died; nor did Hal like the tone in his voice which he had overheard at Bradgate when the admiral was discussing Lady Jane's marriage contract. It seemed to Hal that he was a man with many secret plans and great ambitions.

Lady Jane soon settled down happily at Chelsea. Her lessons with her older cousin gave her an extra challenge, for Elizabeth's tutor described his pupil as 'the brightest star' he had ever taught. Not only did the girls study Latin and Greek, but both were learning to play on the lute and often enjoyed playing duets together. For Hal the long summer evenings gave him plenty of time to himself. Sometimes he would sit with his mother and even began to read to her from his New Testament. Elizabeth Tylney was proud of her boy and tried to answer his questions, but she was worried about him as well, for each time he read to her he looked troubled, as if there was something on his mind.

'What troubles you, son?' she ventured one evening. Hal just shook his head, and said nothing. But the next day as he was reading to her from a place in the Bible where Jesus was saying that unless we forgive those who sin against us, his Father would not forgive our sins,[1] Hal had suddenly snapped the book shut and had run from the room. Elizabeth called after him, but was wise enough to realize that she must leave him alone. With a heavy heart Hal shut himself in his room for the rest of the evening, and one thought drummed through his mind: perhaps his sin against Adrian Stokes meant that God would never forgive his sins. Had he lost any chance of forgiveness? Hal did not know. If only there was someone to whom he could speak! But not even Lady Jane must know what he had done.

Not long after this a preacher arrived at Chelsea Manor whom Hal had never seen before—an old man with pinched features, a heavy moustache and long beard. Wisps of white hair strayed out from under his clerical cap and his strong hooked nose reminded Hal of an eagle. 'Old Father Latimer is going to preach today,' Lady Jane told Hal. 'He has only just been released from prison in the Tower.' Then Hal remembered that he had heard that Hugh Latimer, Bishop of Worcester, used to preach to Lady Katherine's court when she was queen. Then he had been thrown into prison, no one seemed to know quite why. Presumably he must have done something that offended King Henry. Now that Edward was king, the old bishop had been released and was preaching at court once more.

As the preacher climbed slowly into the huge five-sided pulpit, Hal noticed how stooped he seemed. 'He must be very old,' he thought to himself. 'Perhaps he is even noticed the deep wrinkles across Master

---

[1]   Mark 11:26

Latimer's forehead and the worn look on his face, as if he had suffered much in prison. Hal was afraid that he could never be brave enough to suffer in the way that the bishop must have done, or even worse, to face torture and death like Lady Anne Askew.

But as soon as the bishop started preaching, he no longer seemed old at all. His voice was strong; it reminded Hal of a storm breaking on a mountainside. The preacher's eyes seemed to pierce right through him into his deepest thoughts. Master Latimer was speaking about the sins of men and women whose lives are told in the Bible; many had done dreadful things, and yet God had forgiven them.

'They cannot have done anything as bad as I have done,' thought Hal miserably. Then the preacher said something that shone like a bright ray of light into Hal's troubled mind:

> Therefore, let us not despair, but put our trust in God and hope and believe in him ... for he is as merciful as ever he was, and he will pardon and forgive our sins: he is as mighty as ever he was, and therefore can do it; so I will seek him like Mary Magdalene and others have done and were saved.

Now Hal was listening, his eyes fixed on the preacher.

> If God should enter into judgement with us, none are able to stand before his face, neither will any of his saints be found just in his sight, not John the Baptist, or Peter or Paul, no, not even the mother of our Saviour... Therefore, take heed and do not be proud but put your only trust in Christ our Saviour.[2]

'That's just what Archbishop Cranmer said,' thought Hal; he remembered his very words: 'justified freely by faith in Jesus Christ'. If two such preachers were saying the same thing, they must be right. Perhaps there was hope for a fourteen-year-old boy, even though he had nearly caused the death of another boy.

---

[2]   *Sermons and Remains of Hugh Latimer*, Cambridge, 1845, pp.163, 194.

The weeks were passing, and the days were drawing in. Hal found himself homesick for the beauty of the Charnwood Forest in Leicestershire, for the reds and golds of the autumn trees. Low mists hung over the river and stole across the Chelsea Manor gardens, often making Hal feel sad and depressed. Overripe fruit fell heavily in the orchard and Hal would collect it and bring it in for the kitchen staff. As autumn gave place to raw winter days, he would spend time sitting near a comforting old stove in the manor kitchens; sometimes he read parts of his New Testament and often memorized his favourite passages. The accounts of the crucifixion of Christ made him sad, and also very angry with those who had so cruelly killed him, until one day he read some words in a letter written by one of the disciples called Peter which said, 'Christ suffered for our sakes ... and bore our sins in his own body on the tree.'[3] Those words silenced Hal.

Lady Jane meanwhile continued to enjoy her studies with Master Grindal and her cousin Elizabeth. She basked in the love of Lady Katherine, who treated her like her own daughter. Whenever she was free Jane would attend the Bible studies which Lady Katherine organized for her ladies at the court, and Hal was amazed at how much Jane knew about the Bible. She could read it in Greek and Latin as well as in English. Sometimes Hal asked her questions about the meaning of the things he read in his New Testament, but he was shy and usually kept his thoughts and fears to himself.

King Edward and his government were passing many laws to reform religion in England. Hal had seen images, crucifixes and pictures being hacked down and carried out of the churches around Chelsea Manor. Many services were now being conducted in English rather than Latin, which meant that Hal could understand all the prayers that were being said. Both Bishop Stephen Gardiner and Bishop Bonner, who had burnt his first New Testament, were in prison because they had not agreed with the new king's policies. Hal was glad about that—it was no more than they deserved after the dreadful things they had done to Lady Anne Askew and had tried to do to Katherine Parr.

---

3   1 Peter 2:24

During the early spring of 1548, when Jane had been at Lady Katherine's court for nearly ten months, an event took place which changed everything. Quite suddenly the Lady Elizabeth and all her attendants packed up their apartments at Chelsea Manor and left, never to return, or so it seemed. What had happened? Hal never found out exactly, but gossip was flying around among the staff. Lady Katherine, so he learnt, had become increasingly unhappy about the way her husband, Lord Admiral Thomas Seymour, was showering Elizabeth with his affection and, even worse, the way Elizabeth was enjoying his attentions. With no father of her own, Elizabeth was naturally responding warmly to her stepfather, not realizing the dangerous position she was placing herself in. Even Jane had been trying to warn her cousin, but it seemed that she was paying little attention. Then one day, so his mother told Hal, Lady Katherine caught her husband and the princess locked in a close embrace in the gardens of the Manor House. Understandably Katherine was furious, particularly as she was now expecting the admiral's baby—her first child. The only thing to do was to send Elizabeth away immediately before the scandal became public. Had not Elizabeth's mother, Anne Boleyn, been executed on suspicion of a similar offence?

Lady Jane missed her cousin, but was delighted to know about Lady Katherine's expected baby. Perhaps everything would now be all right. But even Jane was growing less certain about the Lord Admiral. He often disappeared for weeks at a time, and no one knew exactly what he was doing. Was he plotting to overthrow his older brother, the Protector, and place himself in a position of supreme power in the land? Everyone knew how much he resented Edward Seymour's authority. Lady Katherine no longer looked happy, but perhaps that was because she was feeling so ill—or maybe she knew something that others did not. Hal himself suspected the admiral's motives more and more each day.

In May 1548, not long after Princess Elizabeth had left, a stocky man with a serious expression alighted from his horse one day and led his tired animal in through the gates of Chelsea Manor. His clerical dress and small cap marked him out as a churchman, and Hal, who was just returning from escorting Lady Jane to her apartments, wondered who it could be.

'Young man, can you tell me the way to My Lady Katherine's apartments?' asked the stranger.

Hal gazed at the speaker curiously. Greying hair and heavy careworn features made the boy think that he must be almost as old as Father Latimer. And his sad, troubled expression suggested that he too had known much suffering in his lifetime.

'Good master,' Hal replied politely, 'you will find her ladyship in her private apartments through yonder archway. Would you wish me to stable your horse?'

The stranger nodded gravely and smiled, a smile that transformed his features. He passed the reins to Hal and made his way through the archway Hal had pointed out to him.

'Who was My Lady Katherine's visitor?' asked Hal when he next saw Jane.

'Why, it is my new tutor and my lady's new chaplain,' Jane had replied. 'His name is Master Miles Coverdale.'

'Master Coverdale!' echoed Hal in astonishment. 'The friend of Master William Tyndale?' Hal knew well that Master Coverdale had helped in the translation of parts of the Bible and had presented King Henry with the first complete Bible in English. Perhaps he could tell him more about Master Tyndale and answer some of his questions in the same way that Jane's tutor in Bradgate, Master Aylmer, had done.

He learnt from Jane that eight years earlier, in 1540, Master Coverdale had fled from his home to the Continent because his life had been in great danger from the same man who had hoped to destroy Lady Katherine, Bishop Stephen Gardiner. The bishop, who at that time had recently gained the favours of the king, was attempting to wipe out men who preached the truths of Scripture, and already Coverdale's close friend Master Robert Barnes had been arrested and burnt to death at Smithfield. Now Hal understood why the stranger showed such marks of suffering in his face. For eight years he had been an exile from his own country, but when Edward became king it was clearly safe to return.

Soon all the questions that Hal had hoped to ask the new chaplain were swept out of his mind as he heard the news that most of Lady

Katherine's household, numbering a hundred or more of her staff, were to move with her from London to a part of the country that Hal had never heard of before—Winchcombe, not far from the old town of Gloucester. There they would stay in a grand country home known as Sudeley Castle which King Edward had recently given to his younger uncle, Sir Thomas Seymour.

Katherine was to remain there until after the birth of her baby, due in three months' time. Lady Jane would accompany her, and of course that meant that Hal and Jane's lady attendants would go too, a prospect that delighted Hal.

14
A great loss

The move to Gloucestershire required days of preparation and Hal was kept busy helping to load the carts, groom the horses and check that all of Lady Jane's belongings were securely packed. At last the long cavalcade of horses and carts was ready for the road. Lady Katherine herself was to travel in a litter carried by four bearers, for her pregnancy meant that riding the bumpy roads might be a risk for her unborn child. Out through the dingy streets at the edges of the city they rode and were soon jogging along country lanes. Hal marvelled at the beauty all around him. With the may blossom weighing down trees and hedgerows, it looked as if it had been snowing in summer. The cheerful song of birds made him want to whistle in harmony with them.

For two weeks they travelled westwards. Sir Thomas accompanied his wife for part of the way, but then said he had urgent business to which he must attend and galloped off into the distance, back towards London. When they stopped for rests by the wayside, Jane delighted to pick bunches of bluebells and wood anemones for Lady Katherine, whom she loved like a mother. Hal would stretch himself out for a nap on the soft grass, knowing that the party was well protected against bandits by an armed guard. If it were not for Lady Katherine's anxious looks there would have been little to spoil the days.

At last the long journey ended as they rode into the village of Winchcombe, threading their way between low thatched-roofed cottages built from the local stone. Many villagers stood outside their front doors, staring in amazement at the colourful procession winding its way along the main street. 'To think I was born in a village like this!' said Hal to Betsy, one of the kitchen maids who was riding on the back of his cart. 'Sometimes I wish I could go back to my own village of Newtown, and just be a village boy again.'

'Then I should never see you any more,' pouted Betsy, who seemed to be enjoying Hal's company.

A sharp right-hand turn led up a narrow winding pathway, and before long Hal's horse was struggling to gain a foothold as it dragged the cart up the steep hill. Hal jumped down to lighten the load and, not surprisingly, Betsy was soon at his side.

At last they came to the magnificent gates of Sudeley Castle and trundled through. Hal gazed in wonder at his new home and found himself hoping earnestly that he might be happy here. Perhaps he might even be able to forget those troubles that so often kept him awake at night: a fear of the unknown and the guilt of his sins.

Life soon settled into an easy routine, and Hal enjoyed a measure of freedom he had not known since he had come into the service of the Marquess of Dorset and his wife. He was often able to roam the beautiful Cotswold countryside, to sit beside the clear, flowing brooks and drink the crystal water. Frequently Betsy found some excuse to accompany him, although her ample figure left her breathless as she tried to keep up with him. Like Meg Saunders back at Bradgate, Betsy seemed to pick up all the gossip from the kitchen staff, and her endless stream of chatter amused Hal, although he sometimes wished she would leave him alone.

For Hal was worried: it seemed as if some terrible thing were about to happen. He had felt the same when he first came to Hampton Court, and he had been right then, for Anne Askew was so shortly to be condemned to the fires at Smithfield. 'But can anything be wrong now?', he wondered. In addition, a sense of his own sins often fell like a heavy black cloud on his spirit. He had wronged Adrian Stokes—he knew that—and Adrian might still find some means of revenge, for Hal was well aware that Adrian suspected him of planting the bracelet in his pocket.

But that was not all. He often felt angry inside: angry against Lady Frances for the way she treated Jane, angry against his circumstances, that he must always remain a poor servant, even angry against God because of the sad death of his father. Deeper still were two other gnawing fears: he was afraid of death—any death, but most particularly a violent death if he should believe those truths he had read in his New Testament. A yet greater fear tormented him: perhaps he had already lost his last chance to believe. Maybe his sins were so great that God would never forgive him even if he wanted to believe.

Such thoughts were running through Hal's mind as he was alone one day working in the Sudeley gardens. Jane was at her lessons with Master Coverdale and, to his relief, Betsy was busy in the kitchens. Suddenly he became aware of soft footsteps and the gentle rustle of a lady's gown across the grass. Looking up quickly, he was amazed to see Lady Katherine herself approaching, and on her own as well, which was most unusual. What could she want with him? To Hal's amazement Lady Katherine seated herself on the grass bank beside him. Despite her own anxieties, she had clearly been waiting for a chance to speak to the youthful page on his own. Seeing him at work in the gardens, Lady Katherine had decided to take her opportunity.

'Master Hal,' she began, 'I owe you a debt of gratitude, for it was you who found the warrant for my arrest and saved me from certain death. I have long observed you and I am grateful for your faithful service to my young friend the Lady Jane, whom I love as my own child.'

By this time Hal was feeling slightly alarmed. Whatever could Lady Katherine wish to say to him? 'But I have noticed too that you look troubled and anxious,' she continued. 'My Lady Jane tells me that you often read the Scriptures when your duties are done. Is that the cause of your concern?'

'Yes, my lady, I do read the Scriptures, but I understand little of what I read,' replied Hal cautiously, not answering her question.

'Is that why you are troubled?' persisted Lady Katherine earnestly. And then she added some words which startled the young page: 'Christ is calling you, Hal. I know that for he also called to me. Even though I was the wife of a king, yet when the Prince of princes and the King of kings did speak many gentle words to me and called to me so many times—more times than I can number—I would not come to him. In spite of all his signs and tokens of love, I hid from him, hoping to escape his sight...'

Tears welled up in Hal's eyes. She could have been describing him. Lady Katherine had noticed this and continued kindly: 'I loved myself better than God and broke his holy and pure commandments.'

'If that could be true of you, my lady, what hope is there then for me?' Hal blurted out in spite of himself. 'For I have done things that I would not care that any should know.'

'Mine was the greater sin, my son,' replied Lady Katherine, 'for I trod under foot my Saviour and his sacrifice for sinners, nor did I think his blood poured out on the cross sufficient to wash me from the filth of my sins. "Only the Bishop of Rome can afford forgiveness to me," thought I. All other sins in the world, gathered together into one, are not so detestable in the sight of God as this.'

'How then did you find mercy?' asked Hal, hardly daring to hear the answer.

'My son,' answered Lady Katherine, turning searching eyes on the boy, 'I almost fell into despair, but then I said, "I will call upon Christ, the Light of the world and only relief for troubled consciences, for he alone can comfort repentant sinners." So by faith I called upon him and I was at last justified in his sight. Now I have tasted of the grace of God.'[1]

Such words from a woman who had once been Queen of England amazed Hal and lifted his spirit with hope and joy. Perhaps there was mercy for a poor peasant lad as well as for a queen. Perhaps his father's last wish that he should not grow up to be 'a bad man like me'

---

[1]   Quotations from Lady Katherine Parr's *The Lamentations of a Sinner*, published 1548

might yet be fulfilled. Lady Katherine rose to go as suddenly as she had come. She had a struggle to stand up again for her baby was soon due. With an embarrassed laugh Hal gave her a helping hand and then looked after her in wonder as she disappeared back towards the castle. Perhaps God had sent her to speak those few words to him, to assure him that there was still hope for him if he too called upon Christ to save him from his sins.

As August 1548 drew to a close excitement intensified at Sudeley Castle. Even Lady Jane chattered endlessly to Hal about the baby so soon to be born. Hal's mother, Elizabeth, had been appointed to care for Lady Katherine during the night and would sit quietly in the corner of the room while she slept. But during the long dark hours Katherine was often restless. Sometimes she spoke to herself in a low whisper. At first Elizabeth thought she might be praying, but then she realized she was talking in her sleep. 'Has he come yet?' she would ask time and time again. Elizabeth knew that she was waiting and hoping for her husband, the Lord Admiral, to arrive. But as day succeeded day Sir Thomas still did not come, even though he was well aware of when his baby was due. Sometimes Lady Katherine would say, 'Oh, may it be a boy...!' Once as she lay awake far into the night, she told Elizabeth that the admiral might be angry if the baby turned out to be a girl. 'And I so want to please him,' she added with a catch in her voice.

As Hal was hard at work in the gardens one day he caught the distant thud of a horse's hooves pounding up the hill towards the castle. Instinctively he knew who it was and hurried to open the gates. Without a glance at the boy who stood to attention as he passed, the Lord Admiral cantered up to the front door and with a graceful swing leapt from his horse, his jewelled cloak gleaming in the August sunshine. And he was only just in time. That very night Hal could hear the sound of running footsteps along the passageways and early in the morning of 30 August a tiny wail could be heard coming from Katherine's room. Shortly afterwards the Lord Admiral had left the room abruptly and had gone to his own apartments: the baby was a girl.

As soon as she woke in the morning Jane rushed to Lady Katherine's room, and gazed in wonder at the tiny bundle in the crib beside Katherine. Carefully Hal's mother lifted the newborn baby placing her in the girl's arms. Jane ran one finger gently across the small wrinkled face, whispering half to herself, and half to the baby, 'You're beautiful.'

But Lady Katherine turned large disconsolate eyes on her young friend. 'He wanted a boy,' was all she could say.

Jane passed the infant back to the midwife and sat down beside Lady Katherine. She slipped her small hand comfortingly into Katherine's. 'I shall love her dearly,' she announced.

Only a few friends gathered around when Master Miles Coverdale baptized the baby not many days later, for the infant, to be called Mary, was far from strong.

Yet even as the baby clung to life, it seemed clear that her mother was not regaining her strength. On the fourth day after Mary's birth Katherine's temperature began to rise, and before long it became obvious that she had succumbed to the dreaded child-bed fever—that frightening condition that took so many mothers to an early grave. Realizing how ill she was, Katherine called for quill and paper to make her will. All her vast wealth, houses, lands and jewels she bequeathed to her husband—one who had shown her little true affection. 'I wish I had a thousand times as much to leave him,' she commented sadly, laying down her quill, for she had loved him truly.

A short while later a loud laugh was heard outside the door, and with a rattle it opened and in came the admiral. After cracking a joke or two he strode across to Lady Katherine's bed, not sparing a glance for his infant daughter. 'How now, my sweet heart?' he roared.

'My lord, I am not well handled,' began the sick woman pathetically, 'for those that be about me care not for me, but stand laughing at my grief. The more good I will to them, the less good they will do to me.' Every eye in the room turned on the admiral, for all knew that he had been heard openly mocking his wife for bearing him a daughter and not a son.

'Why, sweet heart, I would do you no hurt!' exclaimed her husband in an offended voice.

'No, my lord, I think so,' responded Katherine weakly.

She spoke little after that. Each day she grew weaker. Jane scarcely left her bedside, clinging to her hand like a desolate child about to lose her mother. Even when Lady Katherine lost consciousness, Jane remained with her, and on the eighth day after the birth of little Mary Seymour, her mother died, leaving none to care for the infant. Lady Jane too had lost the best friend she had ever known.

Although Sir Thomas wept when his wife died, he was glad to discover that in her will she had left all her wealth to him—his plans required such resources. Without delay he saddled his horse and with a clatter of hooves was gone, for he had pressing business in London and must make arrangements for a grand funeral for Katherine—a funeral he did not attend. Lady Katherine was buried in the castle chapel, immediately adjacent to the house, and Master Miles Coverdale conducted the service in an evangelical style in line with Katherine's convictions.

In the event it was young King Edward himself who insisted that his stepmother must have the highest honours for the occasion: candle-bearers, ushers and six hooded figures to carry the coffin aloft; nothing was lacking except mourners. Only one official mourner attended the funeral—a child of ten, her small face pale with grief, followed the coffin. Lady Jane wore a full-length black dress, and behind her stood her page, Hal Tylney, carrying her long purple train. Behind them walked the household staff in pairs—Mistress Ellen and Elizabeth Tylney together and even Betsy, paired with another kitchen maid, but still gazing admiringly at Hal from a distance.

When the news of Lady Katherine's death reached Bradgate Park in Leicestershire, Sir Henry and Lady Frances insisted that arrangements be put in place for the immediate return of Lady Jane and her attendants. Despite the protests of the Lord Admiral, who wished to keep his young charge in his care, plans for the return journey were soon underway. Hal was glad to be back once more among the quiet woods and hills of Bradgate and to meet again his childhood friend Annie, who was now married to Ben Jacobs and expecting her first child. Jane too was glad to be home, to see her sisters again and to resume her studies with Master Aylmer. Sixteen long months had passed since that May day in 1547 when they had set out for Chelsea Manor. Perhaps life at Bradgate would now settle to a quiet routine.

15
Where Is Master Adrian?

Winter set in early that year. Snow lay like a heavy blanket across the park and bitter winds funnelled along the valley howling like a wolf in pain. Hal saw little of Jane, for much of her time was spent studying high up in her tower chamber. Every day Master Aylmer climbed the spiral stairway to teach his clever young pupil Spanish, Latin, Greek, ancient history and, above all, the truths of the Scriptures from the Great Bible—a translation completed by Jane's former tutor, Master Miles Coverdale.

Jane's unhappy face troubled Hal; he knew she was missing Lady Katherine, but sometimes he wondered whether she was also being badly treated by her mother. Mistress Ellen often looked tight-lipped and angry, but no one dared make any comment. Hal was amazed at how beautiful Jane's younger sister, Katherine, had become. Her long golden-red hair and clear grey eyes attracted comments from every visitor, and she was obviously her mother's favourite. But Hal felt most concerned about little humpbacked Mary Grey, youngest of the family, now five years old. Her poor twisted back meant that she could not run or play like other children. She seemed old beyond her years as she sat in her chair covered over with blankets, her small face wistful and pale. Jane had been teaching Mary to read and people said she was a clever child in spite of her handicap.

Adrian Stokes seemed to have changed the most since Hal had been away. At sixteen years of age, he was now almost six feet in height, a full head and shoulders taller than Hal, and strikingly handsome. His startlingly blue eyes and fair hair, coupled with a merry laugh and ready smile, made all the kitchen maids stare in admiration whenever he was about. But in spite of this, everyone tittered behind his back because Lady Frances seemed to take every opportunity to call in at the stables where Adrian worked. The only person who disliked Adrian was Sir Henry, which Hal thought was not at all surprising.

Apart from a passing remark that 'So you're back,' or words to that effect, Adrian had largely ignored Hal, and Hal was glad. Adrian's main task, in addition to grooming and feeding the horses and checking on the condition of the saddles, reins and other riding gear for the Marquess of Dorset, was to ensure that all was in order whenever a hunt was due. Together with Ben Jacobs, who was now in charge of the kennels, he would plan each detail and, with Christmas approaching, the two youths were kept busy, for there was nothing Lady Frances enjoyed better than roast wild boar on the table for the festive season.

'Hal Tylney,' called a voice which Hal quickly recognized as belonging to Master Jacobs, 'My Lady Frances orders you to take an urgent message to Master Adrian. She wishes all to be ready for the hunt against ten of the clock on the morrow. You are to go immediately.'

Conscious that the message was urgent, Hal hurried to the stable where his own mount was kept and, saddling her up, rode off at once in search of Adrian. Reaching the main stables, Hal glanced round quickly, but there was no sign of Adrian. Horses stamped and snorted impatiently, and it looked to Hal as though they had not been fed. Perhaps he had gone across to the kennels to make arrangements with Ben Jacobs; certainly Adrian's beautiful bay gelding, lent to him by Lady Frances, was missing from his paddock.

But Adrian was not at the kennels. In fact Ben had not seen him since the previous evening. Hal knew a shortcut through the woods, and decided to take that way back to the manor to report that he could not find Adrian. Hungry wild animals might be prowling around at this time of year, but with freshly fallen snow Hal would see their prints if they were nearby. The day was crisp and clear, but as he entered the woods a deep gloom hung over bush and tree. Not a sound could be heard apart from the steady thud of his own horse's hooves. Every tree stump was half hidden by the snow, making the path look unfamiliar and dangerous. Slowly Hal picked his way along, still wondering where Adrian could be.

Quite suddenly he came to a small clearing in the woods and there, to Hal's amazement, standing under the trees was the bay gelding that Adrian always rode—its saddle had slipped sideways and the reins hung loosely. Adrian must surely have fallen from his horse and would be somewhere near, thought Hal. Dismounting quickly, he peered here and there among the bushes, but there was no sign of the young man. Irresolute, Hal stood for a moment, wondering what he must do. The gelding looked frightened and pawed the ground as if in pain. Then Hal noticed that one fetlock was bleeding badly.

Just at that moment Hal thought he could hear a low groan coming from the far side of the clearing. At first he could see nothing, but as his eyes became accustomed to the gloom he saw a figure lying face down, his body half covered by snow, and a small pool of blood staining the whiteness of the snow.

'Adrian!' cried Hal in alarm. 'Are you badly hurt?'

Half opening his eyes, Adrian could only whisper, 'Wolves ... early this morning.' Clearly a pack of wolves had caught the scent of rider and horse. They had been snapping at the horse's fetlocks and, as Adrian tried to beat them off his track, he had fallen from his horse and appeared to have sustained a serious injury.

'I will fetch help,' said Hal simply, throwing his warm cloak around the young man's shoulders. Fearing Adrian might have some back injury, Hal did not dare attempt to move him but, springing back into the saddle, galloped off as fast as he could. Strangely he felt an inner sort of happiness, not that Adrian was hurt, but that he could do something for him, perhaps to make up in some measure for the cowardly way in which he had planted the lost bracelet in Adrian's pocket—an act that had so nearly cost Adrian his life.

Raising the alarm, Hal quickly took two of the men to the clearing where Adrian was lying. While Hal gently led the injured horse away, the others managed to lift Adrian and, carrying him between them, slowly threaded their way through the wood until at last they emerged into the clear winter sunshine. As well as a gash on his head where he had struck a tree stump in his fall, Adrian had damaged his back and was clearly in great pain.

Once again the clever doctor from Leicester made his way to Bradgate Manor and after much prodding and poking, ordered a long period of rest for Adrian but thought that his recovery would be complete in due time.

Lady Frances fussed around the injured young man like a mother hen, ordering the very best delicacies from the kitchen to tempt his appetite. Now and then Hal ventured into his apartments, for he remembered the fearful boredom that he had experienced when he had broken his leg. But there was another purpose behind Hal's visits. In his heart Hal wanted to apologise to Adrian for the incident over the bracelet. Adrian had been truly grateful to Hal for searching for him, knowing well that if he had lain hidden in the woods for much longer, wolves could easily have returned to the scent of blood, even if he had not died of exposure. His manner towards Hal was now much pleasanter and he even seemed to enjoy his company. Perhaps one day Hal would get the opportunity to tell him what had really happened about the missing bracelet—yet it was a terrible risk. What if Adrian still did not believe him? What if he repeated the story to Lady Frances?

At last Hal felt it was a risk he would have to take, for his sense of guilt over the incident hung heavily on his conscience, particularly at night. 'You know, Adrian...,' he began hesitantly one afternoon. But just at that moment there was a sound of swishing skirts on the stairs, and who should enter but Lady Frances herself?

'You may go, Master Hal,' she said curtly. But it was the look on Adrian's face when Lady Frances entered that made Hal realize that it would never be safe to tell him what he had done. It was a burden he must carry with him, perhaps for ever. He must receive forgiveness from God alone if he were to find peace of heart.

Not long after this, as winter slowly released its icy grip, giving place to milder days, Hal saw a stranger cantering up the long drive to the manor house. At first, by his magnificent appearance, Hal thought it was the Lord Admiral. Instinctively he felt anger rising in his mind. How cruelly he had treated Lady Katherine! To Hal's mind she had died of grief, not of infection. But as the rider drew closer Hal could see that it was not the admiral. It was none other than his brother, Edward Seymour, Lord Protector of England. Whatever could he want? Hal had an idea it might be something to do with Lady Jane.

And he was right. The next day Mistress Ellen was beaming. 'Have ye heard,' she told Hal's mother, Elizabeth, 'that my lady is to be betrothed to the Lord Protector's son?' So Jane would not be marrying her cousin King Edward after all, thought Hal. In one way he was glad for, although he knew that Jane had no choice over whom she married, at least she knew and liked young Edward Seymour and had spent time with him during her visits to the royal courts.

As the Protector sat at dinner with Sir Henry and Lady Frances, Hal, who was serving at the tables, noticed how drawn and anxious he was, his eyes heavy with loss of sleep. He noticed too how tearful Lady Jane was looking. Had something terrible happened? As usual it was Meg Saunders who was first with the news. She had heard it from Adrian when she had carried his dinner up to where he lay, and Adrian had of course heard it from Lady Frances.

'They've locked him up in the Tower, they have, and a good thing too, I says,' Meg declared, hands on her hips and bright red cheeks flushed with pleasure at being the one with the news.

'Who did they lock up?' enquired Joan, the new kitchen maid timidly.

'Why My Lord Admiral, who else? And methinks he will lose his head and all. Serves him right, that's what I say.'

'What has he done now?' asked Elizabeth Tylney wearily, who was baking some of the bread that Lady Frances liked.

'Tried to kidnap the king, would you believe it?' replied Meg confidently. 'Why, he comes by night with a forged key, he breaks into His Majesty's bedchamber, shoots his dog dead—poor little creature, 'im as was barking madly to warn his Majesty!—and then lays hands on the poor boy. Was he frightened? Thought he might shoot 'im next, that's what I says. And now he's up for high treason, he is,' concluded Meg triumphantly, as every eye was fixed on her.

When Hal heard the strange story he suddenly realized that this must have been the secret plot that Thomas Seymour had been hatching all along. Now everything made sense. If the admiral could capture the king himself and hold him in his power, then he would have supreme authority in the land. No one would have dared to challenge him for fear of any harm being done to the boy king, who was still only eleven years old. Perhaps the admiral planned to betroth Lady Jane to King Edward once he had him in his control. This was why he was so anxious to keep Jane under his protection after Lady Katherine's death. It seemed the admiral's plans had gone badly wrong. Why else would he have shot the king's pet dog? It also explained why the Protector had ridden all the way to Bradgate. He was anxious to settle Jane's marriage arrangements as soon as possible, so that his brother could not attempt any further harm if he ever regained his freedom.

Some weeks later the sad news filtered through to Bradgate that the Lord Admiral had been tried for high treason and found guilty. His brother had tried to save Thomas from going to the block, but had failed. Another politician, a dark handsome man by the name of John Dudley, whom Hal had seen occasionally at Hampton Court and Whitehall, had insisted that Thomas Seymour must die. Perhaps he was right, thought Hal sadly, when he heard that the condemned man had still been planning ways of raising a rebellion against his brother, the Protector, even at the scaffold. But Hal was becoming wise to the intrigues and plots of these men around the king. Maybe John Dudley too was trying to grab power from the Protector and take it for himself. Who could tell? Certainly, old Father Latimer, who was preaching just after the admiral was executed, felt that there might be more trouble in store. 'A man furthest from the fear of God than any in England' was his description of the dead man. But he had added: 'I wish there were no more in England like him... Well! he is gone! If only he had left none behind him!'

16
The sweating sickness

Hal Tylney had turned seventeen in the late spring of 1551. Now almost as tall as Adrian, he had become a reserved, though conscientious, member of the Marquess of Dorset's Bradgate staff. Recently he had been given charge of a team of gardeners under the overall charge of the head gardener. And in addition he retained his favoured position as Lady Jane's page whenever she was called upon to attend official functions.

Most of the great affairs of state, the rebellions that broke out in different parts of the country and the struggle for power among the men who surrounded Edward VI, seldom disturbed the peace of the woods and hills of Bradgate Park. Hal had already seen enough of the schemes and plotting that went on at court to make him distrust all politicians. But when he heard that John Dudley, the member of the Privy Council who had pressed for the Lord Admiral's execution, had actually seized control of the country, he was indignant and troubled. Not only had Dudley placed the Lord Protector, Edward Seymour, in the Tower, but he had even conferred on himself the title of Duke of Northumberland.

'How dare he?' Hal exclaimed to Lady Jane one day. 'Even your father is not a duke, and John Dudley has not a single drop of royal blood in his veins!' Hal was well aware that this could affect Jane's entire future because she was betrothed to the Lord Protector's son. Nothing more had been said about the arrangements for her marriage to go ahead, and Jane would be fourteen in October. By that age many girls were already married and setting up homes of their own. Clearly the Greys were keeping their options open, watching and waiting to see what the fate of Edward Seymour might be.

Sir Henry and Lady Frances frequently travelled to London to keep in touch with unfolding political events, staying at their town house. When they were not in London, Jane's parents spent much of their time either at the gambling table, chasing ever higher stakes, or pursuing wild animals in the park. Since Jane neither enjoyed hunting nor approved of their gambling activities, it appeared that her mother treated her ever more harshly. Again and again Hal noticed how unhappy Jane looked. How he wished he could help her! If only she would not speak her mind! Life would then be much easier for her. He wished too that he could protect her from the frequent taunts, punishments, even beatings, that she so regularly received from her parents.

Sometimes Jane and her sister Katherine were expected to accompany their parents to London for some state function. On these occasions Hal travelled with her, but for most of the time Jane studied quietly in her tower chamber under the tuition of the chaplain, John Aylmer. There alone she seemed really happy. Rumours flew around among the staff about her brilliance. Some said she was even corresponding with several of the cleverest Reformers in Europe. One thing was certain, and Hal had noticed it more and more in his every contact with Jane: her faith was growing ever stronger and she was not afraid to stand up for what she believed. But for himself, he was scared: scared of what others might say about him, scared of the cost of making any open profession of faith in Christ, scared he might have to suffer a violent and horrible death like that of Anne Askew or William Tyndale.

In the summer of 1551, however, while Sir Henry Grey and Lady Frances were in London, something happened which would change everything for Hal. One bright summer's day a messenger arrived from London. 'My name is Master Jack Sullivan and I wish to see My Lady Jane,' he announced breathlessly. He had ridden hard for five days and was travel-stained and exhausted. While Adrian led his horse away to the stables, Hal conducted the newcomer to the bottom of Jane's tower.

'Heavy tidings, my lady,' said Master Sullivan as he entered her study room, removing his hat and bowing solemnly. 'Your mother, My Lady Frances, lies ill. I fear she may be dying. She calls for you to come and nurse her.'

'What ails my honoured mother, good sir?' gasped Jane in alarm.

'I fear to tell you, my lady, but it is the sweating sickness that has broken out in London. Men and women are dying each hour; some lie unburied in every house and even on the street corners. Our sovereign King Edward has fled to Hampton Court for safety, and all who can escape the town have done so. You are summoned to come with me immediately, for your mother wishes you alone to nurse her.'

'Perhaps she is already dead,' thought Jane, turning white, but answered as resolutely as she was able, 'I will prepare to come straightway.' When Hal heard that Jane had been summoned to London to venture right into the heart of this dreadful infection, he was furious. If Lady Frances should die of the illness that would be grievous enough, but why should Jane die too? Did she wish to destroy her eldest daughter? Jane would surely catch it. Hal was well aware that in previous epidemics which had swept the country it had mainly been young people who had died of the illness.

'She must not go. She will not go!' he exclaimed angrily to Mistress Ellen. 'Does my lady wish to kill her own daughter?'

'Good Master Hal,' replied Jane's nurse, biting her lip in rage, 'she has no choice. We must leave our mistress in the hands of a God of mercy. He loves the puir lassie and will care for her.' So saying she turned away, tears in her eyes, and began to gather Lady Jane's possessions together.

'I too must go then,' replied Hal simply.

'I fear so,' responded Mistress Ellen in a choked voice. 'But Master Jacobs is to follow in two weeks' time to escort the Lady Jane home again—if all is well.'

Hal had little time to think of his own life as he prepared to accompany Lady Jane. But of course he knew that he too would be in grave danger. Early next morning they were all ready to set off. Jane would ride pillion behind Master Sullivan and Hal would accompany them on his own horse. As he gazed around on the beautiful woods and hills that had been his home, Hal wondered if he would ever see them again. Then he tried to banish such thoughts. Surely, his task was to support and encourage Jane. Only thirteen years of age, she faced both the death of her mother and a strong possibility of her own. Yet she was looking far calmer than Hal and, to his surprise, she bent down from her saddle high on Master Sullivan's horse and whispered in Hal's ear, 'Good Hal, trust in God to lengthen your days, but we must live still to die, that in our dying we may inherit eternal life. Do not despair but be strong in faith.' Hal stared at Jane. What a strange girl she was! Yet her words rang in Hal's ears throughout that long ride to London.

Through sleepy sunlit villages they rode, hardly daring to break their journey during the daytime in case they arrived too late. The terrors of the sweating sickness seemed like a distant dream—unreal and imaginary. Perhaps it was all a fanciful tale, designed to trick and distress Lady Jane. But as they neared London things began to change. Loud wailing could be heard from one house after another as they passed through town and hamlet. Here and there a cart rumbled along the deserted street carrying the dead to their graves. Hal shuddered with horror, and tied his cravat across his face so that he would not breathe in the infected air.

At last the travel-weary party reached Dorset Place. 'Does my mother yet live?' asked Jane anxiously, as her father greeted their arrival.

'My child, she lives, but the physician says it is little short of a miracle,' replied Sir Henry slowly. 'You may go to her room after you have dined.'

As soon as she was able, Lady Jane crept up to her mother's room. Wasted and weak, Lady Frances nodded briefly at her daughter, but did not speak. Jane was alarmed to hear that many of the Dorset Place staff had succumbed to the dreadful scourge, and five had already died. Sir Henry had ordered all whose services could be spared to leave the city until the plague had subsided. That was why Jane must come to care for her mother. Hal soon found that he too was needed, both in the kitchens and in the stables.

'You can be dead in three hours,' said Mistress Kirby, head of the kitchen staff, gloomily. 'Mistress Webb, she were carried off in the night, and now I have work to do for two of us.'

'Aye,' added the scullery maid, Anne Burton, 'and it's the young as dies. You shake like a leaf, you go hot and cold; then comes the headaches and the sweat—I know because our Katie, she got it,' and with that the girl began to sob uncontrollably.

Hal could stand no more and went out quickly to the stables. 'Live still to die, that in our dying we might inherit eternal life...'—that was what Jane had said. Hal could remember the exact words. Perhaps they came from Master Tyndale's New Testament, he thought. That night he searched through the pages to see if he could find anything like that. The nearest he could discover was in a story about a man called Lazarus whom Jesus had made alive again after he had been dead for four days. Jesus had said to the man's sister, 'Whosoever liveth and believeth in me shall never die.'[1] Those words comforted Hal a little, although he could not quite understand what they meant.

Much of Jane's time was spent with her mother. She bathed her flushed face, gently combed her hair, fetched and carried anything she required, and after a week it was clear that Lady Frances was gradually regaining strength. Sometimes Jane felt dizzy with tiredness as she undertook tasks beyond her strength. Dizzy spells were one of the earliest symptoms of the onset of the sweating sickness, as Jane well knew. Perhaps she herself was sickening now, she thought with a wave of panic. Hal watched her from a distance, torn between hope and fear as day succeeded day. But soon it was clear that Lady Frances had weathered the dreadful illness. Each day she was leaving her bed,

---

[1] John 11:26

sitting first in an easy chair and then out in the gardens for an hour or two.

At last after two weeks, with a clatter of hooves, Master Jacobs arrived, and for the first time in his life Hal had to admit that he was truly glad to see the older man. But Master Jacobs, now senior servant at Bradgate, had also brought sad news. Word had reached Leicestershire that Lady Catherine Brandon's two boys, Henry and Charles, had both died within a day or two of each other. Hal remembered Lady Frances's half-brothers clearly. Henry was exactly the same age as he was and Charles was only fifteen. Jane too had been very fond of her young uncles, who were really more like older brothers to her. Both had been students at Cambridge, where the sweating sickness had also broken out. Lady Catherine had brought her sons home immediately she heard of the outbreak, but it was too late. Hal felt a lump in his throat as he heard the news. He felt so sorry for Lady Catherine, whom he had met a number of times at Hampton Court. With no one left to inherit Henry Brandon's title as Duke of Suffolk, the dukedom would now pass to Sir Henry Grey, making Lady Frances the new Duchess of Suffolk.

'My daughter, I thank you for your services to your mother,' said Sir Henry to Jane one day. 'All that remains now is for her to regain strength, and tomorrow you may return to Bradgate with Master Jacobs and your page.' Jacobs soon told Hal the good news, and Hal thankfully prepared the horses for the long ride home. Perhaps at last they would be safe.

But it was not to be. Two days after arriving back at Bradgate Park Master Jacobs was dead. He had contracted the sweating sickness during his brief visit to Dorset Place. Waking in the night in great pain with a violent headache, he had shown all the symptoms of the dreaded disease, the drenching sweat proclaiming it only too clearly. By dawn he had gone. The shock of his death was felt throughout Bradgate House, from his wife, Mistress Eliza Jacobs, his son Ben and Annie, his son's wife, down to the youngest maid in the kitchens and scullery and even the garden staff. Not only was it his death that filled everyone with horror, but the fact that the sweating sickness was now likely to spread throughout the Bradgate staff, and to the villages around where many had their homes and families. No one could tell who might be the next to sicken and die?

'Would you believe it? Such a nice wench was our Joan,' proclaimed Meg Saunders, always the first with any bad news, when the youngest scullery maid, only fourteen years of age, died two days later. But when the colourful Meg herself was taken ill no one thought she would pull through. A strong and determined young woman, Meg clung desperately to life and, though sobered by the experience, was back at her duties within three months. Hal's mother Elizabeth kept a watchful eye upon her son—he was all she had and the fear of losing him haunted her night and day, far more than the thought of her own illness and death.

Hal knew well that both he and Lady Jane were at grave risk for they had been in close contact with Master Jacobs throughout the journey back from London. Faced with the possibility of illness and death, an unseen enemy that could strike at any moment, Hal began to pray as he had never prayed before. Each moment that he could steal away from his work, he could be found in some hidden corner in the woodland crying out to God to be merciful to him, to come to him, to forgive his sins and make him ready to die. But still he was afraid: afraid of death, afraid of the opinions of others, afraid of suffering for Christ's sake.

Not long after Master Jacobs' death, Hal was sitting on a log deep in the woods brooding gloomily on the danger he was in. 'Live still to die,' Jane had said. If only he could live in that way, then he was sure he would lose his fears. Quite suddenly, a scene flashed before Hal's eyes. It was of an old man, stooped and wrinkled with a long white beard. He was preaching from a huge five-sided pulpit, and his eyes seemed to pierce right through Hal. Who could it be? Why yes, it was old Father Latimer. His very words came back to the young man's mind: 'Put your only trust in Christ our Saviour.' Surely, that was the answer! That was the answer!

At that very moment and with all the sincerity and earnestness he could muster, Hal cried out to the Saviour, to the one he had learnt to admire through the pages of his New Testament, urgently begging him to take away his fears and cleanse him from the guilt of all his sins. For a few moments he sat absolutely still, hardly daring to breathe. Nothing happened. Nearby a thrush began to sing loudly, its sweet clear melody filling the air. Then he heard a slight crackle in the bushes. Glancing round he saw a fawn gazing at him with its soft brown eyes. It seemed so gentle, so trustful. Gradually Hal became aware of an inner happiness he had never known before. Suddenly he realized that the miracle for which he had been praying had happened. God had heard his prayer and had forgiven his sins for Christ's sake. No voice from heaven had declared it, but God had given him that deep peace for which he had been praying and his fears were swallowed up in joy.

At the first opportunity Hal told Lady Jane of his experience in the wood. Her eyes shone with delight. Now Hal knew that he was not only Lady Jane's page, but one who shared with her in all the blessings of being part of the family of the Lord Jesus Christ. All he longed for now was an opportunity to serve the one who had done all for him.

The next day, as he was turning over the soil in the flower beds ready for more summer plants, Hal suddenly began to feel light-headed. He grabbed hold of his spade to prevent himself from falling. The whole world seemed to be spinning round his head. Surely he was just imagining things... But then he felt an intense stabbing pain in his head—such a pain as he had never known before ... then he knew no more. Hal too had succumbed to the sweating sickness.

When he opened his eyes again he found himself lying on a low couch in the summer room, his mother standing over him, her face distraught with anxiety. She was gently sponging him to try to cool the burning heat of his body. His sheets were drenched with sweat. Then Elizabeth did the most practical thing she could, she wrapped a heavy blanket around her son, to prevent him from catching a chill.

'Mama, I want to live. I want to serve Christ,' murmured Hal.

'You shall live, my son, you shall. I am praying you shall live,' replied Elizabeth fervently, but Hal did not hear. He had drifted back into unconsciousness.

For two days the young man seemed to teeter on the verge of death. Sometimes he lay so still that Elizabeth bent her head to see if she could hear him breathing. Then a slight flicker of his eyelids showed her that her son still lived. Lady Jane was forbidden to come and see him for fear of exposing her to further infection. But each time he regained consciousness Hal said the same thing: 'I want to live to serve Christ.' It seemed he wanted an opportunity to show his love and gratitude to the Saviour—not that his good works would gain him any merit, but out of thankfulness for the mercy and forgiveness he had received.

Other members of the domestic staff became sick, and some died. The threat of death covered the whole household like a threatening black cloud. Everyone was grateful that Sir Henry and his wife were still in London, for there were few who would have been able to serve them. Most were either sick or caring for the sick.

But gradually, very gradually, as the hot summer weather gave place to quiet autumn days, things began to return to normal; no new cases of the dreadful plague had been reported for several weeks. Hal himself was clearly on the road to recovery. Thin and haggard, he was regaining his appetite, and even began to enjoy all the fuss his mother made of him. But, best of all, he knew a joy in his spirit and a sense of peace that made him want to sing and shout for sheer happiness. In fact he had found a verse in his New Testament that described exactly how he felt: 'My soul magnifieth the Lord, and my spirit rejoiceth in God my Saviour ... for he that is mighty hath done to me great things, and blessed is his name!'[2]

---

2   Luke 1:46, 49 (Tyndale's version)

17
Behind the scenes

Six months had passed since the sweating sickness had caused such devastation in the country. Thousands of men, women and children had died in the epidemic, and Hal was deeply thankful to God for saving his life and giving him some opportunity to obey and serve him. Hearing of the young man's experience of God's forgiveness and grace as he prayed in the woods and of his eagerness to learn more of the Bible, Master Aylmer had agreed to teach Hal each week after his duties for the day were over. As the chaplain explained some of the passages of Scripture over which Hal had often struggled, he was amazed to discover that words which had seemed so difficult were now clear and easy. 'But why didn't I understand them before?' he asked the chaplain one day.

'My son,' replied Master Aylmer gravely, 'no one can rightly understand the Bible until the Spirit of God gives him light.' Hal began to realize why people like Lady Anne Askew were prepared to die rather than deny those truths that had become precious to them.

One day early in February 1552 a visitor arrived at Bradgate House wishing to transact some business with Sir Henry. When Hal caught his first glimpse of the newcomer he recognized him instantly. The matted black beard, thick eyebrows and small twinkling eyes were unmistakable. But it was the loud raucous laugh that left Hal in no doubt at all—this must be Master Ebenezer Squires, whom he had met at the Cock and Hen tavern in Dunstable, the owner of the gold sovereign. But why had he come to see Sir Henry? Hal was not long in doubt, for that evening he received a message saying that he must come to the Winter Parlour immediately. Sir Henry and Master Squires were still sitting by a roaring log fire, sipping ale and deep in conversation when Hal entered.

'Now is this the young man you spoke about?' asked Sir Henry with a strange look at Hal. Master Squires rose from his chair and looked Hal up and down. Four years had passed since they had met briefly; Hal had changed from a boy to a young man, and was now at least six inches taller than Master Squires himself. Hal felt himself blushing deeply with embarrassment under his gaze.

'Ho, ho, ho! The very one!' roared Master Squires. 'And how did you spend that gold sovereign, my young friend?'

Hal took a deep breath and then said steadily, 'I bought a copy of Master Tyndale's New Testament, sir.'

'Prithee, would you believe that now? Ho! ho! It's just as I thought,' chuckled the jovial Squires.

'Master Squires is here on several matters of business, one of which is to ask if I would be prepared to allow you to leave my service and to work for him in London instead,' explained Sir Henry. 'As you may know he is now Master of Horse for Sir William Cecil, once secretary for the much-to-be-regretted Protector Edward Seymour, formerly Duke of Somerset. He assures me he needs such as you as his assistant.'

Hal jumped visibly at the strange reference to Edward Seymour, ousted from his position as Lord Protector two years earlier by John Dudley, the new Duke of Northumberland. But he knew he would not be expected to comment. Instead he merely enquired, 'Would not Master Adrian be better suited for such a position, sir?' Hal knew well enough that Sir Henry would not be sorry to lose that young man from his service.

'I too have made that suggestion,' replied Sir Henry sharply. 'But Master Squires appears to have formed a high opinion of you. Think about it, and let me know in the morning. For my part I have valued your service, and have not forgotten your brave act in saving my daughter Katherine at the joust, but the decision is yours.'

At the mention of the name of Edward Seymour, until recently the Lord Protector, Master Squires' cheery face had clouded over. 'Bad days, these, bad days,' he muttered, shaking his big black beard sadly, 'bad days indeed!' He had noticed Hal's reaction and added, 'Have you not heard, Master Hal, of the unhappy fate of the good duke?'

'Why, no, sir; I heard he was imprisoned in the Tower, but no more,' replied Hal.

'I grieve to tell you that, like his brother Thomas, My Lord Seymour was executed five days ago. Accused of high treason, he was, and that without so much as an open trial,' replied Squires, quivering visibly with rage. 'The good duke's blood will make My Lord of Northumberland's pillow uneasy, you mark my words. An innocent man, sir, an innocent man,' he added turning to Sir Henry. 'The good are removed and the evil come to power—bad days indeed.'

'You may go,' said Sir Henry to Hal, who could see how shocked the youth appeared at the fearful news. In that moment Hal had made up his mind. The opening offered him by Master Squires would have improved his social position considerably and set him well on the path to advancement. In addition, he appreciated Master Squires, but nothing would make him return to London, to that cauldron of intrigue and back-stabbing that went on in political circles. No, he would remain quietly at Bradgate House, continuing to benefit from Master Aylmer's teaching and serving Lady Jane when she needed him.

But what would happen now about Lady Jane's betrothal to the dead man's son, also called Edward Seymour? As in all cases of treason, the Seymour lands and estate had been forfeited to the Crown, and the Protector himself stripped of the title of Duke of Somerset. Would Sir Henry and Lady Frances ever let Lady Jane marry the son of a beheaded 'traitor' with no lands, no inheritance and no title? Hal knew the answer, but Jane, not yet fourteen years of age, did not. She still clung to the hope that before long her parents would arrange for her marriage to the young Edward Seymour to go ahead.

As Hal was chopping firewood the next day he was alerted to the sound of hooves approaching from the direction of the manor house. Master Squires was on his way back to London, but seeing Hal he reined in his horse and alighted. 'I respect your decision, my young friend,' he began, but added, 'If ever you change your mind, know well that I would welcome your services.' Then in a low voice he continued, 'Take you good care of the young Lady Jane; I fear for her, that I do; I fear for her. My Lord the Duke of Northumberland will stop at nothing ... nothing...' And without finishing his sentence, Ebenezer Squires leapt back into his saddle and was away off into the distance, leaving Hal puzzled and not a little troubled. Clearly Master Squires knew more than he would say. Perhaps it would be better if Jane married some quiet country nobleman and stayed far from the scenes of treachery and murder that appeared to have seized London society, thought Hal gloomily.

Visitors came and went, and on several occasions during the year the Grey family travelled to London or visited other noble families, including their royal relatives and connections. But no invitation was more eagerly accepted than one from the Lady Mary herself, eldest daughter of Henry VIII and first cousin of Lady Jane's mother, Frances. Now thirty-six years of age, Mary was a bitter and angry woman. She had been shamefully treated by her father and forced to take an oath declaring herself illegitimate and owning him as Supreme Head of the English Church—both things that she vehemently denied. If she had refused she would have been imprisoned in the Tower. Mary had no option but to give in. A fanatical Roman Catholic, she hated the new laws brought in by her brother Edward's government, one of which banned the celebration of the mass. And despite the ruling enforced by Edward himself in a face-to-face showdown with his older half-sister, she continued to celebrate the mass in her private chapels. She had nothing but fierce resentment for all the church reforms introduced since her father's death in order to establish a strong Protestant church. Doubtless she would reverse them if ever she became queen.

But Mary had a tender spot for children. With little hope of having any of her own, she had shown considerable kindness to Lady Jane and her sisters Katherine and Mary. She had sent Jane expensive gifts from time to time, on one occasion giving the girl an exquisite dress made of velvet laced with gold to wear at a special royal function which Lady Jane was due to attend. So when a letter came inviting the family to stay with Cousin Mary at her palace in Newhall Boreham in Essex during July 1552, it was greeted with pleasure.

But Hal was not so enthusiastic. He was well aware, as were all Englishmen, that if anything should happen to the fourteen-year-old King Edward, Mary would become queen. Edward was healthy enough, but there had been a history of early deaths among Tudor boys. Had not the two Brandon boys both died within days of each other in the sweating sickness the previous year? A look in Lady Mary's eyes and something about the determined set of her mouth told Hal that she was a hard woman and would have no mercy on any who disagreed with her on matters of faith.

Lady Anne Wharton, maid of honour to the princess, welcomed the visitors cordially when they arrived and escorted them through the rambling palace to their apartments. 'Take care what you say to your cousin, the Lady Mary,' Hal hissed in Jane's ear as he left her for his own rooms in the servants' quarters. He remembered the warning Master Squires had given and knew that Jane's strong and forthright convictions could easily bring her into serious trouble. Later that evening Lady Mary invited her guests to join her in the Great Hall for dinner. Gorgeously dressed in a purple velvet robe, and decked with costly jewellery, Lady Mary came forward to greet the family. Jane found herself locked in her cousin's embrace, for Mary remembered the girl from the days they had spent together at Hampton Court Palace before the death of Henry VIII. But though her mouth was smiling, her eyes remained strangely hard and cold. Had she already heard of her young cousin's strong beliefs in the truths of that new Reformed faith that Mary so deeply feared and despised?

Hal's warning to Lady Jane was certainly wise, for Jane could be headstrong and outspoken, particularly if some question of her faith were involved. Recently she had been corresponding with one of the great theologians of the Reformation, Heinrich Bullinger, who worked in Zurich, and like him she had strong objections to the Roman Catholic teaching on the sacrament, called the mass. This teaching declared that when the priest offered a prayer of consecration for the bread used in the mass it somehow changed into the real and actual body of Jesus Christ. Although it still looked like bread, smelt like bread and tasted like bread, it had in fact changed and must now be worshipped and honoured as God himself. Jane well remembered that Lady Anne Askew's objections to this very belief had led directly to her martyrdom.

Not many days after the Grey family had arrived in Essex, Lady Jane was walking with Lady Wharton. As they came to the open door of the chapel, the maid of honour suddenly stopped and curtseyed.

'Why do you curtsey?' asked Jane. 'Has My Lady Mary come in?' It sounded an innocent enough question, but the girl knew exactly why Lady Wharton had curtseyed. She had curtseyed because they had just passed the host, as the consecrated bread was called, which was still on the altar in the chapel.

'No,' replied Lady Anne sharply, 'My Lady Mary has not come in. I make my curtsey to him that made us all.' Jane's reply, provocative enough, demonstrated the absurdity of such a statement.

'Why, how can that be,' she asked, 'when the baker made him?' The logic was plain. How could bread made by a baker turn into God? If a baker could 'make' God, he must therefore be greater than God himself. Lady Anne turned scarlet with rage. How dare the girl make such an insulting remark! How dare she question the doctrine of the sacrament in that way! She pursed her lips but said nothing. That very evening as they sat at dinner with Lady Mary, it was obvious that Lady Wharton had reported Jane's indiscreet remark. Mary deliberately ignored her cousin, turning only a stony stare upon her, whenever Jane made some comment. Gone were all the gifts with which the princess had once showered the girl, and Jane was left in no doubt at all that her words had cost her dear—just how dear she could not as yet realize.

18
When Jane said, "I won't"

It would soon be springtime and Hal loved that season at Bradgate. Bluebells sprang up in the woods, stretching as far as the eye could see, their sweet scent filling the air. Primroses shone like golden stars on the banks and the oaks and sycamores were clothed with young green leaves. But at the end of February 1553 Hal learnt to his dismay that Sir Henry, Lady Frances and the family were to leave Bradgate and spend some months at their newly acquired property, Sheen Palace, on the River Thames. Sheen had formerly belonged to the unfortunate Lord Protector, Edward Seymour, but had been confiscated soon after his arrest. The Duke of Northumberland, anxious to curry favour with powerful families like the Greys, had given the property to Sir Henry and Lady Frances, now the Duke and Duchess of Suffolk following the death of young Henry Brandon in the sweating-sickness epidemic.

Hal hated the thought of spending more time in London, and especially at Sheen Palace, even though, like Bradgate itself, the palace was surrounded with wide parkland and woods. It seemed all wrong that the former Protector's family should be deprived of their property. Neither was he any better pleased when he learnt that Adrian Stokes would be joining the party travelling to London. Sheen provided excellent hunting ground and Adrian, soon to turn twenty-one, was now Master of Horse for Sir Henry and Lady Frances.

Sheen Palace[1] stood on the south bank of the River Thames, while at Isleworth on the opposite bank was Syon House, belonging to John Dudley, Duke of Northumberland. Once a monastery, Syon had been transformed into a palatial home where the duke lived with his wife Jane, Duchess of Northumberland, his sixteen-year-old son Guilford and his daughter Katherine. Tall, handsome and already engaged to be married, Guilford was the duke's fifth son and it was well known that his ambitious parents had high hopes for the young man.

No further mention had been made of Lady Jane's betrothal to the former Protector's son; neither did Jane herself dare to mention it, for the young man in question had naturally shared in his family's downfall. But with Syon House lying so close to Sheen, Hal could not help noticing how often Sir Henry and Lady Frances engaged the boatman to ferry them across the river. They spent hours at Syon, and it seemed that the Duke of Northumberland was anxious to gain their support. What was he planning? Hal wondered a thousand times over. On occasions Lady Jane and her sister Katherine were invited to accompany their parents to Syon and at these times Hal was expected to be in attendance on Jane. At other times the Duke of Northumberland, Guilford and even Guilford's older brother, the dashing Robert Dudley, would come across to Sheen to join in some hunt that Adrian was organizing in the park. Lady Jane was reluctant to take part, but as her mother insisted, she had little alternative.

Whenever Guilford was around, Hal noticed how attentive he was to Lady Jane, bowing low and making flattering remarks. Jane did not like it, and complained about it in private to Hal. Surely her parents would soon honour their pledges and arrange for her marriage to young Edward Seymour to go ahead. Hal feared, although he did not

---

1   Sheen Palace stood in the present Old Deer Park adjoining Kew Gardens.

say so, that Sir Henry and Lady Frances might have other plans for their eldest daughter. Perhaps the Duke of Northumberland had new plans for Guilford as well. Hal tried to push such suspicions from his mind. Was not Guilford already contracted in marriage to some well-placed heiress? His mother's favourite, the youth had never been denied anything he wanted in his life, and to Hal he seemed spoilt and petulant.

'Have you heard,' Elizabeth Tylney asked Hal one day not long after their arrival at Sheen, 'that His Majesty King Edward is gravely ill?'

'Why no, mama,' Hal replied with consternation. 'My Lady Jane told me that he had suffered an attack of measles last year. Although his recovery was long and slow, I heard the Duke of Northumberland telling My Lady Jane that her cousin was much improved. The fresh air at Greenwich Palace had given His Majesty new strength.'

'I fear that may not be true,' answered Elizabeth in a low voice. 'I was in the kitchens at Syon House yesterday and I overheard the duchess, My Lady Jane Dudley, speaking of it to her son Guilford,' continued Elizabeth. '"He cannot last much longer...", those were her very words.'

'Perhaps she spoke of some other,' responded Hal, now seriously concerned.

'I fear not, my son,' replied his mother.

'If he is indeed dying,' Hal answered, 'I greatly tremble for this realm, for then the Lady Mary must become queen. Surely, we must give ourselves to prayer for our sovereign king, that God may spare his life.' Elizabeth did not reply. She had noticed her son's new and strong faith and was glad, but for herself she found the deep and passionate debates on religious issues all too confusing... Perhaps one day she would understand. But she too had seen how angry the Lady Mary had become over Jane's remark to Lady Anne Wharton on their visit the previous summer. The future looked bleak indeed.

'My lady,' said Mistress Ellen to Jane one evening shortly after dinner in mid-April, 'your honoured parents wish to see you immediately in the Winter Parlour.' The meal had been a tense occasion with many important guests invited—among them the Duke of Northumberland, John Dudley, his wife and of course Guilford. Other members of the nobility had also been present, including the Lord Treasurer, the Marquess of Winchester and Lord Herbert, Earl of Pembroke, reputed to be the richest person in the country apart from the king himself. Course after course of luxurious food was served: tender venison from the previous day's hunting, dressed peacock, fine beef steak and a variety of sweetmeats. Lady Jane was tired. She had been suffering from a stomach upset and had little appetite for all the dainties she was supposed to enjoy. Guilford, who was seated opposite her, kept pressing her to eat more. Hal was one of those serving at the table and could quickly see that Jane wished for nothing other than to be left alone.

'Why do my parents wish to see me?' asked Jane apprehensively. She wondered whether they had been displeased with her behaviour at dinner.

'I know not, my lady,' replied Mistress Ellen warily, 'but they were deep in conversation with His Lordship the Duke of Northumberland before he departed.'

'Perhaps at last some decision has been made to proceed with my marriage to Edward Seymour,' suggested Jane hopefully, but she did not sound very confident.

Tidying herself up, Jane presented herself in the Winter Parlour. The lamps were already lit, casting strange shadows across the room. The log fire was burning low. Lady Frances was seated on the edge of her chair when Jane entered, her large figure making her look all the more frightening. Sir Henry stood nervously at her side, twisting his silk handkerchief through his fingers.

'You asked to see me, mama and papa,' began Jane nervously.

'Why yes, we did,' began Sir Henry, clearing his throat ominously. 'We have been discussing the question of your marriage.' Jane's face lit up. So they had finally made a decision. 'And we are happy to tell you that by the most gracious kindness of His Honour the Duke of N...'

'But I am...,' interrupted Jane.

'Hold your tongue,' snapped Lady Frances.

'We are honoured and glad to tell you that tomorrow you are to be betrothed to Master Guilford Dudley, son of His Lordship the Duke of Northumberland and Lady Dudley.'

'But mama, papa, I am already betrothed to...,' cried Jane in dismay.

'You are betrothed to no one but Guilford Dudley,' snarled her mother. Jane turned white and then said in a quiet but firm voice, 'Mama, papa, I cannot and I will not marry Guilford Dudley for I am already contracted to...' The words were scarcely out of her mouth before she felt a stinging blow first across one ear and then the other.

'You won't, my girl? You won't?' yelled Lady Frances landing blow after blow on Jane's head.

'You promised me to Edward...,' Jane managed to say as she tried to duck and dodge her mother's brawny arm. 'How can you break your word?' Sir Henry began to swear and curse angrily. Never could he have imagined that a child of his would dare defy her parents in such a way. Regardless of the fact that Jane's lip was bleeding profusely, her nose was bleeding, her hair was dishevelled and one eye was beginning to swell, Lady Frances continued to strike her daughter time after time. Only a slip of a girl compared with her mother's powerful frame, Jane suddenly fell to the floor with a sharp cry, hitting her head on a low table as she fell. She had lost consciousness. Mistress Ellen had been waiting outside the parlour, her face buried in her hands as she heard the shouting and swearing coming from within. Then she heard the crash as Jane fell. Quickly she rushed into the room.

'Take the wretched girl to her bed,' commanded Lady Frances. 'I will have no daughter of mine disobey me in so flagrant a manner.'

Mistress Ellen scooped Jane's small figure up in her strong arms, and carried her out of the room. 'Ah, my puir wee lassie, my puir wee lassie, what have they done to ye?' she moaned over and over again as soon as she was out of earshot. She laid the injured girl on her bed, fetched a basin of warm water and began to bathe Jane's face and back as gently as she could. Hot tears coursed down her honest cheeks, as she carefully removed Jane's dress and slipped a nightdress over her head. By this time Jane was conscious once more, but she did not speak, except to whisper, 'Thank you, Ellen.'

For two days Lady Jane remained in her room. She had an ugly gash on her forehead where she had struck the table; one eye was so swollen and bruised she could not see out of it. Large bruises were appearing on her neck and body where her mother had hit her.

'Ye shouldn't 'a done it, lassie,' said Mistress Ellen kindly. 'Ye well know your mama, how she will no be denied.'

'But I was already contracted to Master Edward,' responded Jane indignantly. She knew she was defeated, however, and would be left with no alternative but to marry Lord Guilford Dudley.

When Hal heard from his mother what had happened to Lady Jane he seethed with inward fury. He had seen it coming. It was all a plot—a wicked plot. Lady Jane was being snared in a plot, and in his mind he linked this turn of events with the king's serious illness. What did it all mean? Hal did not know, but suddenly he found himself thinking of that spider's web that he had seen up in the rafters when he had broken his leg. He remembered how the helpless fly was trapped in the fine silken threads. Was Lady Jane caught like that fly in a web woven by the cruelty of ambitious men and women? Then Hal remembered something else. He had just read in his New Testament some words that Jesus had spoken not long before he died. He had said to his frightened disciples, 'In the world ye shall have tribulation. But be of good cheer, I have overcome the world.'[2] That must mean, thought Hal to himself, that even though Jane may suffer in this world, nothing can happen to her that is not a part of God's plan and purpose. Those words comforted Hal.

Some days passed before Lady Jane was well enough to see Guilford Dudley, and even then her parents had to make the excuse that she had had an unfortunate fall from her horse when riding in the woods. The two young people had little in common. Guilford, tall and good-looking, did not share Lady Jane's love of learning. Although he maintained a belief in those same spiritual truths that the young king, Jane and Hal all held dear—truths that were changing the face of England and for which men and women had been prepared to die—Jane did not know to what extent Guilford felt them in his heart. He could be arrogant and churlish if he did not have

---

[2] John 16:33

things just as he liked them, but on the other hand, he was not unkind... No, Jane could not love him, but then she was not expected to have any such feelings. Duty was all that was required of young women in her position.

The wedding was planned for 25 May 1553, and a grand affair it was to be. Fifteen-year-old Lady Jane was surprised to learn that she was not the only one to be married on that day. Her younger sister, Katherine, still only thirteen, was to marry the son of the opulent Lord Pembroke, and Northumberland's own young daughter, also named Katherine, was to marry at the same time. The groom chosen for her was the son of the Earl of Huntingdon, a near neighbour of the Greys.

Hal puzzled over the choice of grooms for the three girls. Then he began to see a pattern emerging. Each wedding would link the Duke of Northumberland with some rich and powerful noble and ensure that if he were in any trouble politically he could count on the support of these families. But why did he need such backup? Everyone feared him in the way that mice fear a cat, and his violent temper meant that few would presume to cross him. Then something else dawned on Hal. If King Edward died and the Lady Mary came to the throne, the duke might find himself in serious trouble, for he had treated the princess badly, insulting her again and again. Then he would need all the support he could muster. It seemed that Lady Jane still had no idea of her cousin Edward's serious illness, nor did Hal feel he could tell her.

Situated in the Strand, Durham House, newly decorated for the occasion and hung with gorgeous tapestries, had been chosen as the venue for the wedding. Even Jane could not fail to be impressed with all the splendour that would accompany the celebrations. Members of the Privy Council, nobles and their ladies were among the invited guests. But one important guest was missing. Lady Jane was disappointed to hear that her cousin King Edward was not well enough to attend. Perhaps the duke had been wrong when he had said that the air at Greenwich had given him new strength. But Edward did order his Master of the Wardrobe to supply exquisite dresses for his cousins, Jane and Katherine, for he was fond of them, and of Jane in particular. Mistress Ellen, now Jane's senior lady attendant, fussed around the bride, assuring her that she looked charming in her gown of gold and silver brocade, sparkling with diamonds and pearls sewn into the fabric. Dressed in a scarlet doublet and cream breeches, Hal was to carry Lady Jane's train, while Master Adrian was chosen to act as page for her sister, Katherine. Hal was glad of this for he was well aware that Adrian envied his favoured position as a page. The groom, Guilford Dudley, splendidly attired in a cream outfit of purest silk, looked handsome and impressive.

The tables groaned under the weight of the luxurious dishes served for the wedding supper, and Guilford enjoyed himself heartily, sampling all the tempting fare, especially the spiced bridal cakes. Jane ate little, but tried her best to hide her inner feelings of disappointment and anxiety. After the celebrations were complete the duke ordered that each bride should return to her own home rather than to her groom's, a thing which Hal thought most strange. Lady Jane was pleased, however; she dreaded living in Syon House under the watchful eye of the Duke and Duchess of Northumberland, whom she increasingly despised and distrusted. Her young husband, Guilford Dudley, suffered from acute food poisoning that night, as did many other guests, for the unfortunate chef had to admit that he had added a wrong ingredient to the bridal cakes, a circumstance leading to his instant dismissal.

Perhaps he would never return to Bradgate again, thought Hal gloomily as he contemplated the future. Even though Lady Jane was married, he would still be required to act as her page. The outlook seemed uncertain indeed, and only Hal's increasing confidence in the overruling hand of God in all his circumstances gave him an inner peace that he could never have imagined possible before.

19
Strange things afoot

Hal was riding slowly through the woods surrounding Chelsea Manor. It was 6 July 1553 and a hot sultry afternoon. Heavy black clouds had gathered overhead, but Hal scarcely seemed aware of the threatening storm. He was turning over and over in his mind the many strange things that had happened since Lady Jane's wedding day six weeks earlier. The strain of her forced marriage to Guilford Dudley and the depth of her fear and distrust of her new in-laws, the Duke of Northumberland and his wife, had made the young bride ill. After a week or two spent at Syon House with Guilford, Jane was beginning to show alarming symptoms of strain. 'The duke hates me,' she whispered to Hal. 'He is trying to poison me, I know he is.' Nothing Hal could say seemed to reassure Lady Jane. She was scarcely eating for fear that her food contained poison, and insisted that her hair was falling out and her skin flaking—evidence of poisoning, she claimed. But why, Hal queried, should her in-laws wish to poison her? After all, she had only just been married to their favourite son. They would be widely blamed if anything should happen to her.

At last Lady Jane became so terrified that the duke ordered that she and her staff were to go downriver to Chelsea Manor for a rest.

Here Jane had been happy as a child in Lady Katherine Parr's care. Many delightful memories were associated with that beautiful home —another of the Seymour possessions which the duke had taken over after the fall of the former Protector and his family. She remembered days when she had studied with the Lady Elizabeth and when she had joined Katherine Parr's group of ladies-in-waiting to study the Bible. Jane quickly regained strength at Chelsea under the quiet care of Mistress Ellen, Mistress Elizabeth Tylney and now Mistress Jacobs, who had joined her staff after the death of Master Jacobs in the sweating sickness two years earlier. Hal was glad to see Jane looking calmer and happier for he had often prayed that his young mistress might soon feel able to face her new life as Guilford's wife with courage.

Another thing was worrying Hal as he rode through the woods that day. Strange rumours were circulating about King Edward. Not long before they had left Syon House, Hal had overheard an odd conversation between the duke and his wife, the Duchess of Northumberland. 'We cannot let him die yet,' he had whispered. The duchess had responded in a low voice: 'Why not summon the aid of Mistress Agnes? I have heard that her remedies can prolong life in many a case.' What could they mean? Hal was sure they were referring to King Edward, for it had become only too clear to him that the young king was indeed dying. But why 'not yet'? Why prolong his sufferings? The sick youth's pains were so grievous that someone had heard him say, 'I shall be glad to die.' Although Lady Jane now knew that her cousin was gravely ill, she was so distressed by her own circumstances that she did not seem to realize that he could easily die at any time.

'Who is Mistress Agnes?' wondered Hal. He had heard of a woman who claimed to cure desperately ill people, but it seemed that she only kept her patients alive for a short while longer by administering doses of arsenic to slow down the course of their disease, or so it was commonly reported. Surely the duke would not do such a wicked thing to the suffering Edward! Hal kept all these troubling thoughts to himself, and tried to persuade himself that he must have misunderstood the whispered conversation.

A third matter weighed on Hal's mind. If Edward should die, then the Lady Mary would surely become queen. What would happen if she started burning people whom she called 'heretics' as her father, Henry VIII, had done—people such as Anne Askew who, like Hal, believed that only by faith in the death of Christ for sinners could anyone be made just in God's eyes, and not by the merit of good works? He remembered too how angry Mary had been with Jane when it became clear that her cousin did not believe in what the Lady Mary referred to as 'the real presence'—the so-called change of the bread and wine into Christ's actual body and blood after the priest had blessed them. Although Hal truly believed, like Lady Jane, Anne Askew, King Edward and countless others, that this teaching was quite wrong according to the Bible, he was still deeply afraid that he would not have the courage to face cruel suffering and even death for his faith. At present there was a law against burning 'heretics' but Mary might easily have such a law revoked, or so Hal feared.

Suddenly a fierce flash of lightning, followed quickly by an ominous roll of thunder, startled Hal and banished all thoughts except one—how to get back to Chelsea Manor before the rain came. He had ridden further than he had realized and had not noticed that the sky had become black as night although it was still mid-afternoon. Soon crash followed crash, and with each thunderclap Hal's horse reared up in fear. It took all his skill to remain in the saddle. As each blinding flash of lightning tore the sky in two Hal became more and more scared. A tree fell to one side of him; another fell away in the distance—he knew that a wood is a dangerous place in a thunderstorm. Tightening his grip on the reins, Hal soon found to his relief that he was coming to the edge of the wood. Only about two more miles to go, he thought thankfully. But then came the wind and the rain which sheeted down on the young rider. Drenched to the skin and buffeted by the wind, Hal urged his animal onward and as its hooves pounded over the sodden grass, Hal's breeches and hose were soon covered in mud. At last he reached the stables and decided that he must take shelter there until the worst of the storm had passed over.

Crouching in the darkness, damp and shivering, Hal was once more a prey to unhappy thoughts. Perhaps a storm was going to break over England with the death of Edward. Maybe a storm would break over his own life too. Just turned twenty, Hal hoped that when he came of age the following year he might be able to leave Lady Jane's service. Perhaps he could marry and set up a home of his own—but who could tell what the future might hold in these troubled times? When he at last reached the servants' quarters Hal's mother was horrified at the state he was in. She insisted on making him drink a strange mixture of herbs mixed with mustard powder which Hal disliked intensely, but which his mother claimed would protect him against any ill effects of the exposure to the wind and rain.

Three uneasy days followed the day of the storm. Rumours circulated continually around the kitchens. Some said that Edward had already died. Some said that the Lady Mary was even now riding towards the capital with her supporters. No one knew for sure, and certainly no one wished to add to Lady Jane's worries by speaking to her of such things. But late on the evening of Sunday, 9 July, Hal saw a small barge docking in front of Chelsea Manor. As the boatman tied up his craft, a young woman gathered up her long skirts and stepped carefully ashore. Who was it, Hal wondered, and why was she alone? As she drew closer Hal recognized the visitor as Lady Mary Sidney, another daughter of the Duke of Northumberland—a young woman whom Lady Jane had grown to like. Only three years older than Jane, she had recently married Sir Henry Sidney, a close friend of King Edward, who had been spending much of his time with the sick king. If anyone knows the truth, thought Hal to himself, it must surely be Mary Sidney.

'I have an urgent message for My Lady Jane,' the visitor told Mistress Ellen.

'My lady is resting,' replied Ellen firmly. 'Aye, and she has been far from well, so ye may not disturb her. Your message can wait the night.'

'No, no!' exclaimed Mary in a troubled voice. 'I must see my lady.'

'Nay, that ye canna...'

'What is it, Ellen?' asked Jane, who had heard the voices outside the room where she had been sitting, deep in a book.

'My father wishes to see you immediately,' replied Mary instantly.

'Aye, no, my lady is no a-coming,' interrupted Mistress Ellen. 'I will nae have it.'

'But she must come,' replied Mary, now looking very anxious. 'My father will take no denial.'

'What does my honoured father-in-law want me for?' enquired Lady Jane.

'He has something for you—a gift ordered for you from His Majesty the King.'

'A gift?' chipped in Mistress Ellen. 'His Majesty will no be a-givin' of gifts to my lady. Why we heard he were...'

'Mistress Ellen, I will go,' said Jane resolutely, for she could see that her friend was looking terrified at the thought of returning to Syon House without her.

Darkness began to gather over the river as the small barge slipped silently through the water. Syon House lay more than ten miles upriver, and it was quite dark by the time the two young women disembarked and made their way up the path towards the rambling old mansion. Lady Jane began to tremble as they passed under the archway and into the main hall. Not a soul seemed to be about. She wondered whether it was all a trick to force her back to Guilford.

Half an hour or more passed, and still the two waited in the deserted entrance hall, Lady Jane becoming increasingly apprehensive. At last there was the sound of approaching horsemen and a moment or two later Northumberland appeared, accompanied by Lord Pembroke, father of the young man recently married to Jane's sister. With them were a number of other members of the Privy Council, including the Earl of Huntingdon and the Marquess of Winchester, men who had been ruling England until Edward was old enough to take over all the responsibilities of kingship himself. One by one these dignified nobles knelt before Jane and kissed her hand, dutifully saying, 'Welcome, my sovereign lady!' Bewildered and embarrassed, Lady Jane scarcely knew what to make of such behaviour. 'Are they mocking me?' she thought wildly.

'My sovereign lady, will you be so kind as to proceed to the chamber of state?' Jane heard the Duke of Northumberland saying in his most polished manner. As in a dream, Jane followed the duke and, to her astonishment, there waiting for her in the chamber were none other than her parents, her mother-in-law and her husband Guilford. Each of them rose as she entered and bowed or curtseyed before the astonished girl—even her own mother, who had so recently viciously beaten her daughter. Jane looked wildly from one to the other—tall figures towering above the fifteen-year-old who was little more than five feet in height. Then the duke unrolled a document and began to read in a rasping voice:

> I do now declare the death of His most blessed and gracious Majesty King Edward VI. We have cause to rejoice for the virtuous and praiseworthy life that His Majesty hath led...

Edward dead! Jane could scarcely take it in: her cousin, with whom she had so often talked and played when they were both younger, was dead! Tears sprang to her eyes. But why should she be told in so unfeeling a manner? Could she not have been informed quietly in private? She had been genuinely fond of Edward. Was he really dead? But if that had startled Lady Jane, the duke's next words were even more unwelcome:

> His Majesty hath named Your Grace as the heir to the crown of England. Your sisters will succeed you...

The voice went on heedless of the state Jane was in, for all the colour had now drained from her face. It was too much for her. Swaying to one side, she fell on the floor in a dead faint.

No one moved to help the girl. Still they stood there in silence. As Jane came round again she hid her face in her hands and began to sob pitifully: 'So noble a prince ... so noble...' Then suddenly the meaning of the duke's further words rushed over her like a blast of cold wind. 'Me, queen! No, that could never be! Lady Mary is next in line for the throne.' At last she managed to blurt out, 'The crown is not my right, and pleaseth me not. The Lady Mary is the rightful heir.'

A gasp of annoyance broke from all who stood there. This was not what they expected or wished to hear. 'Your Grace doth wrong to yourself and to your house,' growled the duke. Lady Frances scowled at her daughter. How dare she question the dead king's decision to leave her the crown rather than to his half-sisters, Mary and Elizabeth?

'You have a duty to us, your parents,' she hissed. 'You may not refuse.' Jane looked desperately from one to the other. What was she to do? And still they stood glaring silently at her. At last Guilford thought it was time for him to intervene and began kissing and embracing his frightened wife. The memory of the recent beating she had received from her mother was still raw in Jane's mind. Since infancy she had been taught that she had a duty to obey her parents in everything—and not her parents only, but the king who had been appointed by God to govern the people. Perhaps God wanted her to accept the crown. With none to help her, Lady Jane fell on her knees and began to pray silently and urgently to her God for direction at this crucial moment. And still no one spoke as every eye in the room seemed to be trying to pierce through her defences. At last in a clear and calmer voice Jane began to pray aloud:

> If what has been given to me is lawfully mine, may Thy
> divine Majesty grant me such grace that I may govern to
> thy glory and service, to the advantage of this realm.

Controlled and strong again, Jane allowed Guilford to help her to her feet, and then the Duke of Northumberland led her to an ornate but empty seat over which was spread the cloth of estate—a symbol of monarchy. All knelt before her one by one, kissing her hand and promising to be faithful to her, even to death. Lady Jane was now Queen of England.

20
From a throne to a prison

By the light of a flickering candle Hal glanced round a small attic room allocated to him in the Tower of London. It was 19 July. The young man could scarcely believe the change in his circumstances and the astonishing sequence of events that had taken place in the last nine days. Instead of a comfortable mattress to lie on in Chelsea Manor, he now had only rushes on the floor for a bed, with the occasional flea hopping around.

On 10 July, the day after Jane and Lady Mary Sidney had set off upriver to Syon House, had come the announcement of the death of the fifteen-year-old King Edward, kept secret for more than three days. It had happened on 6 July, only hours before that fearsome storm which broke over London when Hal was riding in the woods. That in itself was hard enough to grasp. But to hear that Edward, who was known to have a high respect for his father Henry VIII, had actually disregarded his will and altered the Act of Succession just before he died seemed almost unbelievable. Encouraged by the Duke of Northumberland, the dying king had apparently disinherited his two half-sisters, Mary and Elizabeth, and left his throne to his cousin Lady Jane.

Why had he done so? To Hal, who was well aware of the sharp divisions between Lady Mary's strong Roman Catholic beliefs and Edward's evangelical convictions, the answer was not hard to find. All that Edward had striven to achieve in his short six-year reign would now be undone—wasted—if his sister Mary came to the throne after his death. She would doubtless marry some Catholic prince—perhaps even a Spanish prince, feared and hated by Englishmen of the time— establish a Catholic succession to the English throne, and bring the English church back under the authority of the pope.

Edward could not just disinherit Mary, leaving the throne to Elizabeth. In fact, both his sisters had once been declared illegitimate by Archbishop Thomas Cranmer as Henry's first two marriages were annulled. Legally this meant that both had forfeited their rights to the throne. Lady Jane was therefore the next legitimate heir to the crown. But in view of the Act of Succession passed subsequently by Parliament, and by Henry VIII's will, which named first Edward, then Mary, then Elizabeth as his heirs, few would pay any attention to such conditions.

Crowds had lined the bank as the royal barge, decked with flowers, sailed triumphantly downriver to the Tower to await her coronation. But scarcely a cheer broke from the lips of the onlookers. Dressed in a magnificent gown of Tudor green, studded with rubies, diamonds and emeralds that gleamed in the July sunshine, Lady Jane stood and waved. She looked regal enough, with her auburn hair neatly tucked under her white jewelled hood and wearing three-inch[1] wooden clogs to add to her height. Yet still the faces on the bank were glum. Perhaps, thought Hal anxiously, they were only grieving for the death of their much-loved king, an event that few had expected. But he feared that the real reason might be their respect for Henry VIII's will and the widespread conviction that Mary should be their queen and not Lady Jane.

The things that happened during the following few days had taken place so quickly that they left Hal's brain swimming. As Lady Jane's page—a position of astonishing honour for a country lad from Leicestershire—he had personally witnessed the swiftly changing

---

1   7.5 centimetres

scenes in the royal apartments at the White Tower where Lady Jane held court for a few brief days. Now she was a prisoner. He could scarcely believe it. Past and present seemed to blend together in his mind as he gazed around his small attic room, trying to relive those momentous days. Despite all the professions of loyalty from members of the Privy Council, Hal soon realized that the Duke of Northumberland's plans were rapidly beginning to unravel.

On that very same Monday when Jane had been welcomed to the Tower as queen, a letter arrived from the Lady Mary demanding that she should be recognized as the rightful successor to the throne. Soon her army was advancing towards London and the people were flocking to join it. The duke himself led an army out to meet and capture her; but in his absence members of the Privy Council slipped away one by one to declare their loyalty to Mary—a loyalty they had so recently and solemnly sworn to Jane herself. Although Master Nicholas Ridley, Bishop of London, preached twice at St Paul's Cross proclaiming to a vast crowd the rights of Lady Jane to inherit the throne, his hearers were hostile. Then came the news, almost unbelievable to Hal, that the Duke of Northumberland himself had been arrested even though he too had now declared allegiance to Mary.

And so, just nine days after Jane had been proclaimed queen, came this day, 19 July 1553, one that Hal knew he would never forget. First he thought he could hear the low roar of distant thunder. Then the roar grew louder and yet louder, penetrating the eleven-foot-thick[2] walls of the White Tower. Hal then realized that it was the sound of cheering and singing. Soon church bells began to peal, madly, joyfully, and from the narrow windows Hal could see bonfires blazing in every direction. Lady Jane, who had spent the morning signing some documents as the new queen, was resting under the royal canopy or cloth of estate. But, like Hal, she knew at once that the cheering could mean only one thing: her cousin Mary Tudor, daughter of Henry VIII by his first wife, Katherine of Aragon, had been proclaimed queen instead of her.

---

2   Approximately 3.35 metres

At that very moment Jane's father burst into the room. 'You are no longer queen,' he shouted, and with his own hands began to tear down the royal canopy under which Jane was sitting. Hal stared in astonishment, and then noticed that Sir Henry was trembling all over. Where was Lady Frances? Where was the Duchess of Northumberland? Where was Jane's husband, Guilford Dudley? Was there no one left to support Jane at this desperate hour? 'You must put off your royal robes and be content with a private life,' Jane's father told her. 'I am going now to declare for Queen Mary.'

'Most gladly, my father,' Jane replied, adding, 'I much more willingly put them off than I put them on. Out of obedience to you and my mother I have grievously sinned. Now I willingly relinquish the crown.' Then Hal heard her add words that made the tears smart in his eyes: 'May I go home now?' Go home? Hal knew well that Jane might never go home, for to take the crown unlawfully was regarded as high treason and that carried the death penalty. When Jane's attendants, Mistress Ellen, Hal's mother Elizabeth and Mistress Jacobs, heard the news they looked glumly at each other, then gently helped Jane to take off her royal insignia and put on her own simple dress. But the tears were streaming down their faces as they did so.

The royal apartments were desolate and quiet. Archbishop Cranmer was still there and so was Edward's former tutor Sir John Cheke, but all the members of the Privy Council had gone. Where were they? All had one purpose in common—to save their own lives and to pretend they had never supported Lady Jane, even though they had signed official documents declaring her to be their lawful queen.

Then came heavy steps upon the stairs. In one way it was a relief from the tension in the royal apartments. Sir John Bridges, Lieutenant of the Tower, entered. A tall, burly-looking man with upright military bearing, he spoke kindly enough to Lady Jane: 'My lady, I am commanded to escort you, your lady attendants and your page Master Tylney, to the Queen's House.' Jane shuddered in spite of herself. She knew that the Queen's House, built by Henry VIII twenty years earlier in one corner of the Tower complex, was where Queen Anne Boleyn and Queen Catherine Howard had been imprisoned as they awaited their execution on Tower Green. Would it be the place where Queen Jane, still only fifteen years of age, must also wait to die?

'Where is my husband, the Lord Guilford?' asked Jane.

'My lady, he is already imprisoned in the Beauchamp Tower, together with his mother, and thither I am also instructed to conduct My Lord Bishop Nicholas Ridley,' said Sir John, turning and addressing his words to Cranmer. Silently the party filed down the old wooden stairway of the White Tower and out across the Green to the Queen's House. Ravens strutted around the Green as if they owned it, cawing noisily to each other, and the Yeomen Warders, dressed in crimson and gold, stood to attention as Lady Jane approached. Passing by the Beauchamp Tower, Hal glanced up to see if he could see Guilford. He suddenly felt a sharp pang of pity for Jane's young husband. What had he done to deserve this? Perhaps he, as well as Jane, was like a fly caught in a web spun by the intrigues and ambition of others.

Master Partridge, Gentleman Gaoler of the Tower, bustled out of his half-timbered house next door to the Queen's House to greet his new residents. A fussy little man, he enjoyed the reflected honour of being entrusted with famous prisoners. He scrutinized Lady Jane carefully. Her height and small freckled face made her seem scarcely more than a child, but it was her serious reddish-brown eyes that struck Master Partridge most of all. 'Mistress Partridge will show you to your rooms,' he said with a wide smile that revealed all his teeth, 'and should you wish to dine at our table we will be pleased to see you. Otherwise your staff will care for you.'

'I thank you, Master Partridge,' Jane replied solemnly. 'Know you where my honoured parents may be?'

'I cannot tell, my lady, and I have no orders as yet from my sovereign Queen Mary concerning them.'

Lady Jane's upstairs accommodation was simply, though adequately furnished, but for Hal a three-legged stool was the only item of furniture in his garret room, together with a small box for his possessions. His task, so Mistress Partridge informed him, was to purchase any household goods that Lady Jane might need: quills, parchment and ink for the letters she wished to write, candles for the darker evenings, fuel for the fires and provisions that Mistress Jacobs required for the cooking. He must also sweep the floors and gather fresh rushes from the river to be dried for the beds. But secretly Hal took upon himself a further task: he must do his best to cheer and support Jane. He knew she hoped that she might be released before long, but Hal was far less sure. He had noted the look on Queen Mary's face when Jane had displeased her. Would she have forgotten that and allow her young cousin to have her freedom?

Scarcely had they settled into their new accommodation in the Queen's House before steps were heard on the stairs. Who could be coming? Hal quickly recognized the Marquess of Winchester—the very one who had urged Lady Jane to try on the crown of England for size. 'Your Grace may take it without fear,' he had said smoothly when Jane had refused to try it on. And only a few days later he had switched his allegiance and was now supporting Mary. Standing in a dark corner of the room, Hal soon found out why the marquess had come. He required Lady Jane formally to renounce any title to the crown—a thing she did gladly—but that was not all. He had also come to strip the ex-queen of any symbols of royalty or position. Hal seethed with anger as he watched the marquess confiscating most of the young woman's personal possessions: jewels, hoods, furs, mufflers and even family portraits. As if that was not enough, he accused her of stealing some of the crown jewels. It was useless for Lady Jane to protest; she was nothing now—just a prisoner of the Crown—and so the marquess took his leave bearing away with him almost everything that Jane owned. All that she had left were a few garments, her writing materials, a small book of prayers and her New Testament. Seeing the fury on her page's face, Lady Jane merely asked, 'What more do I need, Master Hal?' Perhaps now she would be left in peace.

As he lay on his rush bed that night, tossing and turning and unable to sleep, Hal could hear the roar of angry lions nearby. Henry VIII had imported the animals into the country and they were kept in the Lion's Tower, not far from the outer bulwarks of the Tower of London. Hal sincerely hoped that they were secure, for only a moat separated them from access to Tower Green.

And what did the future hold? Not only was Lady Jane a prisoner, but with Mary as queen who could tell what might happen to those who clung to the evangelical truths of the Bible? Then Hal realized that he was trying to face a situation that had not yet arisen, so before he blew out his candle, he spent some time looking for words he had read recently in his New Testament. At last he found them—words that gave him courage to face an unknown future: 'Therefore, my son, be strong in the grace that is in Christ Jesus ... endure hardness as a good soldier of Jesus Christ.'[3] Hal was soon fast asleep, unconscious of the hardness of his bed or of the bedbugs and fleas crawling around.

---

3   2 Timothy 2:1:3

21
Mistress Sarah Bridges

From the upstairs window of the Queen's House Hal had a clear view of all the comings and goings at the Tower. But there was one spot on Tower Green, not far from the Chapel Royal, St Peter-ad-Vincula, that Hal tried to avoid looking at. That was where, so the Yeoman Warders told him, high-profile executions had always taken place. Whenever he had to cross the Green, Hal made sure he kept as far away from there as possible. All but one of the six who had been beheaded on the Green had been women, including the seventy-year-old Margaret Pole. She had died only a year before the execution of the beautiful but flighty Queen Catherine Howard on a February day in 1542. Hal remembered well how distressed he had been as a nine-year-old when he had heard of Catherine's death. No other execution had taken place there since then. Yet how easily Queen Katherine Parr could have ended her life in the same way had Hal not found that warrant for her arrest! 'Who will be next?' he wondered, and he tried to push the thought from him. But sometimes as he lay on his bed of rushes at night his imagination seemed to run wild.

Three days after Lady Jane was taken prisoner, Hal saw her father, Sir Henry Grey, Duke of Suffolk, being led towards the Beauchamp

Tower, hands tied behind his back. Hal could hardly bear the sight, for although Sir Henry had urged his daughter to take the crown, he had never been as cruel to her as her mother. Hal was glad that Jane was not near the window at that moment to witness his capture, and only told her the news later as gently as he could.

Not long afterwards the Bishop of London, Nicholas Ridley, was pushed roughly across the Green. He too was to be confined in the Beauchamp Tower. Master Ridley had been appointed to take the place of the cruel Bishop Bonner—the very one who had burnt Hal's New Testament. Unlike Bonner, Ridley was a good and kind man who had done much to benefit the poor and the sick. Hal turned from the window in disgust. What had the bishop done wrong? Nothing except preach fearlessly the truths of Scripture—truths that the new queen rejected. But his open support for Lady Jane now meant disgrace and imprisonment.

Then who should stroll across the Green a short time later but Bishop Bonner and Bishop Gardiner themselves, now released from prison and reinstated to their former positions? Truly these were bad days.

As Hal mixed with the London crowds when he went to the market, he would often pick up scraps of news and carry them back to the ladies in the Tower: news of riots, of celebrations, of the forthcoming trials of those who had supported Lady Jane. He learnt of the uproar among the people when the captured Duke of Northumberland was escorted through the city to join his family in the Tower. Splattered with rotten eggs and pelted with mud and stones, the unpopular duke would have been lynched by the mob had it not been for the protection of his guards.

Jane had been a prisoner for almost two weeks when Hal slipped out of the Tower on some errand only to discover himself caught up in an extraordinary crowd of excited men, women and children swarming around the approaches to Middle Tower, which stood at the main entrance to the Tower complex.

'What's happening?' Hal asked a tall bearded man, clearly in from the country with a basket of vegetables for sale.

'Sooth, man, ain't you heard? Our queen is coming. Why, hark 'ee, cannot ye hear the trumpets a-blowing?' Crushed at the back of the crowd, Hal could hear the chanting, 'God bless Your Grace! God bless Your Grace!' growing louder every minute. Many around him were weeping with joy; others were throwing their hats into the air and yelling themselves hoarse. Then the Tower cannons began thundering out their greetings to their new queen until Hal was almost deafened by the sound. How different from the way that Lady Jane had entered the White Tower scarcely a month earlier! As the crowds parted, Hal caught a glimpse of Queen Mary wearing a long purple dress and riding side-saddle on a handsome stallion. Across the drawbridge that spanned the moat and under the portcullis she proceeded, and on towards the White Tower. Even Hal could not help noticing how much happier Mary looked than when he had last seen her. Beside her rode her half-sister, the Lady Elizabeth, appearing apprehensive and anxious to please. She had changed a great deal since Hal had last seen her, and was a striking figure with her long auburn hair flowing down her back. How like Lady Jane she looked, thought Hal, only much taller!

'Are you not the Lady Jane's page?' asked a quiet voice beside Hal. Hal turned swiftly to see who spoke. A fair-haired young woman of medium height, with the bluest eyes Hal had ever seen, was standing not far from him.

'Why should you think so?' replied Hal cautiously. Certainly it would not be safe to admit such a thing on a day like this.

'Sure I am that I have seen you from the window of my father's house,' answered the speaker.

'Who then are you, may I enquire?' asked Hal politely.

'My name is Mistress Bridges, Mistress Sarah Bridges. My father is Sir John Bridges, Lieutenant of the Tower, and a sorry task it is, caring for the wretched prisoners cast into the dungeons.'

'Then perhaps I ought to tell you that my name is Hal Tylney, and I have served My Lady Jane since I was but thirteen years of age,' admitted Hal at last. 'I find in my heart a deep sorrow for my lady. It was no fault of hers that the crown was forced upon her. Indeed, she has been treated with much wickedness by those who should have cared for her the most.' Hal had blurted out far more than was wise in the circumstances. What if this young woman should report it to her father? Would Hal also be cast into prison?

'I too weep for my lady as I lie in my bed at night,' replied Mistress Bridges unexpectedly, studying Hal's face. 'I pray earnestly that God will give her a safe deliverance from this dreadful place. But my father rebukes me for such sympathies.'

Hal was so surprised by her answer that he could not think of anything else to say, and so merely asked, 'Are you returning now?'

'I am,' replied the young woman. 'This is no time for walking abroad. My father is attending the queen in the White Tower, and will be there for many hours. And ... and my mother is dead,' she ended, her voice choking with emotion. 'She died in the sweating sickness two years ago this very day. I was but sixteen years of age, and my sister Hilda no more than ten. Her loss is one that I still find hard to bear.'

'I too almost died in the great sickness, but God in pity spared my life, and now I have a strong desire to serve him well while I may,' replied Hal, colouring up with embarrassment as he spoke.

By this time Hal and Mistress Bridges had crossed the Green, and she turned to go towards the lieutenant's accommodation, not far from the Queen's House. 'Perhaps we shall meet again, Mistress Sarah,' said Hal shyly as he opened the door of the servants' back entrance, for in fact he felt great loneliness in his present circumstances.

Reaching the dayroom where Lady Jane now spent much of her time, Hal discovered she was busy at the table writing something. She scarcely looked up as he passed, and Hal knew better than to disturb her. After some time Jane called for her page: 'Good Master Hal, I have written a letter to my cousin, the Queen's Majesty, begging her forgiveness for my sin against her person...'

'But it was no fault of yours that the crown was thrust upon you,' protested Hal.

'Master Hal, will you not listen to what I have written and tell me if you think Her Gracious Majesty will pardon my offence?' Seeing that any protest of his was useless, Hal sat down on a small stool at her feet to listen to her letter. It was a long and detailed explanation of the circumstances that had led up to that night at Syon House when she had accepted the crown. She told of her forced marriage to Guilford, of the surprise summons to Syon, of the way she had fainted when she heard of the death of her cousin Edward, of her fear of disobeying the king and her parents, of her certainty that the Duke of Northumberland had tried to poison her, and continued:

> Although my fault be such that but for the goodness and clemency of the Queen, I can have no hope of pardon, nor in finding forgiveness, having given ear to those who at that time appeared to be wise ... I trust in God that as I now know and confess my want of prudence, I can still conceive hope of your infinite clemency.

'Hal, do you think that this my letter will be received by Her Majesty?' Jane asked wistfully, as if Hal might know the answer to such a question.

'I know not, my lady, but your cousin, the Lady Mary, and now our queen, once showed much kindness to you,' replied Hal. 'Even now she is in the White Tower—I saw her a-coming and heard the cheering of the people. Perchance if her heart is full of joy she will receive your letter kindly and I pray she may show mercy, not to you only but to your household.'

'How then may my letter reach the Queen's Majesty?' enquired Jane.

Hal thought for a moment and then exclaimed, 'Why, even today I met Mistress Sarah Bridges, daughter of Sir John! She will surely give it to her father to pass to Her Majesty.'

Jane looked at him sharply, but only said, 'May I then entrust it to you?'

'You may, my lady, I shall carry it in my doublet and pass it to Mistress Sarah when next we meet.'

'Do so, and may God grant me mercy, for he knows my misery and has been to me a strong tower of defence since first I knew his grace,' replied Jane earnestly.

The very next day, as Hal was laying out the newly gathered rushes to dry in the hot August sun, he glanced up and saw Mistress Sarah approaching him. Straightening up, Hal greeted the young woman brightly. 'Good day, Mistress Sarah,' he said, and then added quickly, 'My Lady Jane has written a letter to Her Majesty. Would you most kindly ask your father to pass it to her?'

'Why yes,' laughed Mistress Sarah merrily. 'It seems that I have the part of a courier, for I come to give you a letter written to My Lady Jane from her unhappy husband, My Lord Guilford. He frets much and cannot sleep for fear of some dreadful outcome of these things. He thinks of the cruel axe, and weeps, for this was none of his doing.'

'I know that full well, Mistress Sarah,' replied Hal seriously. 'He is no more than sixteen and has never known hardship afore.'

'He grieves for the comforts of his wife's presence and wishes me to take her his letters,' continued the young woman, and then she added in a low voice, 'Have you heard that my lord duke, his father, must soon come to trial? I fear it will go but ill with him.'

By this time Sarah had sat down in the sunshine not far from Hal as he continued his work spreading out the rushes. Before long the two were chatting like old friends. Hal told her of his childhood home, of the tragic death of his father, although he omitted any details, then of his appointment to serve Lady Jane. He even told her of his discovery of the warrant for Queen Katherine Parr's arrest and of her death in childbirth after having been rejected and taunted by her husband, Lord Thomas Seymour.

'I saw My Lord Thomas die on Tower Hill. I had never seen an execution before; nor do I ever wish to see one again,' said Sarah with a shudder. 'But my father who attended him told me that never had he known a man face death with so impenitent a heart. Why, even in his dying he still plotted the overthrow of his brother, the good duke, our Lord Protector.'

'Tell me, Mistress Sarah, what think you of the faith of our young king, so sadly departed, and of My Lady Jane?' Hal dared to ask at last.

'It is my own,' was Sarah's simple reply. 'When my mother was a-dying she had deep joy in her heart, although she wept to part with husband and children, for she said, "I go to see the face of him who died for me." And to me she said, "Seek him, my child, nor fear those who would deceive you." It was her last wish. For her sake I asked my father to allow me to hear those preachers whose teaching my mother had followed. Even though he was troubled about it, he granted me his blessing. In his heart I think he believes as I do. But he fears to say so.'

'Who then did you hear preach?' interrupted Hal, wondering if it could have been Master Cranmer, or even Master Latimer, whose preaching had touched Hal himself.

'At St Paul's Cross I heard one whose face and eyes I can never forget. Surely, I said to myself, those eyes have looked beyond this sad world, even into the face of Christ. His name was Master John Bradford, and sweetly did he preach Christ crucified for sinners. I heard him say, "Christ Jesus will be a sufficient Saviour even for you that cast yourself on his mercy." And this I did.' Suddenly Mistress Sarah's voice wavered and her eyes filled with tears.

'What ails you, good Mistress Sarah?' asked Hal in concern.

'I grieve to tell you that even now Master Bradford lies in chains in a dungeon deep down below the Bell Tower. Nor has he done anything amiss. Indeed, my father told me he had but tried to calm the crowd who would kill one, Master Gilbert Bourne, appointed by our queen to preach at St Paul's Cross this Sunday gone.'

'But why should they do that?' interjected Hal.

'A great uproar had broken out among the hearers, many of whom were angry with Master Bourne, who had most wickedly denounced the truths of the Bible and of evangelical religion. Some cried, "Kill him! Kill him!" Then one threw a dagger at him, but Master Bradford begged the crowd to hear him in peace.'

'Why then should Master Bradford be imprisoned?' demanded Hal in astonishment.

'My father tells me,' replied Mistress Sarah, 'that our Bishops Bonner and Gardiner accused him of stirring up the mob in the first place. But, indeed, that is false.'

'Then none is safe save those who hold the queen's religion!' exclaimed Hal with a mixture of anger and alarm.

'I fear you are right, Master Hal,' said Mistress Sarah as she wiped her eyes and prepared to go, 'but Christ will strengthen those who love his name and his truth.'

'You sound like My Lady Jane,' said Hal with a short laugh. 'Forget not my lady's letter, I pray.'

And with that Mistress Sarah Bridges was gone. Nor did Hal see her again for several days. Yet, try as he would, he found thoughts of the fair-haired young woman filling his mind. Perhaps one day he would be able to get to know her better. But who could tell what might happen before such a day came?

22
Cowardice and courage

With time on his hands, Hal often wandered along the battlements that linked the individual towers running along the eastern wall of the Tower of London. Mainly used for storage purposes, these towers formed a powerful line of protection for the city of London. In peacetime, however, the servants of prison officials and even those serving important prisoners were allowed to walk along the walls between the towers. Mounting the rough stone steps leading into the dim recesses of the Salt Tower, Hal climbed on and up to the top, then made his way to the next tower, called Broad Arrow Tower. The name fascinated him and in his imagination he could see brave men of past generations defending their city from marauding bands of invaders. Now it was used to store supplies for the royal palaces. Best of all, as far as Hal was concerned, such a walk gave him a view of things that went on far below him, both in the city to one side and within the Tower walls to the other. Sometimes distinguished visitors called to pay their respects to the queen as she awaited her coronation in the royal apartments of the White Tower, and Hal would watch them come and go.

Now and then he had seen Guilford on the battlements of the Beauchamp Tower, where the young prisoner was allowed to take some exercise. Although Lady Jane could walk around Tower Green, she was not permitted to see or speak to her husband. One day, as Hal was standing on the battlements of Martin Tower and was about to turn back the way he had come, being permitted to go no further, the young man gasped with astonishment. Who should be arriving at the White Tower but Lady Frances herself, obviously calling upon the queen? 'Perhaps she has come to plead for her daughter's freedom,' thought Hal excitedly, as Jane's mother entered the precincts of the White Tower. Perhaps she would even come across to the Queen's House to visit Jane. But she did not come. Only later did Hal learn that she had come to beg the cause of her husband, Sir Henry and, indeed, she was successful, for after only two weeks in the Tower he walked away a free man. Hal was glad for Sir Henry's sake, but felt a bitter resentment in his heart against the woman who had brought so much suffering upon her daughter, and yet seemed quite indifferent to her plight.

Sometimes Hal would visit the Lion's Tower, not far beyond the main entrance. To hear the creatures roar as they paced their cages was enough to scare off any intruder, Hal thought to himself. The noise still often kept him awake at night. The Keeper of the Menagerie, a young man called Master Nicholas Platt, was glad to show Hal round. His was a dangerous and dirty job, as he had to clean out the cages and feed animals that had sometimes become wild with hunger. He told Hal of the day when a lioness broke out of her cage and flung herself at him. Only by his fast reactions, and with the aid of a cat-o'-nine-tails to drive the furious animal back to her cage, had he managed to save his life. Visitors paid a fee to come and see the animals, but if they brought a dead creature with them to feed to the lions, they were admitted without charge.[1]

Two weeks after the queen had entered the White Tower, Hal heard an astonishing piece of information. As he mingled among the crowds entering the city through the great Postern Gate bringing

---

[1] The menagerie was moved from the Tower in 1834 to form the nucleus of London Zoo.

cattle and other goods to market, it seemed that everyone was talking of the same thing.

'He must die tomorrow on Tower Hill,' he heard one old woman say in a gleeful voice.

'Aye, but have you heard he has changed his religion?' answered another.

'Like as he thought he might win his life from Her Majesty,' chipped in a third. Hal had no problem in guessing of whom they were speaking. He had already heard that the Duke of Northumberland, John Dudley, had been brought to trial in Westminster Hall and had been found guilty of high treason. He was condemned to be hung, drawn and quartered—the most dreadful sentence that could be pronounced and reserved only for the worst offences. Apparently the duke had begged for mercy and the queen had taken pity on him and commuted the sentence to one of execution on Tower Hill. But what was this about changing his religion? Surely, thought Hal, the strongly Protestant duke had not turned from his professions of faith and become a Catholic once more? What a worthless profession that would be!

Returning from his errand, Hal discovered Lady Jane and her three lady attendants, Mistress Ellen, Hal's mother Elizabeth and Mistress Jacobs, all standing at the window looking across to the Chapel Royal, St Peter-ad-Vincula. They were watching a small group of prisoners approaching the chapel from the direction of the Beauchamp Tower. Leading the way was Bishop Gardiner, his cruel face set in a look of smug satisfaction; as Hal joined the ladies at the window, he had no difficulty in recognizing the tall athletic form of the Duke of Northumberland among the prisoners, once so erect but now looking a frightened, defeated man. He was followed by one of his older sons, also called John, who had actually taken part in the fighting and had been condemned to death like his father. Several others whom Hal did not recognize were also in the party. At the back came Sir John Bridges, Lieutenant of the Tower. They were on their way to the chapel to allow the duke to take mass for the last time and to make a formal renunciation of the Protestant faith before he died. Hal guessed what Jane was thinking and was glad that Guilford was not among that group. At least the young man had resisted the pressure to renounce the faith he had been taught, and which his wife, Lady Jane, held so resolutely.

From first light the following morning the crowds began to gather on Tower Hill to watch the execution take place. Gradually the volume of noise grew greater. Pipers played; girls danced; merchants sold their wares; men swore, pushed and juggled for the best positions; pickpockets were busy everywhere: it sounded more like a public holiday than the occasion of a fearsome execution. The sounds floated across from Tower Hill, the crescendo growing ever louder. Hal's contempt for the duke was such that he was tempted to join the crowd, but his respect for Lady Jane, whose father-in-law Northumberland was, decided the matter, as he busied himself in the kitchen instead. A mighty roar rose from the crowd as the executioner struck the fatal blow and, as was customary, lifted high the dead man's head, crying out, 'Behold the head of a traitor.' Hal wondered if Guilford had heard the cheer and realized what it meant.

Master Nicholas Platt, the Menagerie Keeper, was anxious to provide Hal with all the details, but the young man scarcely wanted to listen. 'And do you know what he said from the scaffold?' persisted Master Platt, 'Why, he warned everyone against teachers of the new doctrine. He said they only pretend to preach God's Word, but really preach their own fancies.'

'That is wickedness indeed!' exclaimed Hal in spite of himself. 'He himself was foremost in advancing such doctrines in our land in the reign of our late good king.'

'What think you of these things, Master Hal? For I cannot tell what to believe,' asked Hal's new friend as he finished describing the duke's death.

'I believe firmly in those truths the duke denied in his dying,' replied Hal steadily. He found it hard to say so, for by nature he was timid. But how could he say he wished to serve Christ if he failed at so fundamental level as this? 'I struggled long and read the Scriptures, but only when I believed in my heart that Christ had suffered for my sins did I find the joy of forgiveness in my soul.'

Master Platt opened his mouth to say something, but then shut it again. At last he said, 'One day you must tell me more,' and then busied himself chopping up a dead dog someone had brought in to be fed to the lions.

Three days after the death of the Duke of Northumberland, as Hal was sweeping the floor of the dayroom, Lady Jane suddenly announced, 'I wish to join Master Partridge and his wife to dine this day. Could you and your mother, Mistress Elizabeth, be ready to accompany me?' Jane did not often eat with the Gentleman Gaoler and his wife, but she was in a bright frame of mind that day, for the news had just filtered through to her that, though she and Guilford would shortly stand trial, it was unlikely that they would face the death sentence. It seemed that Jane's letter to the queen had moved her to show pity on her young cousin, despite the fact that Jane's religious views annoyed her intensely.

No sooner had Jane taken her seat at the head of Master Partridge's table, a place of honour still assigned to her even though a prisoner, than an unexpected visitor entered the room. Startled to discover Lady Jane present, Master Rowland Lea, an official of the Royal Mint, immediately doffed his cap. Feeling more cheerful than she had for many weeks, Jane proposed a toast to the visitor's health and immediately began to ply him with questions. Confined to the precincts of the Tower, she wished to know all about things that had been taking place beyond her prison fortress. Hal listened with interest to the conversation as he stood against the wall ready to serve Lady Jane at the table.

'I pray you, have they mass in London?' Jane wanted to know. The mass had been forbidden by law in the reign of Edward and its restoration in the London churches would be a clear indication of the future religious order that the new queen would impose. Nor was Jane surprised to hear that, although the law had not yet been changed, such services were being held across the capital.

Soon the conversation turned to the execution of the duke and his last-minute change of religious views in order to try to save his head from the executioner's block.

'Perchance he hoped thereby to win his pardon,' suggested Master Lea. Even Hal was astonished at the vehemence of his young mistress's response. It showed him how deeply the sufferings she had already endured had affected her:

> Pardon? Woe worth him! He has brought me and our family into most miserable calamity and misery by his exceeding ambition... Who was judge that he should hope for pardon, whose life was odious to all men? But what will ye more? Like his life was wicked and full of dissimulation [hypocrisy], so was his end thereafter.

Clearly all the pent-up sorrows and anger were pouring out. But then she said something which made Hal jump visibly, for it showed that Jane had already looked the prospects of a terrible death full in the face and had counted the cost of remaining faithful to the truths of God in which she placed her trust:

> I pray God, that I, nor no friend of mine, should die so. Should I who am young and in my few years, forsake my faith for the love of life? Nay, God forbid! Much more should not he [Northumberland]. Life is sweet, it appeared, so he might have lived in chains to have had his life... But God be merciful to us, for he says, 'Whoso denies him before men, he will not know him in his Father's kingdom.'

Jane's courage reminded Hal of that demonstrated by Lady Anne Askew, who had been burnt at the stake for her unwillingness to believe in the Roman Catholic doctrine of the mass. It gave him a new determination to remain true to the Saviour even though he too might face hard days ahead.

Following the execution of the Duke of Northumberland, the queen decreed that her two young prisoners, Lady Jane and Lord Guilford, were to be allowed a greater degree of freedom. For a few weeks they were permitted to meet at the discretion of Sir John Bridges and could walk together around the grounds of the Tower. Hal was glad and during this brief period he noticed that Jane was looking more relaxed than he had seen her since before her marriage. Gradually a measure of true affection was growing between the young couple and both hoped that following their trial, due to take place on 13 November, they might be released. Hal shared their hopes, but strangely had one regret—if he should leave the Tower, any further opportunity to develop his growing friendship with Mistress Sarah would come to an end. He often smiled secretly to himself because he had noticed that whenever he had some errand to fulfil on Lady Jane's behalf which took him outside the Tower precincts, it appeared that Sarah also had urgent business to which she must attend in the same direction. This meant that they often met up apparently by coincidence—but perhaps it was not coincidence. Was Mistress Sarah noting his movements from the window of her father's house?

During their brief conversations waiting at some market stall, or even at the tallow merchant's shop, Mistress Sarah gave Hal news of different prisoners which she had learnt from her father. 'Today I saw an old man, a bishop of the church, being brought into prison,' she informed Hal one day in early October. 'His hands were tied behind him with ropes, his beard was matted and he walked with difficulty— but his eyes were bright and sharp. My father knew him, for he had been here as a prisoner many years earlier.' From Sarah's description, Hal knew instantly that it must be 'old Father Latimer.' The thought pierced through him like a knife.

'Good Mistress Sarah, what can My Lord Bishop Latimer have done to anger the queen? Is there no justice left in our land? He is but an old man. I fear that if he is thrown into the dungeons it will kill him.'

But Hal's alarm and anger reached a new height when he saw Archbishop Cranmer himself being hustled into the Tower two days later. Both these men had served their God and young King Edward with loyalty and faithfulness.

'Oh, when will God arise and avenge his righteous cause?' he demanded, with despair in his heart, when next he met Mistress Sarah.

'I cannot tell,' she replied, 'but this I know, that if the man Christ Jesus was cruelly abused and crucified, how can his servants expect to pass through this world without suffering?' It was a thought that had not occurred to Hal. He knew she was right, but that did not stop him grieving for these good men so harshly treated. Now Master John Bradford, Bishop Ridley, Bishop Latimer and even Archbishop Cranmer were all prisoners of the Crown—their future most uncertain.

As the golden October days crept past, a season that Hal loved, he thought wistfully of the autumn trees at Bradgate. How he wished he could wander in the woods or by the river, hear the cries of the rutting stags, and trace the shining cobwebs in the hedgerows! Even in so sad a place as the Tower of London the spiders seemed to vie with each other to decorate the old grey battlements with their webs. But inevitably there would be a fly, or even more than one, caught helplessly in the filaments. And who could tell what the future might hold, not just for the bishops but for Lady Jane, just turned sixteen, for Guilford, and even for himself and Mistress Sarah? Weren't they too like flies caught in a web?

23
Condemned

Hal sat on the wharf not far from a flight of steps leading down to the riverside from the Queen's House. He gazed idly at the boats as they passed up and down the river. He heard the cries of the boatmen, but they scarcely seemed to penetrate his troubled mind. It was 13 November 1553, and Lady Jane and her husband Guilford, together with two of Guilford's older brothers, Ambrose and Henry, and also the Archbishop of Canterbury, Thomas Cranmer himself, had just returned from standing trial at the Guildhall.

Lord Chief Justice Richard Morgan had presided over the trial and had declared Jane guilty of high treason. She would either be burnt alive or, if the queen felt merciful, would die on Tower Hill under the executioner's axe. Hal's mother Elizabeth and Mistress Jacobs had attended the trial, but Hal, who was not required, could only wait back at the Tower for the verdict. All the accused had been found guilty: Guilford and his brothers were condemned to be hung, drawn and quartered. Hal felt sick and very angry when he heard of the sentences. Even the archbishop, who was forced to change his plea from one of 'Not Guilty' to one of 'Guilty' was sentenced to death. Hal escaped from the dayroom where his mother, Mistress Ellen and

Mistress Jacobs were all sobbing uncontrollably because their young mistress had been placed under sentence of death. The only one who was not crying was Jane herself. 'Remember I am innocent and did not deserve this sentence,' she declared bravely, but added, 'yet I should not have accepted the crown.'

A water rat scrambled up the bank and flicked its tail cheekily as it scurried past Hal. Still he sat motionless, confused and distressed. He had spent the time of the trial praying earnestly that Jane and Guilford at least might be declared innocent and acquitted. No one knew either when, or even if, the death sentence would be carried out. But the very fact that it had been passed meant that at any moment, and without further jurisdiction, Jane could be beheaded or even burnt. The thought was too terrible to contemplate. It was unjust; it was cruel; it was wicked. Hal fought back his own tears as he thought about it. Then he remembered that just two days earlier he had overheard Jane praying in her room. Her exact words had been imprinted in Hal's memory:

> Suffer me not to be tempted above my power, but either be a Deliverer to me out of this great misery, or else give me grace patiently to bear thy heavy hand and sharp correction... Shall I despair of thy mercy, O God? Far be that from me. Give me grace therefore patiently to bear thy works... I refer myself wholly to thy will...

Hal bit his lip and bowed his head. If Jane could face the possibility of a terrible death—and she was only just sixteen—then surely God would also give him strength and grace to submit to his will, however hard it might be to bear. Numbly he rose to his feet and stumbled back towards the steps leading to the Tower. As he came to the door of the Queen's House he saw Mistress Sarah at the window of the lieutenant's accommodation.

Hal's ashen face and set expression told Sarah all she needed to know, but her bright smile and cheery wave comforted him as he mounted the stairs back up to the dayroom.

And these were strange days. Not only had Queen Mary's first parliament revoked all the laws of religious reform passed under King Edward's government, but also the Book of Common Prayer which

Archbishop Cranmer had compiled had now been declared illegal. Would anyone who still clung to the forms of worship used only a few months ago be safe? More than this, it was rumoured that the thirty-seven-year-old queen now planned to marry. 'That is a good thing,' thought Hal to himself; 'perhaps she has chosen some English nobleman to help her govern wisely.' But he soon learnt otherwise, for one day as he went out to buy provisions in the marketplace he heard some worrying comments flying around.

'No Spaniard is a-goin' to come to these shores,' declared one. 'Aye, and if she marries him there will be a rebellion,' added another. 'You mark my words.'

'England for the English,' chipped in a third. 'The Spaniards will take our land and make us their slaves.'

'I'd sooner die than see my queen marry one of 'em,' threatened another voice.

Clearly there was trouble afoot, and Hal soon learnt that it was because the queen had announced her engagement to Prince Philip of Spain, son of the powerful Holy Roman Emperor Charles V, whose desire to annexe England and add it to his own vast domains was well known among the people. Englishmen had long feared and disliked the Spanish, and rumours of the atrocities of the Spanish Inquisition were passed from mouth to mouth. Would they treat the English in that way too? Even tradesmen were alarmed lest their own businesses should be undermined by Spanish enterprise.

Back in the Tower Sir John Bridges soon informed Lady Jane that she would no longer be able to walk freely in the Tower grounds, nor see or speak to Guilford. She was to be restricted to her rooms in the Queen's House. 'Perhaps Queen Mary fears that there might be an attempt to overthrow her and set Jane back on the throne,' thought Hal. As November turned to December, Jane was clearly becoming ill and depressed. The days were overcast and grey and little daylight penetrated the rooms in which she was confined. The only scraps of news that reached the prisoner were those that Hal or one of her three lady attendants picked up as they left the Tower from time to time. 'Why do Sir Henry and Lady Frances never visit Jane?' thought

Hal angrily. And still rumours of a forthcoming rebellion sparked by the queen's marriage plans grew ever stronger.

Much of Jane's time was spent sitting at the window reading her Greek New Testament. Hal looked in amazement at the strange symbols on her page and wondered how she could possibly understand them. A small book of prayers which belonged to both Jane and Guilford also seemed to bring her much comfort. Sometimes Jane wrote letters, very long ones on occasion, and Hal had to make sure she had a supply of quills, paper and ink and that her letters reached her correspondents safely.

Guilford too was finding the days hard. His father was dead and he and his four brothers were all under sentence of death. Often Jane wrote notes to him in reply to his, always trying to encourage and strengthen his resolve. She would remind him that the Saviour had promised a crown of life to those who were faithful to him even to death. Mistress Sarah was willing to act as the go-between, and as Hal and Sarah met when letters were exchanged, they would often discuss the troubling situation. On occasions they even spoke of their own futures, perhaps together, should Lady Jane ever be released from prison.

But it seemed that Jane herself had begun to lose hope. One day Hal discovered some strange writing on the wall of the dayroom. It had been scratched with a pin. He could not read the words and wondered if Jane had written them in another of those strange languages she seemed to be able to read. Certainly they were not like the words in her Greek New Testament. He spelled out a few of the words: '*Post tenebras lucem spero*.' At last Hal asked Jane what the writing meant. 'It is Latin,' she said simply. 'I will read you that one; I think it is the best. it says, "After the darkness I hope for light." One day, Master Hal, it will be light for me again, but I begin to feel it will not be in this life.'

'My lady's spirits are sadly discouraged,' said Hal to Mistress Sarah one day. 'If only she were able to leave her rooms and walk abroad once more! I fear she will but waste away if nothing is done.' When Sir John learnt that his prisoner was ill, Jane was allowed out once more for brief periods of exercise, but never without the watchful eye of Master Partridge or some prison official. And still, as that grievous year of 1553 slipped away and 1554 dawned, the news that filtered through to the prisoners continued to be disturbing. People spoke of a forthcoming rebellion against the queen, and reports of an attempt to put the Lady Elizabeth, or possibly Lady Jane, on the throne instead of Mary increased daily.

Hal tried his best to shelter Lady Jane from the rumours which were growing more alarming all the time. But as the short days of January wore on, even he could not prevent her from seeing all the bustle and activity in the Tower. Cannons were being wheeled into place to protect the city from any approach along the River Thames, while heavy ordnance was moved out of storage and placed at strategic points along the walls. News that a four-pronged attack on the capital was imminent reached the prisoners in the Tower towards the end of the month, and now Lady Jane realized that whether she lived or died depended on the outcome of the rebellion.

'I have this day heard that My Lady Jane's father, the Duke of Suffolk, has joined the rebels,' whispered Mistress Sarah to Hal one evening. Recently Hal and Sarah had been meeting secretly in the disused Salt Tower when their day's work was complete. Hal's heart sank when he heard her words. This was indeed a certain death sentence for Lady Jane should the rebellion fail. That her own father, so recently released from prison by the queen, should be among the rebels showed to Hal his utter disregard for his daughter's life. 'He has marched to Coventry to raise the city against the queen, and plans to bring a force from Leicestershire to the capital,' added Sarah, who picked up news from reports brought to her father, Sir John. Should Hal tell Jane this grievous information? He scarcely knew what to do, but decided that she must be allowed to prepare for the most desperate eventuality, and if she did not know of her father's involvement it could be a cruel kindness to keep it from her.

Late in January came news that the rebellion had actually begun. Thousands were marching up from Rochester in Kent, armed with any implement they could find, and chanting, 'We are Englishmen! We are Englishmen!' These were led by Sir Thomas Wyatt, son of one of England's best-known poets. Along the way the people were streaming out of their homes to join Wyatt's makeshift army. But any information about the troops coming from Leicestershire was hard to come by. Even worse were the reports that rebels from Wales and the West Country had already been routed by the queen's forces.

Hal kept his visits to the market to a minimum, for there was talk of a siege of the Tower, with demands that the queen should voluntarily surrender her throne to avoid bloodshed. But when Hal did venture out on 30 January, he discovered the market deserted; he could hear women screaming with fear, saw shops being boarded up in every direction and panic written on all faces. 'They are camped on Blackheath Common,' yelled someone. Even as Hal listened he could hear the sounds of bugles and shouting coming from the direction of Blackheath. As he hurried back to the Tower, Hal nearly bumped into Master Nicholas Platt, Keeper of the Menagerie. He had a squealing piglet under each arm, which he had stolen from a farmer who was hurrying to get back out of the city before the gates were closed. 'Else the animals in the Menagerie will starve,' he told Hal by way of excuse.

By early February it looked as if victory for Master Wyatt and his men might be in sight, for now his troops were advancing towards Southwark and would soon stream across London Bridge. From there they would march to Whitehall Palace, where they would demand that the queen should either agree to abandon her marriage plans, or surrender her throne. But at that critical moment Mary herself arrived at the Guildhall and made a rousing speech, stirring up her people to rise in her defence. And so they did. Just as Wyatt and his men arrived at London Bridge, the queen's troops managed to raise a blockade so that none could cross. His men, now hungry and tired, had no alternative but to march many miles upriver to the next crossing point at Kingston. From the Tower the sound of gunshot could be clearly heard. All in the Queen's House were nervy and silent. Then the noise died away as the rebels began their long march to Kingston. From that moment the battle was effectively lost.

On 5 February there were a few renewed skirmishes around St James's Park, but most of Wyatt's forces had either deserted or had been picked off as they struggled to march back downriver once more towards Westminster. The expected reinforcements from Wales, the West and Leicestershire never came. By 6 February prisoners were being led into the Tower in droves. Lady Jane could see them coming

—some being dragged in, others coming quietly; some wounded; all with a look of defeat on their faces. Where was her father? No one seemed to know. But one thing was now certain: Lady Jane could not have much longer to live. And the next day, 7 February, the queen signed her cousin's death warrant. Both Jane and Guilford were to be executed on Tower Hill on 9 February.

24
A better coronation

Hal saw him first. A small rotund figure dressed in clerical robes was crossing the Green, heading in the direction of the Queen's House. Perhaps, thought Hal, he has been visiting the bishops, Masters Latimer, Cranmer and Ridley, and Master John Bradford. Sarah had told him that these four leaders of the Protestant church had all been thrown into one small cell, owing to the sudden influx of prisoners after the rebellion. Crowded they might have been, but Hal imagined that it would give these suffering servants of Jesus Christ much joy to be together. But no, the priest was clearly coming to visit Lady Jane. What could he want with her? She would have no wish to see a Catholic priest, of that Hal was sure.

A heavy knock on the door below alerted the women in the dayroom to the arrival of the visitor. Lady Jane recognized him instantly. This was none other than Dr John Feckenham, personal chaplain to Queen Mary, and recently appointed Dean of St Paul's. Mounting the stairs and entering the dayroom, Dr Feckenham immediately turned to Lady Jane, his usually jolly face grave and troubled. 'Madam, I lament your heavy case...,' he began. Hal gasped. All that he most dreaded lay in those few words. He could hardly bear to hear the rest of the sentence. The words fell like hammer blows on his reluctant ears: 'You are to be executed tomorrow on Tower Hill together with your husband, My Lord Guilford Dudley.'

What would Jane do? Would she faint, weep, fall at the priest's feet and beg for mercy? Or would she protest her innocence? To Hal's astonishment the girl did none of these things. Instead she addressed the priest in a steady, measured tone: 'As to my heavy case, I thank God I do so little lament it; rather I count it a manifest declaration of God's favour towards me than ever he showed me at any time before.' What an extraordinary thing to say! How could she regard the news of her forthcoming execution as a sign of God's favour? That seemed incredible to Hal.

But Feckenham had not come just to bring Jane notice of the death warrant that had been signed. He had a second purpose, and the young Tudor ex-queen knew very well what that was. He had come to put pressure on her to turn from her evangelical faith and become a Roman Catholic instead. Even if her body must perish, so the queen had said, he must try to save her cousin's soul. 'You are welcome to me, sir, if your coming be to give me Christian exhortation,' Jane continued in a guarded fashion. Taking her words as his cue, the priest began to raise the points of difference between Jane's firmly held beliefs and his own. Although Lady Jane had been courteous enough to Feckenham when he arrived, she had no wish to prolong the discussion. If she must die the next day, she wanted to spend all the time she had left in preparing herself for the ordeal she must face and in seeking the grace and forgiveness of God. 'My time is short,' she told Feckenham. 'Leave me, I pray you, that I may seek my God for his mercy before I die.'

Seeing he had been unable to engage Lady Jane in discussion, Feckenham turned and left the room. As he closed the door the three women who had cared for Jane so faithfully burst into loud cries. But where was Hal? He was nowhere to be seen. In fact he had climbed up to his attic room and was sitting on his three-legged stool, head between his hands—overwhelmed by grief and horror. If only he could die instead of Jane—it was all too dreadful to contemplate.

Feckenham may have gone, but he had certainly not given up his attempts to convert Lady Jane to the Catholic faith. If only he had a few more days, he was sure he could succeed, he told the queen, urging her to give him more time. But even Feckenham was astonished at Mary's response. Yes, she would allow Lady Jane three more days to live and, even more amazing, she would cancel the death warrant against her young cousin if she would accept the Roman Catholic faith. Clearly if Jane became a Catholic, the Protestants would no longer wish to put her on the throne. Jane would therefore pose no further threat to Mary. Hurrying back to the Tower, Feckenham was in high spirits. All Lady Jane must do was to turn away from her faith, and her life would be secure! Surely this was good news indeed! But Jane's heart sank when the priest gave her the queen's message.

'Alas, sir,' she said in dismay, 'it was not my desire to prolong my days. As for death, I utterly despise it, and Her Majesty's pleasure being such, I willingly undergo it.' The priest looked totally stunned, as Jane continued: 'I assure you, since the time you went from me, my life has been so tedious to me, that I long for nothing so much as death. Neither did I wish the queen to be solicited for such a purpose.'

At last Hal began to understand Jane. All she had suffered over the last six months, and even from her earliest years, had made her long for nothing more than a deliverance from the sorrows of earth, and an entry at last into that land where all tears are wiped away for ever. A violent death was indeed terrible, but it had become a preferable option to the continuance of the life she had known, especially in the light of those joys in store for the Christian in heaven. To postpone her death by a further three days, now that the queen had signed her death warrant, could only extend her present sufferings.

'Ask Her Majesty, I pray,' begged Jane as Feckenham turned to go once more, 'that the day of my death be not delayed.' But the hours dragged by and still the priest did not return. Not until the following morning, the day first proposed for the execution, did Feckenham once more knock at the door of the Queen's House. No, the queen would not allow Lady Jane her wish. The execution would still take place on 12 February. But she did make one apparent concession. Lady Jane would not die on Tower Hill, which was open to the public gaze, but rather on Tower Green—in that very spot where Anne Boleyn and Catherine Howard had perished. Even now Hal could hear the rhythmic banging of hammers as workmen began to erect the scaffold in full view from the window of the Queen's House. 'This change of place is no act of kindness,' thought Hal angrily. 'Her Majesty knows full well that if two innocent young people should be executed where all may watch, a riot might easily ensue.' Only Guilford would die on Tower Hill, the exact spot where his father had so recently ended his days.

'My lady, I desire you to attend a public debate on those few matters of difference between us,' continued Feckenham, 'and may I remind you, madam, that Her Majesty, our most gracious queen, has promised that you shall live, if you do but concede your error in these things. Your father-in-law, the honoured Duke of...'

But Jane wished to hear no more. Interrupting him, she snapped, 'Such disputation may be fit for the living, but not for the dying. The truest sign of your compassion for me, which you have strongly professed, will be to leave me undisturbed to make my peace with God.'

Still Dr Feckenham would take no denial. To him this seemed the last chance to save this young woman's life. As he looked at Jane, so petite, so young, so highly intelligent, he could not help grieving that she should prefer to face the scaffold rather than to accept the Catholic faith. Seeing he would not be refused, Lady Jane at last consented to face a panel of Catholic theologians in the Chapel Royal of St Peter's the following day.

Hal wondered whether Jane would give way under such intense pressure. In his heart he knew that she should not and, indeed, that she probably would not, but his affection for Jane, dating from that time when he had found the four-year-old child sobbing, hidden in the undergrowth at Bradgate because her mother had beaten her yet again, made him waver.

'Master Hal, I need your support. Will you accompany me to St Peter's?' asked Jane.

'I too shall come, my lady,' insisted Mistress Ellen. Although Hal's mother, Elizabeth, shrank back from such an ordeal, Mistress Jacobs, sturdy, red-faced and angry, also insisted on coming. She was determined to support Jane to the last. The sorrow and pain which these three faithful women, who had loved and served her all her life, were enduring made it no easier for Jane.

The next day, shortly before Lady Jane was due to face the clerics, Hal was suddenly alerted by shouts from Tower Green. Looking out of the window, he was horrified by what he saw. A bedraggled, ill-looking man, unshaven and dejected, was being dragged across the Green towards Beauchamp Tower. At first Hal did not know who it was. Then suddenly he looked again. Surely not! It could not be! With a gasp of recognition, Hal realized that the prisoner was none other than Jane's father, the Duke of Suffolk. Whatever could have happened to him that he should be in that condition? There went a man who had carried the sword of state at the coronation of Edward VI—one of the highest nobles in the land—reduced to such a pitiful wreck. The young man fought back his tears, and was only glad that Jane was still in her bedchamber, and had not seen him pass.

The scaffold was almost complete when Jane and her small company, guarded by Sir John Bridges, crossed the Green to go to the Chapel. Stark and menacing it stood, as if it were saying to the prisoner, 'This is what awaits you if you will not give up your faith.' Mistress Sarah Bridges had urged her father to allow her to attend, and Hal glanced quickly in her direction as he passed by the panel of the dignified clerics in their long priestly robes, all gathered to oppose one young woman of sixteen years of age, condemned to die if they did not succeed in their persuasions.

Dr Feckenham opened the proceedings: 'I am here come to you at this present, sent from the queen to instruct you in the true doctrine of the right faith, although I have so great confidence in you that...' It almost sounded as if he thought that at last Lady Jane would capitulate. Hal glanced across at her. He knew well enough by the set of her face that Feckenham and his priests did not have an easy task before them.

Not surprisingly, the two issues that were endlessly debated that day, first by one and another of the priests and then by Feckenham himself, were the two great areas of dispute between evangelicals and Catholics: the teaching concerning the mass and the grounds on which a sinner may be justified before God. Back came Lady Jane's answers, time and again, always respectful, yet always firm. When the priest asserted that good works must be added to faith before a man can be justified, Jane retorted:

> I deny that. I affirm that faith only saves, but it is right for a Christian to do good works ... but when we have done all, we are unprofitable servants, and faith only in Christ's blood saves us.

Hal found himself marvelling at Jane's answers.

At last, almost in despair, Feckenham threw one final accusation at Jane: she based her faith on human teachers, not on the church. Hal wondered what she would say to that. Her answer was clear and certain:

> No, I ground my faith upon God's Word and not upon the church, for the faith of the church must be tried by God's Word, and not God's Word by the church.

And then with a final devastating sweep, for she was now in full flow, she added:

> And I say, that it is an evil church ... that alters the Lord's Supper, and both takes from it and adds to it. To that church, say I, God will add plagues, and from that church will he take their part out of the Book of Life.

Dr Feckenham had the last word, and a long and tedious speech it was; but it became clear that, even with all his learning, he was defeated. As those clever men filed out of the chapel, Hal's heart swelled with a new admiration for his young mistress, yet a new sorrow that felt like a crushing weight rested on his shoulders. Now he knew for certain that Jane must die in two days' time. As she said her final farewell to the priest who had tried hard to save her life, he heard her asking Feckenham to accompany her to the scaffold and support her to the end. Clearly she had learnt a true respect for Dr Feckenham, who had treated her with unusual kindness, despite their disagreements. Yet even then she added: 'But I fear we shall never meet again unless God turn your heart, for I am sure that unless you repent you are in an evil case.'

The next day was a Sunday—the last day of Lady Jane's life. Sir John Bridges himself came up to the dayroom to see her. A man hardened to the sufferings of his prisoners, and one who had witnessed brutality many times, he had been touched in a strange way by his young captive's courageous bearing. He had come for two reasons; the first was to bring a message from Guilford, also condemned to die the following day. 'My Lord Guilford is in grievous distress,' he began. 'He weeps and begs most earnestly that he may see you again before he suffers that he may bid you farewell, my lady.' Despite Jane's unwillingness to marry Guilford, a bond of affection had been forged between the young couple, as both had suffered together because of the ambition of others. Lady Jane now thought carefully about Guilford's request. She feared it could be the one thing that would undermine her resolve, and his as well, in their last moments of life. Kindly, yet firmly, she sent back a message to Guilford:

> The tenderness of our parting will overcome the fortitude of us both, and will too much unbend our minds from that constancy which our approaching end requires of us.

But she did agree to stand at the window to see him pass on his way to the scaffold on Tower Hill, to encourage him during that last bitter walk to remain constant and cast himself on the mercy of God.

And Sir John had one more request. Surprisingly, he asked Lady Jane for some memento of herself, a small reminder to him of his brave young prisoner. This she promised him and in turn asked him to take her last messages of love and forgiveness to her father—so near yet never to see her again. Pulled unceremoniously out of a hollow tree after three days in hiding, Sir Henry now presented a pathetic figure. And to that father, whose action was the direct reason for her death, Jane had now written, assuring him that 'Nothing can be more welcome to me than from this vale of misery to aspire to that heavenly throne of all joy and pleasure with Christ our Saviour.'

Late that night Lady Jane was writing a last letter to her sister Katherine. Her lady attendants had gone to bed, unable to bear any more sorrow. Hal alone sat with her in the semi-darkened room. Too

197

grieved to sleep, he did not wish to leave Jane alone. If she were suddenly overwhelmed by fear, she might need someone at hand to comfort her. Jane had no paper left and was writing to her sister on some blank pages of her Greek New Testament. Unexpectedly she looked up and said, 'Hal, I thank you with all my heart for all your loyal service to me. There is but one more thing I ask of you. Could you take this my book and the letter therein to my sister, Katie?'

'Gladly will I do that, my lady,' replied Hal, 'for I hear that your sister weeps much for the things that have come upon your family.'

'Listen to what I have written,' continued Lady Jane, 'for herein lies my last message to you as well as to Katie.' And then by the flickering light of the candle, the girl destined to die by the cruel axe within a few hours began to read her letter to Hal:

> Trust not that the tenderness of your age shall lengthen your life; for as soon (if God call) go the young as the old. Defy the world, deny the devil and despise the flesh and delight yourself only in the Lord. Be penitent for your sins, yet despair not... Rejoice in Christ, as I do. Follow the steps of your Master, Christ, and take up your cross; lay your sins on his back, and always embrace him. And as touching my death, rejoice as I do that I shall be delivered from this corruption and put on incorruption... I pray God grant you to live in his fear, and to die in the true Christian faith, for which in God's name, I exhort you that you will never swerve. Farewell, and put your only trust in God, who only must help you.

'My lady, I shall never forget your words, and may God grant me grace to be faithful to his name, even if I should also be called upon to face such a death.' These were perhaps the hardest words Hal had ever spoken, for they touched on the one thing he had always dreaded: the possibility of having to endure a cruel and violent death for Christ's sake. But Jane by her courageous example was pointing out the way. 'My lady,' he added, 'will you not now take some rest? And may Christ comfort and sustain you to the end.' His voice wavered unsteadily as he said those last words, for he scarcely knew how he could bear to watch Jane die.

The morning of 12 February dawned cold and overcast. Hal was up early, raking out the ashes of the fire. If he could do no more, he could at least see that the room was warm and comfortable. Lady Jane, neatly dressed in a long black gown, with a scarf at her neck, stood at the window, for soon Guilford would pass on his way and she had promised to support him as he kept that final severe appointment. Before long the fair-haired young man came into sight, escorted by Sir John and one or two others. He had obviously been crying and looked very frightened, but as he passed the window he glanced up and smiled. Jane had kept her word, and the sight of her gave him fresh courage. She remained at the window after he had gone, as still as a statue. So soon, so very soon, they would return for her. And within fifteen minutes the rattle of a cart bearing its sad bloodstained burden for burial at St Peter's could be heard approaching across the Green. Leading the way was the Constable of the Tower, with the executioner following behind.

'O my puir, puir child, do not stay,' cried Mistress Ellen, trying to protect Jane from the ghastly sight. But Jane still stood at her post, until she suddenly turned, and for the first time Hal saw that the tears were streaming down her face.

'O Guilford, Guilford...' was all she was heard to murmur, as she began to write something in a book that lay on the table.

By the time the Constable had mounted the stairs of the Queen's House and arrived in the dayroom, Lady Jane had composed herself, but her three lady attendants were sobbing bitterly as they emerged into the bleak February air. Hal followed. He dared not look at Jane in case he too lost control. Dr Feckenham was awaiting her and, slipping her hand into his, Jane crossed over to the black-draped scaffold. As she went she was reading from her small book of prayers. Hal was grateful to see that Mistress Sarah had summoned enough courage to come and support Lady Jane, even though her eyes were red and her face swollen with crying. Hal gave her hand a comforting squeeze as he took up a position at the foot of the scaffold together with prison officials, soldiers and others who had been allowed into the Tower to witness the execution. The three ladies and the priest mounted the scaffold with Jane where Sir John and the executioner were already standing.

'May I speak what is on my mind?' Jane asked Sir John.

'Yes, madam,' came the terse reply.

'Good people, I am come hither to die,' began Jane in a clear voice as she confessed that she had been wrong to accept the crown, but declared boldly that she had only done it because others had told her to and she had assumed that they knew the law better than she did. 'I do wash my hands thereof in innocency before God, and the face of you, good Christian people...,' she continued. Reaffirming the grounds of her faith, Hal heard Jane say, 'I do look to be saved by no other means, but only by the mercy of God, in the blood of his only Son Jesus Christ.' But most of Jane's words passed over Hal as if he were caught in the middle of some fearful nightmare. As in a dream he heard Jane repeating a long psalm begging God to forgive her sins. He even heard her thanking Dr Feckenham for his kindness to her, and giving the customary pardon to the executioner for the dreadful deed he was about to perform.

But what happened next would be engraved on the young man's memory for the rest of his life. Again and again he would wake at night in a cold sweat as the whole scene flashed before his eyes. Jane had passed her gloves and a small handkerchief to Mistress Ellen, a token of her gratitude for the love that Ellen had shown throughout Jane's sixteen years. She gave her book of prayers to Sir John, the promised memento; then Hal's mother Elizabeth stepped forward to give Jane a handkerchief to tie across her eyes, but all three women were too broken to do much to help her. Then Hal heard the executioner say, 'Stand upon the straw, madam.' Jane edged forward a little, mesmerised by the sight of the block and the huge axe. Then she struggled to tie the handkerchief over her eyes.

But she had misjudged her distance from the block and now she was groping wildly in the air, trying to find it. Then Hal heard her cry of distress: 'Where is it? Oh, where is it?' Not a single person moved. No one could bear the responsibility of helping an innocent victim to die. 'What shall I do?' she cried—a terrible, unforgettable cry of anguish. It seemed to tear Hal's whole being in two. Then, with a heart breaking with pain and love, he bounded up the steps, took both of Jane's small hands in his and guided them gently towards the block. 'Be of good courage, my lady,' he whispered in her ear. Jane knew well who had helped her in her last desperate ordeal.

'Lord, into thy hands I commend my spirit,' she called out in clear triumphant tones. Then all was over. With one cruel, dreadful stroke her head was severed, her short life ended. But in that moment the young uncrowned Queen of England was granted a better coronation —crowned with the crown of life, promised to those who are faithful unto death.

25
A gift for Katherine

For some hours Jane's small body lay unattended on the scaffold while officials disputed over where she should be buried. Some argued that, as a heretic, she could not be buried in the Roman Catholic chapel of St Peter's. Others, however, reasoned that, as a daughter of one of the noblest families in the land, even a queen, if only for nine days, she deserved an honourable burial. At last, with objections overruled, her body was hastily laid in a rough coffin and buried in St Peter-ad-Vincula between the remains of two other former queens of England, Anne Boleyn and Catherine Howard, and not far from the spot where Guilford had also been buried.

Jane's weeping lady attendants were back in the dayroom, trying to pack up their few possessions, for they could no longer stay in the Tower. Mistress Jacobs would return to Bradgate House, where she could take up her position once more as head of the kitchen staff. Mistress Ellen was also needed to care for little humpbacked Mary Grey, still only ten years of age. For Elizabeth Tylney, however, the future was bleak: she had no home in Newtown Linford and it seemed her services would no longer be necessary at Bradgate. Almost certainly Sir Henry would also face the death sentence for his part in the uprising, and as for Lady Frances, she was apparently serving the queen at the Palace of Whitehall as one of her matrons of honour.

But where was Hal? No one had seen him since Jane's death, and now the shadows of night were beginning to draw in on that sad February day.

Distraught with grief and anguish at Jane's death, and burdened with horror at his own part in it, Hal had walked along the riverbank until he found some lonely spot where he could sit unobserved. There he broke down and sobbed until he could sob no more. All the pent-up distress of those anxious months leading to the death of an innocent young woman found a release at last. Jane had been helplessly trapped in a web of intrigue and wicked ambition, woven by unscrupulous people and by the religious intolerance of a queen whose bigotry robbed her of compassion. Yet Jane's trust in the pity and mercy of her God had never wavered.

Despite the darkening sky, Hal still sat staring straight ahead of him with unseeing eyes. So preoccupied was he with his misery and anger that he failed to hear light footsteps approaching. Sarah sat down beside Hal and placed one arm across his shoulder. She did not speak; indeed there seemed little she could say. Together they sat side by side, finding consolation in a shared sorrow. At last Hal began to weep once more. 'I helped her die. I helped her die. How can I ever forgive myself?' was all he could say.

'It was your last and greatest service of love,' replied Sarah quietly. 'She needed you more at that moment than in all her life before.'

'I wish I too could die. How can I go on living?' responded Hal in a low voice.

'Come, Hal,' replied Sarah. 'What about your mother? She has none but you to support her. And what about me?'

'You?' Hal whirled round and looked the girl full in the face. Sarah's long fair hair was matted, her eyes still red with crying. Suddenly he realized that he had been selfish in his grief. 'Mistress Sarah, you are right. My Lady Jane needed me very much at the last... and... and... I... I love you, Sarah,' he stammered, 'but I can never marry you. I have no means of supporting you, and now that Jane is dead I will no longer be needed at Bradgate. Your father would never allow us to wed unless I could support you.' For reply Sarah merely slipped her hand into Hal's and together they walked back along the riverbank into the gathering gloom.

Back in his attic room Hal carefully opened Jane's Greek New Testament which he had pledged to take to her sister, Katherine. He ran his finger reverently over the strange symbols which Jane could read but he could not. 'She no longer needs the consolation of these words,' he thought to himself, 'for now she sees the face of the one whose words they are.' Then he turned to the letter at the back, closely written in Jane's neat hand. 'This book will lead you to the path of eternal joy, good sister Katherine.' It was a path Jane herself had trodden, thought Hal to himself. Then he saw some other words which reminded him of something Jane had said to him long ago: 'Live still to die, that you by death may purchase eternal life.' Clearly Jane herself had long lived with eternity in view and weighed all the events of her life in its light. It reminded Hal of a verse he had discovered in his own New Testament which asked the question: 'What shall it profit a man if he should win all the world, but lose his own soul?'[1]

The next day Hal knew that he must try to put the terrible events of the last few days behind him, and make arrangements for his mother and himself. But first he must say farewell to Master Nicholas Platt, the Keeper of the Queen's Menagerie. Master Nicholas was sorry to see Hal go, but suddenly said, 'My mother has a room to spare in her house not far from the Postern Gate. Pray, will you and your mother not stay with us until you find some more suitable place?' Hal accepted the offer with gratitude and discovered that Madam Platt's plump motherly personality and cheerful chatter were just what he needed most at that time. Nor would he be too far from Mistress Sarah, at least for a few days.

On the Wednesday morning, two days after Jane's death, Hal set out on the long walk across the city to Whitehall Palace, where Katherine served as a chambermaid to the queen. He wished he had

---

1   Mark 8:36, Tyndale version

enough money to hire a boat, for everywhere he turned gruesome corpses were hanging from trees and posts, the vicious punishment of those who had taken part in the rebellion against the queen. The sight was appalling. After reaching Newgate Prison, Hal picked his way along Fleet Street and down the Strand. Memories of these places came flooding back, but he pushed them resolutely from his mind. He must find Lady Katherine quickly. At last he reached the palace, all so familiar to him, and was soon enquiring the way to Katherine's apartments.

Suddenly Hal stopped short. Who should be approaching him but Lady Frances herself, and behind her none other than the tall figure of Master Adrian Stokes? Adrian cast his eyes downward when he saw Hal, and Lady Frances enquired sharply, 'What is your business here, Master Hal?'

'Madam,' replied Hal bowing slightly, 'I would wish to tell you how much I sorrow for the death of your daughter, My Lady Jane.'

'Foolish girl,' muttered her mother under her breath, 'throwing away her life!'

'Madam,' persisted Hal, 'I promised my lady not long before she suffered to bear a message to her sister, My Lady Katherine. Can you tell me where I might find her?' He did not mention the New Testament in case Lady Frances should claim it. In reply, and without a word of enquiry as to the welfare of Hal's mother Elizabeth, Lady Frances jerked her thumb in the direction of some rooms at the end of the corridor.

'Weeping as usual, I'll not doubt,' she said, adding, 'She does nothing but cry all day. And what good that will do her, none can tell.'

'Good day, madam,' replied Hal politely and set off in the direction Lady Frances had indicated. Sure enough, when Katherine responded to his knock, Hal could see she had been crying. 'I too have wept,' said Hal sympathetically, although it soon became clear that Katherine was not grieving over the death of her sister, but over her own circumstances. 'Did you not hear that my marriage with My Lord Pembroke was annulled? Now I fear I will never wed more.' And Katherine began to cry again. How like Jane she looked, thought Hal to himself, with the same auburn hair and bright-looking eyes, but how unlike her in character and personality!

'My lady, I bring you a gift from your honoured sister, My Lady Jane. It is her Greek New Testament from which she received comfort the night before she suffered. In the back she has written a letter to you.'

'Thank you, Master Hal,' said Katherine, wiping her tears with the back of her hand. 'I would do well to heed my sister's words, for I hear she died strong in the faith. And who can tell in these evil days how long any of us may live?' Hal smiled faintly. That certainly sounded more like Lady Jane's spirit. Bowing courteously, he left the fourteen-year-old to unwrap her gift, and made his way out of the palace, glad that Lady Frances and Adrian were no longer in sight.

Hungry after his long walk across London, Hal stopped to buy a newly-baked pie from a stall in Fleet Street, and then set off back towards the Tower. How strange it felt after years of caring for Lady Jane to have no responsibilities, no one to whom he must answer! Men and women passed backwards and forwards on their business and there was an uneasy calm in the city. Everyone now realized that their queen was determined to marry the Spanish prince, but what that would mean in the future, no one could say.

Hal knew that he must urgently seek for work in order to support his mother, but what could a country boy do in the great city with none to help him? He did not know the answer. Perhaps he could find work on Billingsgate Market. At least he might still see Mistress Sarah from time to time if he did, for she sometimes came to the market to purchase her fish...

But just as Hal was approaching the city walls at Newgate, he saw someone walking towards him whom he instantly recognized: a short, stocky figure with a heavy black beard, small twinkling eyes and bushy eyebrows.

'Good day, Master Squires,' said Hal politely.

'Why, bless me, and who are you?' enquired Master Squires, squinting into Hal's face. Then with a roar of recognition, he exclaimed, 'Now who would have thought it? Why if that isn't Master Hal from Bradgate, then my name's not Ebenezer Squires.'

'You will have heard why I am here,' said Hal steadily.

'Why yes, and I have heard a lot more too. My friend Sir John Bridges has told me of your courage, young man. A bad job, that were, a very bad job,' he added lowering his voice, 'caught like a rat in a trap, that young woman. My heart breaks to think of so wicked a deed. Bad days these, I say, bad days.'

'I shall never forget her,' responded Hal quietly, 'never.'

'Tell me, young man, and what are you going to do now?' enquired Squires.

'That I cannot tell, sir,' replied Hal, 'but I had thought I might find employment in Billingsgate Fish Market, for I must support my mother.'

'Tush, man, smelly things, fish,' retorted Squires. 'What do you know about property management?'

'Nothing, sir, but I could learn,' answered Hal eagerly.

'Where are you living?' asked Squires.

'We have lodgings with Madam Platt, not far from the Postern Gate, but that is only until I can find work and permanent lodgings.'

'In that case, you shall live with me. As it happens, the manager of Sir William Cecil's properties is now too infirm to continue his employment. So a position is vacant from next week. But,' he continued, speaking in little above a whisper, 'Sir William has to take care not to offend the queen any more. Although he was not in favour of King Edward's change to his father's will, he did sign the document granting the throne to My Lady Jane. Right bad job it were, a bad job.'

'I would be glad to take up the position, sir, but what about my mother?' enquired Hal.

'I need another cook,' snapped Master Squires. 'And I shall be round to collect you in three days' time. Good day, young man.'

It had all happened so quickly that Hal could hardly believe it. For the first time since Jane's tragic death a small flicker of hope began to spring up in Hal's heart. And if he could earn a good wage, perhaps one day he could return and claim Sarah Bridges for his own.

26
An unexpected reward

True to his word, Master Ebenezer Squires arrived three days later, leading a horse for Hal to ride, with his mother riding pillion. 'Now before we go,' he announced in his booming voice, 'I wish to have a drink with my good friend Sir John. And when I return, we will be off. So if there is anyone to whom you wish to say farewell, this is your time.' That was a strange comment, thought Hal. Could Master Squires possibly know of his friendship with Sarah? But then if he were friendly with Sir John, it might be that Sarah had told her father.

While his mother gathered their few possessions together, Hal raced over to the secret meeting place in the Salt Tower where he and Sarah had so often sat and chatted in the evenings. She might just be there. And, yes, she was. She appeared to be reading a book when Hal hurried up the old stairway. 'Mistress Sarah,' he gasped, for he was out of breath, 'I have good news; Master Ebenezer Squires has offered me work, and although I have come to say farewell, it may not be for long.' Sarah smiled delightedly, for she had heard all about Hal's earlier encounters with Master Squires. 'And, Sarah, when I have saved up enough money, I will return and ask your father for your hand in marriage.'

With shining eyes the young couple embraced, but just as Hal turned to go, Sarah said, 'This is the book that My Lady Jane bequeathed to my father on the scaffold. See here is her message to him.' Hal recognized the small red book instantly, for he had often seen it in Jane's hand. In the half-light of the Salt Tower it was not easy to read the message, but Hal gradually made it out:

> Forasmuch as you have desired so simple a woman to write in so worthy a book, good Master Lieutenant, therefore shall I as a friend desire you, and a Christian require you, to call upon God, to incline your heart to his laws to quicken you in his ways and not to take the word of truth utterly out of your mouth...

And then Hal gasped—for coming next were the very same words again that Jane had written to Katherine: 'Live still to die, that by death you may purchase eternal life...' Perhaps God was engraving that message on Hal's heart. Perhaps he would need it one day. He too might have to suffer for his faith. Who could tell?

'My father was moved by those words; I think he does believe, but he is afraid,' said Sarah. 'It grieved him deeply to see her die. And, Hal, there is something more I must tell you. Sir Henry was brought to trial three days ago, and must die on Tower Hill on 23 February. See here,' she continued, 'Jane had also written a message to her own father in the margin of this book. My father took it to show Sir Henry, and he seemed cheered by it.' Nor was Hal surprised to see that Jane had sent a similar message to her father:

> I trust that we [she and Guilford], by losing this mortal life, have won an immortal life; and I, for my part, as I have honoured Your Grace in this life, will pray for you in another. Your Grace's humble daughter, Jane Duddley.

It almost seemed as if Jane were standing in that semi-darkened room with Sarah and Hal, speaking to them. 'I think she would have been glad to know of our love,' whispered Sarah.

'I think she did know of it,' responded Hal. And then giving Sarah a quick hug, he tore himself away. 'I will be back,' he promised.

'Whither are we bound, Master Squires?' asked Hal as they turned the horses along Drury Lane and on into Eastcheap. 'Sir William Cecil lives in Canon Row, in Westminster,' answered Squires, 'and that is where I work. But you, Master Hal, you will find yourself on many a journey. Ho, ho! Are you still sure you will work for me? My master has properties as far north as Lincoln, and but three years since has acquired the Manor of Wimbledon.' Hal did not reply. A cold February wind was blowing sharply in his face, but his real reason for not answering was that he was saying to himself, 'Let me go anywhere, anywhere, as long as I can soon return and claim Mistress Sarah for my own.'

Arriving at Canon Row, Hal and his mother were soon following Master Squires, cantering down the long drive leading to Burleigh Place, where Sir William lived with his wife Lady Mildred Cecil and two small daughters. Sir William cast a long, sceptical look at Hal when Master Squires introduced the twenty-year-old as his new property manager. Hal's close connection with Lady Jane was not an asset at that time, but Squires' enthusiasm for the young man was a recommendation that it was hard to ignore. 'Humph, we'll see,' was his only comment, and then as an afterthought he added, 'I did hear of your courage at the Lady Jane's execution, but I would ask you not to mention the name of that young lady in this place.' Hal felt an inner surge of anger at this, but a warning glance from Master Squires checked him. Instead he merely said, 'It will be an honour to work for you, sir. I have travelled much and am a quick learner.'

'I go to attend the execution of Sir Henry this day,' announced Squires several days later. 'Well do I remember him as a young man jousting with his father-in-law, Sir Charles Brandon. I grieve much that his days should end in so sad a fashion. While I am gone, I will direct Master Rogers to instruct you in all the work you must do in respect to Sir William's estates.' Hal was grateful that Squires did not suggest that he should accompany him to Tower Hill, for indeed, it would have been more than Hal's spirit could bear.

When Squires returned later that day he drew Hal aside, and said in a low whisper, 'My Lady Jane would have been justly proud of her father this day, for in spite of his sin against her, he spoke good words on the scaffold. He said, "I die in the faith of Christ, trusting to be saved by his blood only (and not by any trumpery) the which died for me, and for all them that truly repent and steadfastly trust in him." Could she have wished better?'

'No, sir,' replied Hal. 'But may I ask you whether My Lady Frances supported her husband at the end?'

'Lady Frances? Ho, ho, ho!' roared Squires. 'Much too taken up with that fancy boy of hers. You know his name?'

'I do, sir. It is Adrian Stokes. I know him well.' Hal turned away in disgust. At almost forty years of age, what was Lady Frances doing courting the attentions of a youth of twenty-one while her husband and daughter were dying dreadful deaths? Remembering Sir William's warning, Hal did not say any more about the Grey family. Who could tell what might happen if he mentioned some of the things he knew? A mere three weeks after the execution of her husband, Hal heard that Lady Frances had married Adrian Stokes, a marriage that could no longer be delayed for she was already carrying his child.

Hal learnt quickly, and within a few weeks he was beginning to ride as far as Lincoln and out to Northamptonshire, to check on Sir William's properties. Daily life at Bradgate had already taught him much of the routine of staffing and supervising a stately home and of collecting rents from tenant farmers. Sir William even nodded his approval when Hal passed him in the corridor one day, which gratified Hal. Gradually Hal was beginning to save some money, a thing he had not been able to do in all the years of serving Sir Henry and his wife. Elizabeth too was being better paid and she added whatever she could to Hal's growing account. She knew of her son's love for Sarah Bridges and was anxious to help him in any way she could.

On a beautiful day late in spring when the may blossom hung like white clouds on bush and tree, an official-looking visitor galloped up the drive leading to Burleigh Place, saying he had business with Sir William. After an hour or more he cantered off again. Hal had scarcely noted either his arrival or departure, but then a surprising thing happened: Sir William sent a messenger requesting to see Hal. Never had he exchanged more than a few words with his young employee before, and Hal hurried to Sir William's office, hoping that all was well.

'I have just had a visit from Sir James Stepney, the attorney-general,' he announced. 'He has been handling the affairs of the late Sir Henry Grey. Apparently Lady Frances is anxious that her previous husband's will should be dealt with as speedily as possible. Why that should be so, I cannot tell. But there is a clause in the will that you may be able to explain:

> To Master Henry Tylney, who as a boy saved the life of my infant daughter, Lady Katherine Grey, at the jousting tournament in 159-9-, I bequeath the sum of £100.00 sterling.

Can you explain that to me?' Sir William gazed at Hal, carefully watching his face.

'I can, sir, but it was nothing,' said Hal in astonishment. 'The infant Katherine managed to escape from her nurse and was running to her father's horse as it galloped towards Sir Charles Brandon's mount. I managed to grab her just before the horse struck her, but my own leg was broken in the incident.'

'It seems you are well known for acts of courage,' commented Sir William Cecil dryly. 'Sir James had trouble tracing the one named in the will, but Lady Frances said she had heard of you, and directed him to me to trace your whereabouts. My only fear is that with such an endowment you will no longer wish to fulfil your employment in respect to my estates.'

'Oh. yes, sir,' responded Hal quickly. 'I am wanting to marry, and perhaps this legacy will help me to win the approval of the bride's father.'

'And who, may I ask, is the young woman you have in mind?' asked Sir William, and Hal could not help noticing a slight twinkle in his eye.

'It is Mistress Bridges, sir, Sarah Bridges, daughter of Sir John, Lieutenant of the Tower.'

'Then as your employer I shall be glad to wish you well, for I have met the young woman you mention, and indeed you seem to know how to make a fine choice.'

Covered with confusion and delight, Hal left Sir William's office, his heart racing with joy and excitement. £100! He could scarcely believe it. It was as much as his father would have earned in twenty-five years. It seemed like a fortune to Hal, although he was well aware that in terms of the worth of Sir Henry's vast estates it was indeed a modest sum. All that now remained was for the money to be accredited to him, and then he would be able to cross London once more to ask Sir John Bridges for the hand of his daughter.

One morning in early June, some four months after Jane's death, Hal asked Master Squires' permission for some time off work. 'And where might you be going this fine morning?' boomed his bushy-eye-browed friend.

'I go to visit Sir John,' replied Hal guardedly.

'Give my good friend the greetings of old Ebenezer Squires,' replied the other jovially, 'and tell him he could do a lot worse. Ho, ho, ho!'

Hal felt himself colouring up; there did not seem to be much that Master Squires did not know. However, he smiled cheerfully, saddled up his fine grey mare, an animal lent to him by Master Squires, and set off across London. Even the reflection of the sky and clouds in the puddles looked beautiful that morning, and he could not help thinking how happy Lady Jane would have been for him. The remembrance of her brought a wave of sadness across his buoyant spirit. 'But at least she is beyond the web of intrigue and wickedness so tightly woven around her by ambitious and unscrupulous people,' thought Hal, drawing a measure of comfort from the recollection.

Hal could no longer slip in and out of the servants' back entrance to the Tower, but, like any other visitor, had to cross the moat and call for admittance by way of the Middle Tower. He shuddered at the sight of the grim fortress and wondered if Archbishop Cranmer, good Master Bradford and the Bishops Ridley and Latimer still suffered in those dark dungeons. How glad he would be to take Mistress Sarah away from this depressing place! 'I have business with Sir John,' called

Hal as the gate attendant demanded a reason for his visit. The rusty portcullis was slowly raised and Hal dismounted and led his mare through and onto Tower Green. He was deeply thankful that the scaffold had been dismantled, and as he crossed over to the lieutenant's apartment, Mistress Partridge bustled to the door of her house, obviously very curious to know what had bought Hal back to the Tower.

Sarah herself answered Hal's knock, and the delight on her face when she saw Hal brought tears to his eyes. 'I have kept my promise,' he said simply. 'Is your father about?'

'My father is due back shortly,' responded Sarah. 'Come within, and wait.' Hal had never been inside before and glanced round, almost in a daze. 'Tell me, quickly,' whispered Sarah. 'What has happened? I could never have thought you could be back so soon.'

'Sir Henry Grey has left me a legacy of £100,' returned Hal, 'and I come to see if your father will consider that I am able to support his daughter...' Just at that moment heavy footsteps were heard approaching, and the tall figure of the lieutenant entered, bowing his head to avoid striking it on the lintel. He had seen the handsome mare tethered to a post outside the house and wondered who his visitor might be.

'Well now, Master Hal, what brings you back here?' enquired Sir John.

'I come, good sir, to ask the hand of your daughter Mistress Sarah in marriage,' replied Hal with a nervous gulp.

'Do you indeed?' said Sir John raising his eyebrows in surprise. He glanced from one young person to the other, and suddenly barked, 'Go to your room, Sarah. Master Hal and I must talk business.' As Sarah left the room, Sir John turned to him: 'I find it hard to imagine how you propose to support my daughter.' He drummed his fingers tentatively on the table as Hal told him first of the wage he was now earning, then of Sir William Cecil's confidence in him and, lastly, of the legacy he had received. Sir John wanted to know about the incident that had occasioned the legacy and whether there would be adequate accommodation at Sir William's London home for Sarah.

'And may I ask you, honoured sir,' enquired Hal, 'of the nature of the dowry you would be able and willing to provide for your daughter? For ... for I love her with all my heart.' It was all so different from anything he had planned to say. And now a silence that could almost be felt descended on the room. For a full five minutes Sir John sat gazing at the rush mat on the floor.

Suddenly a titter from the door alerted both, and the cheeky face of Hilda, Sarah's twelve-year-old sister, peered around the door. What would Sir John say to such an intrusion? To Hal's surprise, the lieutenant looked up and said, 'Come, Hilda.' Lifting the girl onto his lap, he said, 'Master Hal here would like to marry your sister. Shall I let him or not? What do you think?' Hilda, a demonstrative young person, suddenly flung her arms around her father's neck. 'Yes, papa, and I'll look after you instead. I will soon be thirteen and can care for you as well as Sarah. Besides, Sarah never stops talking about Master Hal. It would break her heart if you said "No."'

'Well that decides it, Master Hal. You may return in seven days' time and we will finalize the arrangements. Hilda, go call your sister.'

A glance at Hal's face when she entered the room told Sarah all she needed to know. Hal stood and said gravely, 'I owe you much thanks, good sir, and I will care for Sarah to the very best that I am able.' Sarah grasped Hal's hand joyfully and accompanied him on his way out of the Tower.

27
Entangled in the web

The wedding took place in Sir William Cecil's private chapel early in July 1554. Hal wore the richly embroidered breeches and scarlet cloak which he had previously worn for court occasions, and Sarah was neatly dressed in a dark green kirtle, with a small French hood over her fair hair. The service was conducted in Protestant style, with vows exchanged in the main body of the church instead of at the door as in Catholic services, for no law had yet been passed reverting to the former procedures. All knew, however, that it was only a matter of time before the heavy hand of the law would try to compel all to conform to Catholic ritual.

Hal had spent a gold sovereign on a ring for Sarah, and felt a thrill of elation as he put it on her finger. After all the sadness he had known this was a day of true delight, and few were happier on that occasion than Hal's mother, Elizabeth. She thought back to the day when as a seventeen-year-old girl she had married Matt, a country lad who cared for the livestock at Ulverscroft Priory. How little could she have dreamed of such an unlikely future for herself and her firstborn child! Master Squires insisted on acting as host for the wedding feast, and paying for all the sumptuous wedding fare. Even Sir William found time to call in and raise a cup to wish the bride and groom well for the future.

One of the first decisions that Hal and Sarah made was to buy a complete Bible to read together. Hal had a New Testament, but the purchase of an entire Bible would have been far beyond his means, apart from the legacy he had just received. Sarah was the better reader of the two, for her father had made sure that both his daughters received a good standard of education—something that was still unusual for most girls.

'I bought my New Testament in a bookshop in Chancery Lane,' Hal told Sarah. 'Tomorrow I will go and see if they can sell me a Bible.' Hal found the shop easily, remembering how he had walked that same way clutching his gold sovereign—the one he had tried to return to Master Squires all those years ago. More than six years had passed since then, and Hal had recently turned twenty-one. He recognized the cheery-looking shopkeeper, older now and plumper, but when Hal asked for a Bible, the kindly man's face grew grave: 'Have you not heard, good sir, that a law has just been passed forbidding the reading and possession of the Bible? If I sell you a Bible I put you in breach of the law of the land.' Hal stared at the speaker in unbelief. This was surely Bishop Bonner's doing. Not once, but now a second time, Hal felt the chill darkness of the bishop's shadow cast across his way. Should he risk the purchase or obey the dictates of one who would rob him of the privilege of reading God's Word? Standing irresolute in front of the counter, Hal suddenly seemed to be back in a semi-darkened room late at night in the Tower of London. Lady Jane would die the next day and she was reading him the letter she had written to Katherine:

> This book is worth more than precious stones; it is the Book, dear sister, of the law of the Lord bequeathed unto us wretches which shall lead you to the path of eternal joy... It shall teach you to live and learn you to die...

'If you will sell me the Bible, I will take the risk of possession,' said Hal steadily, sounding much more certain than he felt. The shopkeeper glanced nervously all around. No one was in sight. With a quick movement he dived under the counter and at a speed that astonished Hal, wrapped up the coveted book, cleared his throat and said, 'That will be eighteen shillings and six pence, sir.' Slipping his packet under his doublet, Hal said, 'Good day, master, and I thank you for your kindness.' And then he was off at a smart pace.

As Hal and Sarah adjusted to life together, they learnt yet more troubling news. Apparently Bishop Bonner had sent out an edict to all members of the clergy within the city of London and the surrounding vicinity, saying that every adult must attend mass and confession at least once a year, and most particularly at Easter. Then came the alarming words:

> We will and command you to note the names of all such
> as be not confessed unto you and do not receive of you
> the said sacrament before the sixth day of April ... so
> that we, knowing who did not come to confession or
> receive the sacrament, may proceed against them.

Although no laws had yet been passed forbidding Protestant worship, Bishop Bonner was setting up what was effectively a ring of spies and informers. No one was safe. It would be impossible to know whom you could trust; and Hal had good reason to recollect in what way Edmund Bonner would 'proceed against' those who would not conform. Had not this same man been one of those who had most cruelly tortured Lady Anne Askew and had her burnt to death?

For the present they were safe, but no one could tell what might happen by next Easter. Sir William Cecil, himself a Protestant, made no attempt to force his employees to attend mass, although how long even he could protect them, Hal did not know. The marriage between the queen and Prince Philip of Spain had taken place three weeks after Hal and Sarah's own marriage and, with a Catholic husband at her side, Mary's second and third parliaments repealed all the remaining Protestant legislation introduced during Edward's reign and reunited the English church with Rome, under Pope Julius III. But in December 1554 an Act of Parliament was rushed through in six days which reintroduced a law allowing for the burning of 'heretics'— or, as Hal observed to Sarah, giving the bishops liberty to burn to death anyone with whom they or the queen had any religious difference.

Sarah turned worried blue eyes on Hal. She was already four months pregnant, and could see immediately that both she and Hal would be in grave danger if they continued to read the Bible together and especially if they were absent from the celebration of the mass next Easter. But her strongest fears were for others. 'I tremble greatly for Master Bradford—he who first showed me Christ as a Saviour for my soul,' she admitted. Master Bradford had been moved from the Tower, so her father had told her, and was now locked up in the King's Bench Prison, under what dreadful circumstances, she hardly dared to think. The other three captive bishops had all been taken to Oxford, where they were facing repeated and abusive trials.

It was about this time that Hal first noticed Master George Jakes. He had worked as an undersecretary for Sir William Cecil for the last ten years, and throughout Edward's reign had kept a low profile, for he was a diligent if not fanatical Catholic. A quiet-spoken man, he walked with a limp, and seemed to have a cast in one eye, so it was never easy to tell in which direction he was looking. On several occasions Hal noticed that Master Jakes was watching him in a strange, rather unnerving way. 'Is he looking at me,' Hal wondered, 'or is it someone else nearby?'

'Be on your guard as to what you say to Master Jakes,' Ebenezer Squires warned Hal one day. 'He does not like you.'

'But why? What ill have I done him?' enquired Hal anxiously.

'Naught, my son,' replied Master Squires, 'but he wanted your position when Master Rogers became too old for the task. I overlooked him, knowing well that he could not fulfil the demands. He could not manage a day's ride with that leg of his even if I gave him the best horse in the stables. He resents your presence here, and as for your beautiful wife, he wishes she were his.'

'Thank you, Master Squires. I shall avoid him as if he carried the sweating sickness,' replied Hal with a wry laugh, but inwardly he felt disturbed and angry. The presence of a jealous, fanatical Catholic who also had an eye on his wife was certainly a cause for uneasiness in the present religious climate, when men were being invited to spy on others and report 'heretics' to the priests. Despite his efforts to keep away from Master Jakes, there were a few occasions when Hal was obliged to speak to him, particularly when he wished the undersecretary to record some problem he had discovered as he inspected Sir William's estates.

The year 1555 dawned cold and grey. A new fall of snow lay on the ground and a bitter wind whipped it in Hal's face as he rode back home from Wimbledon, after securing the services of a new chef for the kitchens at Sir William Cecil's manor house. In fact, Hal was considering transferring his mother from Westminster to Wimbledon, for at least she would be safer there, away from the watchful eyes and ears of those who might betray any who read the Scriptures or failed to attend the mass.

Reporting to the office on his return, Hal discovered that Master Jakes was on duty that day as Sir William's permanent secretary was ill. Hal kept his comments and suggestions as brief as possible, but just as he was leaving, Jakes put down his quill, and fixed his good eye firmly on Hal. 'Hast heard that my lords Bishop Gardiner and Bishop Bonner are trying seven heretics at Southwark on the morrow?' he asked, with a gleam of satisfaction in his eye. 'Methinks they will burn unless they recant,' he added casually.

'I had not heard, Master Jakes,' replied Hal cautiously, anxious not to give Jakes any clue as to his own feelings in the matter. 'Dost know their names?' It was unwise of Hal to ask, but Jakes was eager to pass on the information, and reeled off their names in a rush: 'Indeed, I do, they are Master John Rogers—even he whose labours completed the work of that arch-heretic Master William Tyndale, spreading the English Bible throughout our land, Bishop John Hooper of Gloucester, Master John Bradford, Master Rowland Taylor of Hadleigh, Master Saunders of Northamptonshire, Master Barlow that was Bishop of Bath and Wells and Master Edward Crome of Cambridge.' The news horrified Hal, and George Jakes watched his expression carefully. Sorely tempted to respond with some remark that revealed his feelings, Hal merely nodded and wished Jakes good day.

Heavy at heart, Hal found Sarah and told her the news he had just heard. 'Who can tell where this will end?' he concluded in a troubled voice. 'Aren't these among the best and most noble men in our land? I fear Master Jakes rejoices in such cruelty. Surely, false religion robs a man or woman of all humanity!'

'We can only pray that God will in pity spare their lives,' responded Sarah, 'or send them his grace to endure to the end. How are times changed since our good king died, scarce eighteen months ago!'

Only two weeks later, on 4 February, John Rogers, father of eleven children, the youngest just a baby in his mother's arms, was led out to Smithfield to die. Sarah, whose own first child was due in April, wept bitterly at the news. How she grieved for that mother left alone with none to support her or her children! The condemned man, found guilty because he would not accept that Christ was physically present in the bread used in the mass, had begged earnestly for a chance to speak to his wife, Adriana, before he suffered. But even that simple request was refused, although Adriana and her family managed to stand near the roadside as Rogers passed by and they shared a brief farewell.

On 8 February, just four days later, Lawrence Saunders, a well-known Protestant preacher under Edward VI, was taken to Coventry to die; and the following day Rowland Taylor, vicar of Hadleigh in Suffolk, was burnt on waste ground outside the town. Almost his entire congregation came to support their well-loved vicar at the last.

That same day Bishop John Hooper of Gloucester suffered most grievously in the fires. His agonies, prolonged and terrible, angered and distressed Hal and Sarah beyond measure, and not them alone. What sort of queen had the nation put on the throne who could inflict such torture on her people? Four of the accused men that Master George Jakes had named had now died within one week. Two, unable to face the terrors of such a death, had recanted, and though stripped of their clerical office, had escaped with their lives. Only Master John Bradford was left—and Hal understood that he had been sent back to prison. Perhaps the queen feared a riot among the people if she added the death of yet another godly and sought-after preacher to the appalling sum of her brutality.

It seemed that Hal's worst fears were coming true. How often he had trembled at the prospect of suffering a violent death himself!

How often had his faith almost failed under so fearful a burden! With Easter approaching, Hal guessed that Master Jakes would surely be watching to see if he would attend mass. Sarah's baby was nearly due, and Hal realized that she too was afraid of the future, for his sake and for that of her unborn child. She tried to put her fears to rest and each night she and Hal read together from the Bible. Many were the times that words from the Old Testament gave courage to the young couple as they faced uncertain days.

'Listen to this, Sarah,' said Hal one night. 'See here it says, "Be strong and of good courage; do not be afraid, nor be dismayed, for the Lord your God is with you." So be at peace, my dear one. Nothing can happen to us but our God will strengthen us. Now sleep well.' But Sarah did not sleep well that night, for in the early hours of the morning Hal found himself hurrying along the London streets to summon the midwife, who only just arrived in time to deliver the baby—a beautifully formed little daughter with a shock of black hair and an unmistakable resemblance to Hal himself.

With their newborn infant safely strapped up in swaddling bands according to the custom of the times, and the various lady attendants gone at last, Hal and Sarah looked with shining eyes at each other and at the baby.

'What shall we call her?' asked Sarah, even though she had already made up her mind.

'I would much like to call her Jane in memory of one whom we both loved and respected,' answered Hal quietly.

'Did you know that was my wish also?' asked Sarah. Hal merely smiled to himself. He had not been sure, but had thought that such a choice was highly probable.

As soon as Sarah was stronger again, Hal had another suggestion to make. In view of the terror of the days, he thought his wife and child would be safer back under her father's roof in the Tower. No one would dare to touch her there, for Sir John was held in the highest respect in royal circles and, whatever his thinking about the truths that Hal and Sarah believed, he kept it to himself and conformed with prevailing opinion for the sake of his position.

But for Hal himself the web of fanaticism and intrigue which had finally destroyed Lady Jane's life was now entangling him as well, and growing ever tighter each day. He had a reason for not attending mass at Easter as Sarah's baby was born that very day. But was he going to have his child baptized in accordance with Catholic ritual? One man was certainly watching his every move, and Hal knew it.

28
Betrayed

'I hear your wife has presented you with a daughter,' said Master Jakes, with something between a sneer and a smile, as Hal concluded some business with him early in June 1555. 'Pray what are you naming her, and when is her baptism? For I should hold it an honour to attend.'

'My daughter's baptism will be private,' replied Hal firmly, 'and no date has yet been fixed for the occasion.'

'Aha ... I see,' responded Jakes. 'I only enquired because My Lord Bonner was concerned to know. He is anxious that all within the London diocese should fulfil the desires of our sovereign Queen Mary and His Grace, King Philip.' Hal felt a cold chill run down his spine. Was this man drawing him into a trap? Baby Jane was now eight weeks old, and most children were baptized within three or four weeks of birth. But Hal and Sarah were determined that they would not submit their child to the Catholic baptism ritual. They had indeed been planning a private ceremony. This was to be conducted by Master Aylmer, Lady Jane's former tutor, who had recently arrived in London, awaiting a ship to flee the persecution which was breaking out with ever greater intensity on all sides.

'I bid you a good day, Master Tylney,' concluded Jakes with a gleam in his one good eye that Hal found disturbing.

Two days later Hal was cantering back to Westminster from the Tower after visiting Sarah and baby Jane, for he had now arranged for them to stay with Sarah's father until times were safer. Suddenly he was alerted to the sound of horses' hooves swiftly approaching him from behind. He quickened his pace, but soon the riders were abreast of him. 'Whoa there! Halt, Master Tylney!' called a voice. Reluctantly Hal reined in his horse and turned to see who was addressing him. A young man with a spotty face dressed in clerical robes and with his hair styled in a priest's tonsure, spoke first: 'His Lordship Bishop Edmund Bonner requires your presence on the morrow, Master Tylney.'

'He has heard reports concerning you,' continued the second, an older man whom Hal was sure he had seen before somewhere, 'regarding your non-attendance at mass on Easter last, and your failure to bring your infant for baptism.' Hal suddenly remembered that this was one of the men whom he had seen pushing Bishop Nicholas Ridley roughly across Tower Green not long after Lady Jane had been imprisoned.

'Inform his lordship that I have good reason for both omissions,' replied Hal. 'My wife gave birth at Easter and I was unable to attend mass. Moreover, the baptism of my child is to go ahead shortly. Good day to you, sirs.' And with that he spurred his horse into a gallop and disappeared into the distance. But his heart was thumping with fear. All he had most dreaded since he had first understood the truths of the evangelical gospel and received those same truths as his own spiritual conviction was gathering over his head like an angry and threatening cloud.

As Hal went to fetch his horse from the stables the following day, he heard a voice behind him that he instantly recognized. 'Master Hal, my good friend,' said Ebenezer Squires, 'I would have you set off for Lincoln immediately to attend to Sir William's property. You must go without delay.' Hal could not fail to detect the note of urgency in Squires' voice.

'I am in trouble, Master Ebenezer,' said Hal, wiping his hand across his face. 'Hast heard that Bishop Bonner is asking for me?'

'I have,' replied Squires, and there was no longer a twinkle in his eye. 'I fear you must stay from London as long as you are able, and I will do all in my power to answer for you. I will inform Sarah where you have gone.'

Without further delay Hal set off on his long ride to Lincoln. The beautiful June weather and the fresh young green on tree and hedgerow did nothing to lift the burden resting on Hal's troubled spirit. At every inn where he stopped for a meal or to spend the night the conversation all around him was the same. It seemed that young and old, learned and ignorant, rich and poor were all being sacrificed in the fires of the queen's religious fanaticism.

'Aye, and they burnt poor old William Pygot, the butcher from Braintree,' said one, 'and all because he said that to worship the real presence in the mass was idolatry.'

'Didst hear about Thomas Wats, the draper from Billericay?' asked another. 'They burnt him at Chelmsford but two days gone. He refused to recant even though they made him fair promises.' At this Hal slipped quietly from the room. He could bear no more.

For two weeks Hal prolonged his enquiries and surveys of Sir William Cecil's Lincoln property. At last he knew he could extend his business no longer, and reluctantly turned his horse's head south once more. Crossing the Thames at Kingston Bridge, Hal called at Wimbledon Manor, where he spent some days checking up on the condition of the property and visiting his mother, Elizabeth, who now worked there. Perhaps this would be the last time he would see her.

Distressed at the news of Bishop Bonner's summons to Hal, Elizabeth urged him to attend mass to save his life. 'It can do no harm, and God well knows your heart, my son,' she begged with tears streaming down her face. 'You may serve your God by life more than by death. Think too of your wife and daughter.' The shock of witnessing Lady Jane's death had left Elizabeth broken and fearful.

'I think My Lady Jane would grieve sore if I should do so, and does not our Saviour say, "He who loseth his life for my sake, the same shall save it?"' Hal answered, as he kissed his mother tenderly. Begging her prayers, he leapt into the saddle once more to ride back to London and to a doubtful future.

Hal crossed back over the Thames, this time at London Bridge, and called at the Tower to see Sarah and baby Jane before returning to Canon Row in Westminster. Almost ten weeks old, the baby was full of delightful smiles as Hal cradled her in his arms. 'My mother would have me attend mass that I may live to serve my God here and to care for you and for our child,' Hal ventured, clasping Sarah's hand.

Despite her tears, Sarah merely shook her head and whispered, 'Lady Jane would have said, "Live still to die that we by death may inherit eternal life." And did we not read together those words, "Only be strong and of a good courage"? Surely our God will watch between us.'

Hal nodded dumbly, laid the baby carefully back in her cradle and clasped Sarah in his arms. 'Let us then be faithful unto death, my Sarah, that we too may receive the crown of life,' he said. And with these words he tore himself out of his wife's arms, mounted his horse and rode away before his resolution failed him.

Darkness was falling by the time Hal reached Westminster. Heading down Canon Row, he soon clattered into the yard and was about to close the stable door behind him when he heard footsteps approaching. Looking up apprehensively, Hal was relieved to see that it was Master Squires. 'I have heavy news, Master Hal', he began. 'The bishop's men have called here every day since you left. I have told them that you are away on business, but I doubt not they will return, for they will not be denied.'

'I feared as much,' Hal replied. 'I come from the Tower, where my dear Sarah urges me to be "strong and of a good courage."'

'You have ever been a brave young man, Master Hal, and I pray God keep you safe, my son,' said Master Squires sincerely.

'I wish you a good night, Master Squires,' Hal replied, and with that he unlocked the door of his apartment and went into his lonely room, but not to sleep. It could be his last night of freedom and he wanted time to pray to seek strength from God for whatever might await him. He must prepare answers to the questions he knew Bishop Bonner would ask and he wanted time to write a letter to Sarah—a letter that she could keep in remembrance of him if he should lose his life. It was past midnight before Hal eventually lay down to sleep, but not before he had discovered some words in his New Testament which Christ spoke just before he suffered and died. He had said to his frightened disciples: 'Peace I leave with you, my peace I give unto you. Let not your hearts be grieved, neither fear ye.'[1] And with those words ringing in his mind, Hal slept soundly.

The very next morning Hal was awoken by a hammering on his door. The spotty-faced cleric, whose name Hal learnt was Nicholas Harpsfield, was back, together with his older companion. 'My lord bishop demands to know why you did not answer his first summons,' said the older man.

'Because I had nothing for which to answer his lordship,' replied Hal, 'and my business demanded my attention.'

'Such will not please his lordship. I fear it may be worse for you if you do not accompany us now,' growled Harpsfield threateningly.

'I come,' responded Hal, 'but let me first inform Sir William Cecil of your orders.' Hal knew well that this would be a wise move, for even the bishop would not lightly cross Sir William. With Queen Mary's uncertain health, a day might come when Hal's employer could be restored to a high position in the country under the Princess Elizabeth, now heir to the throne. Bishop Bonner would certainly be aware of that.

'We have secured the person of Master Henry Tylney, your lordship,' said Harpsfield, who apparently acted as Bishop Bonner's secretary and assistant. With a slight snigger he pushed Hal roughly towards a large oak table behind which the round-faced bishop was sitting. Rolling his eyes at Hal, Bonner merely said, 'Aha, Master Tylney, I have heard much of you.'

'Indeed, sir?' was Hal's only reply.

---

1   John 14:27, Tyndale version

'Were you not page to that arch-heretic and traitor, the Lady Jane Dudley?' Hal had not expected this, nor could he stand any slur on the character of Lady Jane.

'My Lady Jane was no traitor, your lordship, nor was she a heretic. She believed those truths from the Bible that His Majesty our late noble King Edward lived by and died by.'

Unwilling to defame the character of the king publicly, Bonner changed the subject. 'Master George Jakes informs me that you have not submitted your daughter for baptism. Why is this?' Hal had guessed rightly. Master Jakes had betrayed him, but he had his answer ready.

'My lord bishop, the baptism is but delayed that one who has been my tutor and friend may conduct the service.'

Again the bishop changed the subject: 'Your late mistress, the Lady Jane, denied the real presence of Christ in the sacrament. This is surely abominable heresy. What say you?'

Hal knew that he was now caught like a fly in a web. As steadily as he could he answered, remembering the very words Jane had used before the tribunal of clerics just before she died. 'The bread of the sacrament, when it is broken, puts me in mind how that for my sins the body of Christ was broken on the cross.'

The bishop had now risen from his seat, his face purple with anger. 'Man, you are a heretic. You have not answered my question. Is Christ really and actually present in the bread as our Holy Mother Church teaches, or is he not? Answer me.'

'When Christ was nailed to the cross his body was whole, nor had it been eaten by his disciples at the Supper of our Lord...'

'How dare you think to teach me!' roared the irate bishop. 'Have him away. Sir William Cecil's man or no, you shall surely burn for this, unless you recant.'

And without further ado, Hal was hustled out of the room. With his hands tightly tied behind his back, he was dragged away in the direction of Newgate Prison, his riderless horse led back to Canon Row and returned to the stables. As Ebenezer Squires saw the mare being stabled, he did not need to ask the whereabouts of Hal himself.

Looming up in front of him, Hal saw the grim gates of Newgate Prison. How often he had trembled at the thought of the dreadful sufferings of men and women in those dark dungeons that lay beyond that entrance! They seemed like the gates of death itself, for out of them prisoners passed on their last journey: some to the gallows in Old Bailey, some to Tyburn, where common criminals were hung, and some to Smithfield, where the fires were lit to consume heretics.

Slowly the portcullis was raised and the new prisoner pushed inside. An appalling stench greeted Hal—the stench of death and disease, for more than 300 prisoners rotted in these dungeons, many dying of gaol fever before the day of their execution had arrived. From all around Hal could hear the groans and cries of desperate, broken men and women. The prison was built around three sides of a courtyard with various doors leading off. Accompanied by Nicholas Harpsfield and a large, red-faced jailer, Hal was dragged through a door and pushed roughly down worn stone steps, vile and slippery. Along a dark, damp passageway they went until the jailer stopped and from a bunch dangling at his waist produced one large key, rusty with age. Opening a cell door, he thrust Hal inside.

The dungeon was gloomy and dirty. Two other men were slumped in corners, lying on filthy, flea-ridden straw. Rats scurried around, searching for scraps of food. 'Stay there until you learn how to answer his lordship, our merciful bishop,' said the spotty-faced cleric with a sneer. Yet, strange to say, and beyond Hal's understanding, an unusual peace, even an odd sort of happiness, filled his mind. Could this be that peace which Christ had promised— a peace unlike anything the world can give? Hal thought of Sarah. She was safe, and baby Jane was being well cared for. More than that, he knew that his brave wife would be glad that he had not given in under the bishop's hostile questioning.

29
Carrying Christ's cross

At first it was hard to distinguish between day and night. But gradually Hal could tell when the dim light of day filtered into the dungeon through a small iron grid. Each morning some water, a small piece of bread and occasionally some dried meat or pulses would be pushed through a slot in the wall, but otherwise only the heavy groans of his fellow prisoners broke the silence. Unknown to his jailer, Hal had placed his New Testament into the pocket of his doublet before his arrest and now had it with him in the dungeon. He could just manage to read, but he must not let the other prisoners see it in case his precious book was confiscated.

After only two nights in the prison Hal was sleeping fitfully on his bed of filthy straw when he heard the loud clanging of a handbell outside the door.[1] 'Prepare to meet thy God,' boomed the raucous voice of the jailer. Then Hal remembered having been told that at midnight on the day before men were taken out for execution they

---

1   The bell may still be seen. It is kept in a glass case in St Sepulchre's Church which is built near the site of the old Newgate Prison near the Old Bailey

were roused from their sleep in this grim way. Was it for him that the bell was now ringing? Hal slept little after that. In the morning he heard the great rusty key turning in the lock and then Hal's two fellow prisoners, men so dejected that Hal had not even learnt their names, were taken away—where they were going, he could easily guess.

Hal found it hard to tell how many days passed as he lay in the dungeon. He thought he must have been a prisoner for about two weeks when he heard the key rattling in the lock once more. Even though the bell had not rung, perhaps it was his turn now. Would he be taken out to the fires of Smithfield? 'Give me courage to bear whatever I must endure,' he prayed earnestly. Instead of calling his name, however, the jailer pushed two other men into the cell. 'And tomorrow you burn,' he said callously. Who could they be? Hal quickly saw that one man was young, probably about his own age, or even a little younger. He had a fresh, open face and seemed a country lad like himself. The other was an older man, probably in his mid-forties, with gentle features and a small beard. But it was his eyes that struck Hal. Even in the poor light of the cell, Hal thought they were the most wonderful eyes he had ever seen. They reminded him of something Sarah had once said. What was it? Then he remembered: she had told him of a preacher who had 'eyes that seemed to look beyond this sad world, even into the face of Christ.' Yes, he recollected now, she had been speaking about Master John Bradford. But surely, this could not be Master Bradford?

The older man was the first to speak. 'My young friend here, Master John Leaf from Yorkshire, and I must seal our testimony for Jesus Christ in the fires of Smithfield ere many hours have passed. I thank God for it. The Lord make me worthy thereof.'

'O sir,' answered Hal quickly, 'pray what is your name? For I too suffer for that same cause.'

'My name is Master John Bradford,' replied the other. Hal could feel the tears smarting in his eyes. How great was his privilege to meet this man, one who lived so close to his God and was beloved by all the people! Why even now Hal could just make out the shouts and cries of men and women hurrying past the prison gate on their way to Smithfield to support the preacher to the last.

'Oh, let me tell you, good sir,' Hal gasped, 'that my wife, daughter of Sir John Bridges, Lieutenant of the Tower, once heard you say, "Christ Jesus will be a sufficient Saviour even for you that cast yourself on his mercy," and she found mercy through Christ that very hour.'

'Right glad am I to hear of it,' responded Bradford. 'Sir John was good to me. He too told me that his daughter believed as I do. And you, young sir, did I not see you at the Tower with My Lady Jane?'

'You may indeed have done so, sir. My name is Hal Tylney and I was her page. She taught me that I must so live as to be ready to die. And now I know that I too must suffer the fires unless I recant.'

'Be of good comfort, Master Hal. John Leaf and I shall have a merry supper with our Lord before tomorrow's sun has set. And if our Saviour call, you too shall rejoice with us ere long. Only be faithful. Carry Christ's cross willingly as he shall lay it on your back. A better life awaits those who believe through the merits of his dear Son Jesus Christ.'[2]

With these words Master Bradford fell silent, but Hal could tell that he was praying and preparing himself for that last ordeal which he must face so soon—his final farewell to this world, and his entry into that better one to come. Once more the clanging of the bell startled Hal, but certainly his fellow prisoners had no need of the jailer's crude exhortation for they were both spending their last fleeting hours in prayer.

Early the following morning, Master John Bradford and Master John Leaf were led out of Newgate to die. Hal looked wistfully after them. 'A merry supper with the Lord...' If only he could look beyond the sufferings of death to the joys of heaven! But for the present the rat-infested cell, the dirt and the disease seemed to fill his perspective.

Not many days later a new jailer was appointed to the block of cells where Hal was imprisoned. A jolly, round-faced man, he seemed to enjoy his wretched employment, even gaining a measure of satisfaction from the sufferings around him. But he was more communicative than the previous jailer and often brought news to Hal of what was going on.

---

2   From *The Writings of John Bradford*, vol. 1, Banner of Truth Trust, 1979.

'Many a bonfire is being lit these days, my son,' he announced heartlessly one morning as he brought Hal his food. 'Our queen will burn all the heretics in the land ere long, you mark my words. Hast heard of Master Robert Samuel, vicar of Bargholt and Master Robert Glover of Coventry...?'

'I have no desire to know, Master Jailer,' Hal snapped, at which the jailer slammed the heavy door once more and took his departure.

Gradually one day merged into another, one week into another for Hal. Prisoners came and went—some cynical, some angry, some distressed. To one or two Hal spoke of a hope beyond the grave through the mercy of Christ's sacrifice for sins, but most were unwilling or unable to listen. Sometimes he was allowed to take a short walk in the prison yard for exercise, but the sights and sounds of human suffering that greeted him on all sides made him almost thankful to return to the dim solitude of his cell. Most of all Hal longed for news of Sarah and of his infant daughter. Were they safe? Was Sarah grieving for him? What was baby Jane doing now? Was she beginning to crawl? Had someone else been employed to take his place to oversee Sir William Cecil's property? But no answer came to Hal's many questions until at last one day late in October 1555.

Almost four months had passed since Hal's arrest and brief hearing before Bishop Bonner. Wasted in body and despairing in spirit, Hal whiled the long hours away attempting to read his New Testament or just sitting staring into space wondering endlessly when the summons might come for him to die. Often he thought back to Lady Jane's brief life and death and gained some consolation as he remembered the strength of her faith and her constancy in the face of her impending execution. But one day Hal heard the heavy steps of the jailer approaching his cell. Perhaps he was bringing other prisoners to join him. It often seemed strange to Hal that though others came and went he was never summoned. Little did he know of the pressures being placed on Bishop Bonner behind the scenes for his release. Hal looked up as the key turned in the lock and the jailer entered. 'Take this,' he said urgently, 'and if it is ever known that I delivered a letter to you, why, I will join you in the cells.'

'I give you thanks,' said Hal wonderingly. 'And who gave this to you?'

'A small man with a black beard has well repaid me for the risk I take.' And with that the jailer rapidly disappeared.

Hal turned the envelope over and over. Could it really be a letter from Sarah? He had guessed rightly, and the hot tears ran down his cheeks as he recognized the well-loved writing: page after page, each closely written. Clearly Sarah had been adding to her letter daily for many weeks. With hungry eyes Hal devoured its contents. Sarah herself was safe and well and baby Jane could sit up on her own and delighted to talk to herself. No, his post with Sir William Cecil had not been filled. Master Squires himself was overseeing the properties as much as he could.

But the news that shook Hal most of all was of the martyrdom of Master Latimer and Master Ridley in Oxford on 16 October. He read with breaking heart how the old man had declared just before the faggots were lit, 'Be of good comfort, Master Ridley, and play the man; we shall this day, by God's grace, light such a candle in England as I trust shall never be put out.' Stroking his face with his burning hands, the courageous preacher, to whom Hal owed so much, had soon succumbed to the flames. But as he learnt of the sufferings of his fellow martyr, Nicholas Ridley, whom the fires had taken so long to consume, Hal could hardly bear to read on. The cruelty with which these men of God were destroyed seemed almost more than Hal's weakened spirit could sustain. And soon after, so Sarah told Hal, yet another brave man, William Dighel, had died in the fires at nearby Banbury. 'Such things will fill you with fears, my own dear Hal,' Sarah had written, 'but God will give you grace to bear Christ's cross should he call you so to suffer for his name's sake. In the meantime my father and Master Squires are doing all they can to obtain your release.'

'We shall this day light such a candle...' The words rang over and over again in Hal's mind. Perhaps his death, although far less significant than that of the bishops, might add to the glow of that candle which would one day pierce through the darkness that now covered the face of the land as a fanatical queen tried to extinguish the light of truth in England. But Hal wondered what had happened to the former archbishop, Thomas Cranmer. Sarah had only told him that he was still being held in prison in Oxford and had faced torment and spiteful questioning at his trial.

Hal read and reread his letter from Sarah many times over until its pages became worn and the words blurred and smudged with his tears. And still the weeks dragged by. Hal thought wistfully of the reds and golds of autumn at Bradgate. Perhaps he would never again see the splendour of the trees as they changed colour. As winter set in, Hal shivered in his cell, and drew his thin coat closer around him, until one day the jailer unexpectedly delivered a warm blanket to his cell, no doubt bribed once more by Master Squires. Even so, severe fevers sometimes struck the prisoner down, weakening his body and undermining his will to endure to the end. In addition, the round-faced jailer seemed to enjoy lingering in Hal's cell, passing on information about other prisoners, and especially making a point of telling Hal if any man or woman had broken down under their trials and sufferings, and had recanted their faith, so gaining their freedom. No doubt he hoped that Hal would follow the same course.

Torn with longing to see Sarah, sick in body and often despairing of ever regaining his liberty, Hal found himself increasingly bombarded with temptations to submit to the pressure and recant his faith. When five men and two women were led out from Newgate to die in a single fire at Smithfield towards the end of January in 1556, Hal broke down and wept. No, he could not endure much longer. His spirit was at breaking point. Gradually he felt the fragile threads of his resolve beginning to snap one by one. Now he scarcely had the energy to read his New Testament, and even when he did discover promises and comforts within its pages, they seemed meant for others, but not for him.

Times and dates meant little to Hal, for one day was exactly the same as another. But as the bitter cold of winter began to give place to brighter days, Hal heard footsteps approaching his cell. The jailer had concluded his rounds, so who could it be? As the door swung open, Hal was alarmed to see the spotty face of Nicholas Harpsfield, the cleric who had first arrested him. 'Our merciful bishop, His Lordship Edmund Bonner, requires your presence,' he announced. 'Perhaps you will have learnt better manners by now,' he added in a low voice. Hal did not reply. With difficulty he rose to his feet for he was weak and ill. By the time he reached the bishop's palace he was quite exhausted.

The rotund and heartless bishop was sitting behind the same table almost as if he had not moved in the last seven months, for it was now March 1556. 'Aha, Master Henry Tylney,' drawled Bonner, 'we hope you have a civil tongue in your head after your sojourn in Her Majesty's jail.' Still Hal did not reply. 'I have here a statement written by one who was once a heretic like yourself, none other than Master Thomas Cranmer. Methinks you would like to hear it.' Hal grasped the table in front of him, his head spinning. He had guessed what was coming. Without changing his tone, the bishop began to read from a paper he had in his hand:

> I, Thomas Cranmer, do renounce and detest all manner of heresies and errors of Luther and all other teachings which be contrary to sound doctrine... I confess one holy catholic church without which there is no salvation... and as concerning the sacrament, I believe and worship in the sacrament of the altar the very body and blood of Christ being contained most truly under the forms of bread and wine, the bread through the mighty power of God being turned into the body of our Saviour...

Hal gasped in spite of himself and gripped the table still harder, his mind in a turmoil of dismay and confusion. Hadn't the good archbishop laid the foundations of the evangelical and Protestant church by his leadership and courage? There must be some mistake. But still the hateful voice droned on: 'And listen further, Master Tylney:

> And God is my witness that I have not done this for favour or fear of any person, but willingly, and of my own mind, as well as the discharge of mine own conscience as to the instruction of others.

What think you of that, young man?' asked the bishop with a gleam in his eye. 'Do you still say that the bread of the sacrament does not change into the real and actual body of our Lord? Are you a heretic still, or, like the good Master Cranmer, can you now see the folly of such wicked notions?'

Weakened and debilitated as he was by long months in prison, such a recantation from one whose faith he had admired so deeply broke the last frail strands of Hal's determination. If Master Cranmer could have been mistaken, who was he, Hal Tylney, a mere layman and little taught, to disagree? At that critical moment the thought never even crossed Hal's mind that such a confession might have been wrenched from Cranmer under desperate duress after more than two years' imprisonment—extracted at a time of total weakness, despair and fear. He could only think of his own desperate longing to see his wife and child again. Deliberately banishing from his mind thoughts of Lady Jane, of Master Bradford, of Latimer, Ridley and the many courageous men and women who had already gone to their deaths in the fearsome fires of persecution, Hal merely nodded dumbly and eventually whispered, 'I give in.'

With a sardonic smile on his lips, Bishop Bonner looked in triumph at the broken young man in front of him. Then he roared, 'Aha, Master Tylney, good sense at last, I see! Right glad I am to hear of it.' To Harpsfield, who was standing in the background, he roared, 'Take Master Tylney back to Burleigh Place and report to Sir William Cecil that his man has recanted.' And to Hal he added, 'Make sure you are in attendance at mass this Easter Day soon to come.' So Hal was taken from the bishop's palace, and a horse hired to carry him back to Canon Row as he was too weak to walk any further.

30
A broken man

Sarah had remained at her father's accommodation in the Tower of London during Hal's imprisonment, but as soon as news of his release reached her she returned to Burleigh Place with her baby, who was now almost a year old. The sight of Hal's emaciated frame and haggard appearance distressed Sarah almost as much as anything that had happened in the intervening eight months. Clinging to each other, both wept—in Hal's case, tears of joy at seeing Sarah once more, but mingled also with tears of shame at the circumstances of his release. Sarah's tears were more those of relief that her husband was still alive. For the moment neither spoke of the abject surrender wrenched from Hal in a moment of utter weakness and dismay over Cranmer's recantation.

Hal gazed with unbelieving eyes at the change in his young daughter. With dark hair like his and Sarah's blue eyes, she was a beautiful child. Smiling shyly at the father she did not know, little Jane quickly buried her face in her mother's lap. Too weak even to pick her up, Hal had to content himself with watching his baby's antics from where he lay on the couch. Pulling herself up against the furniture, she would crow with delight at her achievement, before collapsing heavily on the floor again.

Hal had not been back more than a day before there was a loud rattle at the door. Sarah ran to see who it was. They were not surprised to discover that Master Squires had called. 'Well, well, well, my young friend,' he boomed, 'we will soon have you back on your feet again. Why, a bit of good food is all you need, and then you can take over this job once more. Right glad I am to have you back.' Like Sarah, Ebenezer Squires did not refer to those final words spoken by Hal which had secured his release.

For his part, Hal merely shook his old friend's hand warmly and said simply, 'I thank you, good Master Squires, for your kindness to me. Without it I am sure I would have died in that dark cell.' Then Ebenezer Squires hurried from the room as suddenly as he had come, for in spite of all his bluster he was a man of deep feeling. The sight of Hal in his weakened condition was almost more than he could bear.

Gradually, under Sarah's watchful care and with better food, Hal began to regain strength. But nervously and emotionally he remained a broken man. Night after night he awoke, often crying out in fear or horror. Sometimes he thought he was back in the rat-infested cell in Newgate; at other times he would relive the tragedy of Lady Jane's last moments; but above all he was burdened by the weight of guilt on his spirit. He had denied the Saviour; he had failed to carry Christ's cross as Master Bradford had urged. Never could he forgive himself, and he feared that God might not forgive him either. Even the promises and consolations of Scripture seemed only to mock and condemn him.

One night, as Sarah lay asleep beside him, Hal found himself tortured by accusing thoughts and unable to sleep. At last he rose from his bed, lit a candle and began to flick listlessly through the pages of his Bible. At the back, bound together with his Bible, was the Book of Common Prayer, compiled by Thomas Cranmer himself and designed to be used in services of worship. Now that the book was banned under the new queen's government, it had become an offence to be found even reading such words. Almost despite himself Hal began to glance at some of the prayers. One in particular attracted his attention: 'May it please thee to bring into the way of truth all such as have erred and are deceived,' he read. And it continued, 'May it please thee to raise up them that fall and finally to beat down Satan under our feet.' Hal read and reread the words. Would God hear him if he prayed like that? He did not know. But wasn't he a God of mercy and forgiveness? Burying his face in his hands, Hal whispered the words over and over again in the darkness. Even though he did not yet know the way back, his troubled conscience found a degree of peace that he had not experienced since before his release. Soon he returned to his bed and was able to sleep.

It was 21 March 1556. A loud knocking on their apartment door alerted Hal and Sarah to another visit from Ebenezer Squires. 'Hast heard about Master Cranmer?' he asked as he bustled in. 'All London is talking about it.'

'What has happened, Master Squires?' asked Sarah anxiously.

'Even though he recanted our queen still ordered his burning. By my troth, it seems she must away with that good man, whether he recants or not.'

'And have they burnt him after all?' enquired Hal, his voice breaking with distress.

'Aye, my friend, burnt him they have, but God be praised, Satan was beaten down under his feet!'

'What do you mean?' gasped Hal, for weren't these the very words he had found in his Prayer Book a few nights earlier?

'Why, they thought that he would read out his recantation of all the truths he has taught us before they lit the fires for the burning, but he did not. Rather he repented him of his weakness, and instead declared the very faith of the Scriptures. "The pope," says he, "I refuse as Christ's enemy," and as for the sacraments, he began to declare his true beliefs, but those around did shout him down.' Hal had turned pale and sat staring into space as Squires continued, 'Yea, more than that, he declared that the hand that had written those false things must suffer first when he came to the fire.'

'And did he do that?' asked Sarah who had sat down beside Hal, fully knowing how he must be feeling.

'"This hand hath offended," cried the brave man as he held his right hand in the flames until it was quite consumed. And in his dying he cried out as did the martyr Stephen as the stones were falling upon him, "I see heaven open and Jesus standing at the right hand of God." Surely we may say that even today truth has triumphed over falsehood. Yea, God be praised!' Hal remained shaken and silent long after Master Squires had left the room. His last mental refuge for his own failure had been stripped from him.

As Easter Sunday approached, Master Squires made arrangements for Hal, Sarah and the baby to travel to Sir William Cecil's country seat in Wimbledon for Hal to convalesce. Hal's mother, Elizabeth, still worked in the kitchens in the manor house, and would be anxious to see her son again. But more importantly, it was vital that Hal should be away from the watchful eyes of Master George Jakes or of any others who might betray him to Bishop Bonner if he should fail to attend the mass on Easter Sunday. The fresh country air and his mother's cooking soon restored Hal to health again, but nothing could quite remove the burden resting on his spirit. To him it seemed that one moment of weakness had swept away months of courageous endurance and suffering for Christ's sake. Even though he did not attend the mass, Hal felt little relief of conscience.

'I am worse than Peter,' he confided to Sarah one night. 'I fear I am like Judas, who betrayed his Master for earthly gain? Wasn't Judas called the son of perdition?'

'Come, Hal, think not so,' answered Sarah kindly. 'Is not our God a God of forgiveness to those who weep for their sins as did the woman of whom we read but yesterday, she who washed the Saviour's feet with her tears and wiped them with her hair?'[1]

Hal smiled faintly. He was grateful for Sarah's understanding but in his heart he knew that he could never gain release from oppression of spirit until he was prepared, if the occasion arose, to own Christ and his truth publicly and confess his fall. And this he felt he could not face.

As the weeks passed Hal was able to return to work overseeing the properties of Sir William Cecil. Sometimes, when Master Squires was not available to do so, he accompanied Cecil on his travels for he had

---

1   Luke 7:44

become a trusted man in his service. Occasionally Sir William wended his way north on secretive visits to Hatfield House in Hertfordshire where the Princess Elizabeth lived under what virtually amounted to house arrest. For many years Cecil had acted as financial adviser to the princess—a fact that now cloaked the underlying reason for his visits. All knew that Queen Mary was in poor health and Cecil's plan was to keep Elizabeth abreast with political developments and prepare her for the day when she would become queen. Hal would not accompany Sir William during his interviews with the princess, but sometimes he gained a fleeting glimpse of the auburn-haired young woman, who reminded him so strikingly of her cousin, Lady Jane. Perhaps she would soon replace Mary, he thought wistfully; then his anguished conscience would at last be at rest, for all knew that Elizabeth secretly supported the Protestant cause. Yet Hal recognized in his heart that this was not the real answer to his problems.

And still the burnings went on. That June four young men from Sussex appeared before Bishop Bonner. Master George Jakes, not satisfied with having betrayed Hal himself, now had all the details which he passed on to Hal with a measure of glee: Thomas Harland was a carpenter; John Oswald a farm labourer; Thomas Avington operated a lathe for cutting wood; Jakes did not know what the fourth, Thomas Read, did for a living. Three of the four had stood firm, denying the crucial doctrine of the real presence. Thomas Read had recanted, so Jakes informed Hal, but in a dream soon afterwards had seen himself shut out of heaven, for his clothes were filthy, whereas those of his companions were shining white. Grieving for his weakness, Read had retracted his confessions and he too was burnt, tied to a single stake with the other three in Lewes. Jakes, who had greeted Hal warmly when he heard of the circumstances of his release, watched the young man's face carefully as he elaborated on the sufferings of these martyrs. A look of vindictive satisfaction spread across his features as he noted the obvious distress that his gruesome account was causing.

Throughout the summer and autumn of 1556 men and women, high and low, young people and old alike, were being hunted down, brought before the bishops, interrogated and as soon as they denied cardinal Roman Catholic teaching were condemned to a cruel death at the stake. Hal tried to busy himself in his work, hoping to suppress the accusations of conscience, but without success. Each martyrdom increased his inward agitation and the last words of the martyr John Bradford would ring again in his ears: 'Only be faithful. Carry Christ's cross willingly as he shall lay it on your back.' But he, Hal, had not been faithful, nor had he been willing to carry Christ's cross to the last. Sarah watched him anxiously, knowing well his secret misery. She was pregnant once more and could foresee yet another crisis looming if they refused Catholic baptism for their second child.

As 1556 drew to its close Hal and Sarah looked into the new year with wistful hope. Perhaps their queen, whom everyone knew to be depressed and ill, would decide that she had sacrificed enough of her citizens in the fires of persecution; perhaps she would realize that her people would love her more if she became more tolerant of any who differed from her. But early in February 1557 they were sadly disappointed, for the queen, together with her husband Philip of Spain, published a long edict ordering bishops, clergy and others in authority to far greater diligence in rounding up and burning 'heretics.' They were to search all ruined churches, all vicarages, chapels, derelict buildings and waste ground for the small groups of men and women who might be worshipping in secret. If any appeared 'obstinate or disobedient' in clinging to their views they were to be handed over to the local sheriffs to be dealt with according to the law—and Hal had good reason to know what that meant. As the searches intensified the prisons became overcrowded, for more and more were being thrown into dark and damp cells, some to die of disease or starvation as they awaited their trials.

Four days after this proclamation came the third anniversary of an event that Hal could neither forget nor recall without pain. On 12 February 1554 Lady Jane had ended her short life at the hands of the public executioner, even though a denial of the truths of the faith could have saved her from such a death. He remembered his last whispered words as he had guided her hands towards the block: 'Be of good courage, my lady.' Lady Jane had endured to the end, faithful and brave. As he remembered these things, Hal did not weep. No, God called for more than tears. God called for repentance for his own weakness, and courage to remain firm to the end if he should be called upon to take a stand for the truth once more. It was a defining moment for the young man, marked only by a whispered prayer: 'May God give me grace, cost what it may.'

Soon after this as Hal was returning home after a visit to Lincoln, he heard a conversation in one of the taverns which appalled him.

'Hast heard of them from Colchester as have been caught?' enquired one lanky farmer with sharp blue eyes and a long beard.

'Aye, that I have, twenty-three of 'em, so I hear say,' replied another. 'Seems that Master John Kingston of Colchester came upon them a-worshipping in an old barn and that after the old ways, not according to the faith of our queen.'

'Methinks they are being brought to London to trial by our lord Bishop Bonner,' added the first. 'I fear they will burn for their folly— eight women too, so I am told. Ah! When will our Elizabeth take the throne? Has this our queen a heart of stone, that she should burn old women so?'

Hal listened in silence to the conversation, but inwardly his mind was in turmoil, and even more so when he caught up with the sorry band the following day as he neared St Albans. To his disgust he saw that there were indeed old men and women among the group. Footsore and weary, they were all tied together with ropes. Hal seethed with inward anger at the sight.

And yet in a strange and inexplicable way he envied them. They had not denied the Saviour as he had done. These were people who had clung to their beliefs despite the constant threat of an agonizing death. Coming level with an elderly woman at the rear he saw that she was struggling to keep up the pace. He leant from his horse and whispered those words of the martyr John Bradford: 'Only be faithful. Carry Christ's cross willingly as he shall lay it on your back.' The prisoner looked up and a quick smile lit up her worn features as she whispered, 'I thank you, good sir.' At that moment Hal noticed that a young priest escorting the group was nearby and must have heard the exchange for he was staring curiously at him. Then Hal recognized him. It was none other than the spotty-faced cleric, Nicholas Harpsfield, Bishop Bonner's secretary and assistant, who had arrested

Hal himself. Was Hal now caught in the web of intrigue and betrayal once more?

The incident was soon forgotten, however, for as Hal unlocked the door of his apartments at Sir William's manor in Canon Row, a high-pitched infant's cry startled him. Surely not! Could Sarah have given birth to their second child during his absence? The baby was not due for another two weeks, or else Hal would never have left home.

Bursting into the apartment, Hal hurried up the stairs only to be greeted by his mother, Elizabeth, at the door. 'Be quiet, my son,' she warned, 'for Sarah sleeps at last. Your babe was born but two days since, and I was summoned to care for your wife.'

When Sarah woke several hours later, she smiled weakly at Hal. It had been a difficult confinement and at one point it was feared that both she and her baby boy would die. Kneeling by her bedside, Hal gathered his wife in his arms, tears of thankfulness streaming down his cheeks. It might be some weeks before she regained her strength but it now seemed that she would recover. Two-year-old Jane was fascinated by the tiny form with a puckered red face and a loud wail that lay in the crib beside her mother. When Hal and Sarah were alone together they decided to call their new son John. 'And may he grow up to be like Master Bradford, that holy man of God,' whispered Sarah.

31
Out of weakness made strong

As Easter was approaching Master Squires again arranged for Hal, Sarah and the children to spend a few weeks at Wimbledon Manor. Elizabeth would be on hand to help Sarah, who was still far from strong, but, more importantly, it would remove Hal from the ever-watchful eyes of men like Master Jakes, who would be waiting to see if he neglected to attend mass. But this time it was different. Previously Hal had been weak after his long imprisonment, distraught with failure and unfit to face any fresh challenges to his faith. Now, however, he felt more able to fix his eyes on an uncertain, even ghastly, future with a steadier gaze.

Hal had heard of some who had deliberately invited martyrdom by provoking the clergy to capture and condemn them. To him that seemed wrong, for as God had given him a wife and two infants, he felt a responsibility to care for them while he could. No, he must not follow such a course. But if called upon to suffer he could only pray that this time he might not falter, but persevere to the last. A few days earlier he had discovered some words in the Bible that he had never noticed before—words that lifted his spirits and gave him fresh courage. 'Rejoice not against me, O mine enemy,' the prophet had said, 'for when I fall, I shall arise; when I sit in darkness, the Lord shall be a light unto me.'[1] Yes, he too had fallen, but with God's help he would rise up again from his weakness and shame. And if he were cast once more into the darkness of some gloomy dungeon, then the Lord would give him light in his soul. Hal did not share these thoughts with Sarah, for he feared that in her present condition the possibility that he might be captured again could be too great a burden for her to bear.

Leaving his wife and children in the safety of the Tower once more, under the protection of Sarah's father Sir John Bridges, Hal returned to his employment at Sir William Cecil's home. But every day he was conscious of being watched. Wherever he went he could imagine there were some lurking in the corners of taverns, or serving at roadside stalls, who seemed to be on the lookout for 'heretics.' He had only to make one false move, speak one careless word, and he could be convicted of heresy once more. Again Hal found himself thinking of the spider's web he had once seen as a child in Bradgate Manor. The spider was hidden in a corner of its web waiting for the fly to zoom accidentally into the fine filaments and be helplessly trapped.

Sometimes when Hal went to see Sarah at the Tower he confided his fears to her. If he thought she had not anticipated such a situation, he was wrong. Again and again as she lay alone at night Sarah struggled with her fears that Hal might be recaptured. Her only consolation was in words she read in Hal's New Testament, the very copy he had bought with Master Squires' sovereign many years ago. Their daughter Jane was a delightful toddler; each time her father called she would clasp his legs, and beg to be lifted onto his lap. Her devotion made it no easier for Hal to contemplate the future.

Early in August 1557 Hal was travelling to Northampton, where Sir William Cecil also owned property. The midday sun beat down on him and nearing Northampton Hal was grateful to see the sign of the

---

1   Micah 7:8

Fox and Hen swinging lazily in the light breeze. Cantering into the yard, he reined in his horse. He had to duck to avoid striking his head on the lintel of the low doorway as he entered the thatched tavern. Inside it was cool and gloomy and it took a few moments for Hal's eyes to become accustomed to the poor light. Served with a large mug of ale, he sat down at one of the wooden tables and began to sip the refreshing drink thoughtfully.

Hal was halfway through his mug of ale before he noticed a man seated at a nearby table. He looked strangely familiar. As he was sitting sideways to Hal, it was not possible to see his face clearly, but both men finished their drinks and rose to their feet at about the same moment, emerging into the bright sunlight. Only then did Hal realize that his fellow drinker was none other than Adrian Stokes, now Sir Adrian, one-time stable lad from Bradgate, who had married Lady Jane's mother, Frances Grey.

'Master Tylney! How comes it you are here?' asked Adrian in surprise. 'Why, we heard you were cast into Newgate for your heretical views. Methought you had burned long since. Perchance you recanted of your heresies against our church and our queen?'

'By the mercy of God I was released,' replied Hal carefully. 'I wish you a good day, Sir Adrian.'

'Why so hasty, good Master Hal? Tell me more, I pray. Did I not warn you that if you held to the follies of My Lady Jane, you would suffer? Right glad I am to hear you have now a right mind.' A look of secretive triumph had crept over Adrian's handsome face. It reminded Hal of the way he had looked when he discovered the younger boy searching for his missing New Testament stolen from under his mattress long ago.

'Did you hear of those six burnt at one stake outside Colchester but two days since?' Adrian carried on, regardless of the fact that Hal had not answered. 'Ere long we shall have no heretics left in the land. Will that not be a good day, Master Hal? Three of them were women, and one with child, so I am told—two heretics burnt at once there, if I may be so bold as to say so.'

Such heartless and repugnant words were more than Hal could bear. Anger overcame his fear as he replied in a low voice: 'Have you ever thought, Sir Adrian, that a fire that cannot be quenched, even the fire of hell, awaits those that act so wickedly, thus casting poor women into the flames?'

'Sooth, man, you are a heretic yet!' exclaimed Adrian with a mixture of triumph and disgust in his voice. 'How grieved will My Lady Frances be to hear of it, she who waits daily on our gracious Queen Mary, whose mercies you have trampled underfoot! I suggest you mend your ways ere it be too late.' And with that Adrian Stokes swung into the saddle and galloped off into the distance towards London, leaving Hal stunned and dismayed. Slowly he mounted his horse and rode on towards Northampton to complete his work, fully aware that Adrian had every intention of betraying him, not merely to Bishop Bonner but to the queen herself.

Completing his assignment, Hal returned with heavy heart towards London and rode straight to the Tower. He must tell Sarah of what had happened. Little Jane ran out to greet her father with outstretched arms, and even baby John crowed delightfully as Hal swung his infant into the air and caught him again. As Hal told his wife of the circumstances of his unexpected meeting with Adrian Stokes, she slipped her hand into his, and whispered. 'It is even as I feared. I know not which of the two of us will suffer most, for every minute of every day that you are afflicted I grieve with you. Were it not best that we die together in the fires?'

'Nay, my dear one,' replied Hal, gazing lovingly at his brave wife. 'God calls you to care for our children, and if he wills, I shall be released to you again—I cannot tell how. But if not, like Daniel's three friends of whom we read in the Holy Scriptures, a fourth will stand with me in the flames, even our Saviour, Christ. Pray for me, that God will make me bold to suffer for his name's sake.' With difficulty Hal wrenched himself from Sarah's arms and rode off towards Westminster.

Scarcely had Hal begun his work the following day before two soldiers cantered up the drive and shouted noisily for Master Henry Tylney. Out bustled Master Squires, demanding to know their business.

'We have orders from Her Majesty for the arrest of Master Tylney,' snapped one impatient soldier. 'He is to be conducted to the Bishop of London without delay.' Ebenezer Squires had been watching Hal over recent weeks and knew in his heart that his young friend, still only twenty-four years of age, could not long remain a free man. Nothing he could do would now save Hal from the fires. No pardon was ever afforded to a man who had once recanted and then reverted to the truths which he had held at the first. At best Squires might be able to pay for better prison conditions. He could possibly even present arguments for postponing any execution with the hope that the death of the queen, anticipated by many, would bring the fearsome burnings to an end.

'I find it hard to believe that you should once again prove so false to our Mother Church and to our gracious and merciful queen,' snarled Bonner as Hal was led into his presence, hands securely tied behind his back.

'Your lordship, I am as loyal a citizen as ever Her Majesty had,' responded Hal steadily. 'Nor have I ever spoken aught against the faith or person of our queen.'

'My lord bishop,' said a voice from the back of the room, 'I heard the accused offering sympathy to one whom we have burnt for her treachery and wicked notions, even old Mistress Glover.' Hal turned to see who spoke and was not surprised to discover Nicholas Harpsfield, the spotty-faced cleric, standing there.

'Hold, Master Harpsfield!' thundered Bonner. 'We will hear his heresies from his own mouth.'

'What think you of the mass, Master Tylney? Does the bread of the sacrament become the very flesh of the Lord Christ or no? Did he not take bread, break it and say, "This is my body?"'

Carefully Hal began, still remembering Lady Jane's own answer to such a question: 'I own our Saviour said so, but did he not say, "I am the door"? Nor was he a door for all that, but ...'

'Answer my question, man,' roared the irate bishop. 'How much longer must I endure your impudence?'

Knowing that he stood no chance of avoiding imprisonment and death, Hal took a deep breath and answered, 'My lord bishop, I hold the mass to be an idolatry. I may no more worship bread, be it what it may, than fall down before an idol of wood or stone.'

'Have him away! Have him away!' exclaimed the bishop. 'What further need have we of hearing such words of blasphemy?'

Thrown into a filthy dungeon in the Marshalsea Prison in Southwark, Hal had two consolations. The first was that God had given him a further chance to prove the reality of his convictions—now at last his conscience was at ease. Also the location of his prison was not far from his beloved Sarah and the children at the Tower. Only the width of the river lay between, and even though he could never see them, the knowledge that they were so near was a comfort to the prisoner.

Strangely, however, after only a week in the Marshalsea—a week when Hal had expected at any moment to be taken out to Smithfield, to suffer at the stake—he heard heavy steps approaching his cell and the very soldiers who had arrested him stood at the door. 'This must surely be the end,' thought Hal nervously. But to his surprise one of them snapped, 'We have orders from the bishop to move you to the Fleet Prison.' Hal shuddered with fear. The Fleet was situated close to Smithfield—that awful place where the fires seemed to burn perpetually as men and women of spiritual conviction were destroyed without mercy. Surely this must be in preparation for his burning.

Even older than Newgate Prison, the Fleet Prison stood beside the east bank of the River Fleet, and in case any bold prisoner should attempt an escape, a moat had been dug around it, with trees growing on the banks.[2] To Hal's surprise, however, he was not thrown into the lowest dungeon, dark, damp and below ground level, but was commanded to ascend the old wooden stairway until he reached the topmost floor. Opening a heavy door, the soldier pushed Hal into a cell with little ceremony, and bolted the locks behind him. Hal gazed around in surprise. Light filtered in through a small window protected by iron bars high up near the ceiling, and through that

---

2   Farringdon Street now marks the line where the old prison and moat once stood.

window he could catch a glimpse of the tops of the trees with a patch of sky beyond. Tears of joy sprang to his eyes as he realized that conditions here were a big improvement on those he had endured at Newgate. Surely, he thought, God knew how much he could bear and had eased his circumstances. Perhaps he was not to be taken to Smithfield yet. Hal discovered too that with a small bribe the jailer could be persuaded to buy paper, ink and quills so that he could write to Sarah and to his mother to ease their distress about him. Also he could record his thoughts and experiences—helping to pass the long hours when he must sit with little to do.

Week after week crept by, and still the prison warden told Hal that no date had yet been fixed for his execution. Other prisoners came and went, but Hal remained. Gradually the leaves on the trees turned to autumn gold; then the strong winds of November blew them off, leaving only the bare branches which creaked and swayed outside Hal's window. Soon snow covered the branches, and the sky beyond became heavy and leaden. Why was there no change in his circumstances? Why was he left, while others, sometimes men and women of faith like himself, were transferred to Newgate before being taken out for burning? What Hal did not know was that Ebenezer Squires was paying a handsome bribe to Bishop Bonner to delay the burning. Each week that he agreed to postpone Hal's appointment with death, the sum of money increased, making it worth the corrupt and cruel bishop's interests to leave Hal in prison. And always Squires hoped that the queen might soon die and Elizabeth come to the throne instead.

For over a year Hal remained a prisoner in the Fleet. Like Joseph he obtained favour with the jailer, and even the jailer's wife hastened to add small luxuries to Hal's meagre diet from time to time. Often he was allowed to exercise in the prison yard and sometimes found he could talk to fellow prisoners. As spring turned to summer during 1558 Hal's cell grew unbearably hot and often he felt sick with longing to see Sarah and the children again. Would he be left here for ever? Perhaps Bishop Bonner intended him to die in jail. And still the burnings went on. The jailer brought Hal news of those who had been the latest victims, although he knew that there could be no mercy for Hal, even should he recant again.

'I hear an old woman by the name of Kathleen Tynley waits in prison to be burnt in Canterbury. Perchance it is your grandmother, young man?' enquired the jailer with a smirk one day in early October.

'Nay, master jailer,' replied Hal, 'my name is Tylney, and not Tynley. Howbeit, I grieve more than I can tell that such an one should end her days so. Glad I am that a better world than this awaits those that do look to Christ alone for their salvation.'

'I hear say,' whispered the jailer some weeks later, lowering his voice, 'that Master Nicholas Harpsfield, him that serves our Lord Bishop Bonner, is travelling to Canterbury this very day, where Mistress Tynley and four others wait to be burned. He fears lest our queen should die ere such sentence can be carried out.'

'Is our queen a-dying then? enquired Hal.

'May her soul rest in peace,' replied the jailer fervently.

'Think you then that if the Lady Elizabeth become queen, such as Mistress Tynley will be pardoned?' asked Hal tentatively.

'That I know not,' replied the jailer, 'but in case you think to be pardoned, Master Hal, I must tell you that Master Harpsfield has ordered these cells to be cleared of heretics. Ere long Her Majesty will reap the rewards due for her zeal for truth, and that before the great Judge of all. Each heretic burned must surely add to her reward.'

Hal scarcely knew how to answer such a comment. But now he knew for certain that his death sentence could not be long postponed. Winter had set in, and again the November winds tore through the trees stripping them of leaves. The rain lashed down continually.

'A terrible time to die,' thought Hal gloomily, for he knew well that if the kindling faggots were wet, the fires would be slow to burn, prolonging the sufferings of the poor victims.

Only a week after this, Hal heard hurried footsteps on the stairs. The key turned and in burst the jailer's wife. 'O Master Hal, Master Hal,' she cried in alarm, 'I bring you heavy tidings indeed. Even now the fires are being built. I fear ere tomorrow night you must away.'

'Mistress jailer, grieve not for me,' replied Hal, who had been expecting such news. 'Grieve rather for those whose wicked deeds rise up before God and will not go unpunished. But, ah! I beg your prayers for my poor wife and infants.'

At that moment the jailer himself entered Hal's cell. 'It is as I feared, Master Hal,' he said, for he had grown fond of Hal in his strange way. 'Bishop Bonner and Master Harpsfield wish to clear this jail lest our queen should die before all the condemned heretics be burned. Indeed I must escort you to Newgate this very night for at 9 o'clock on the morrow you are appointed to the fire.'

'I thank you, master jailer,' replied Hal solemnly. 'it is even as I thought, and my God will give me grace. You have ever dealt well with me and I pray God send you his light ere long. One favour I ask. Could you give this my Bible to my dear wife Sarah and tell her to be of good courage and that I have ever loved her well?'

'That I will do, Master Hal,' responded the jailer. 'Only hasten now, for we must be gone.' Soon Hal was being hurried through the rain-drenched streets, walking the short distance from the Fleet to Newgate. Again the sounds and smells appalled him as he passed under that heavy gate, but to his amazement he did not feel as afraid as he had imagined. A strange peace, even a sense of exhilaration, seemed to flood his mind.

Grabbing his prisoner by the arm the jailer of Newgate opened the door of a cell and pushed Hal inside, 'And be ready against the morrow,' he warned in a flat voice. Turning around, Hal saw that another young man was also in the cell. As his eyes grew accustomed to the dim light, Hal looked more carefully at his fellow prisoner. Only then did he realize who it was. 'Master Nicholas!' he exclaimed in astonishment, 'how came you hither?'

'As you did, my good friend,' replied Nicholas Platt, the young man who had kept the menagerie at the Tower and who had once asked Hal about his beliefs. 'After My Lady Jane's death I thought much about the truths for which she was prepared to suffer. Nor could I find rest in my spirit until I too had cast my soul upon Christ for mercy. And when I learnt from your wife that you also were in

Newgate for those same truths, I became bold for the faith. So now we die together, good Master Hal.'

Through that long last night those two young men shared many thoughts. Sometimes they fell silent as each prayed urgently for strength to face a lingering and agonizing death. At midnight both were startled by the noisy clanging of the bell. 'Prepare to meet thy God,' cried the jailer in his usual harsh tones. Nicholas had learnt a verse from the Bible, one that Hal did not know, and this he recited to his fellow prisoner: 'When thou walkest through the fire, thou shalt not be burned, neither shall the flame kindle upon thee.'[3]

'Such words give me new strength to suffer gladly for my Saviour,' responded Hal. 'Even today I remember my Lady Jane's words: "Live still to die that in dying we might inherit eternal life." Now at last I understand them. And right glad I shall be to join my lady and Master Bradford in that merry supper with our Lord ere many more hours have passed.' Both young men decided to try to snatch a little sleep so that they might be stronger to face their fiery ordeal.

The morning of 17 November 1558 dawned cool and grey. Hal was the first to wake and spent time seeking the help of God. All his life he had feared such a death, but now that the reality awaited him he found a gladness of heart he could not explain. Yes, he had indeed been caught in a web, a web woven by a bigoted and fanatical queen and her cruel churchmen. But hadn't God caught up his life in another web—a web of his mercy and loving kindness to a poor sinner, a web of his providence and care?

Nicholas had now woken and after a breakfast of bread and ale the two men waited for the signal that meant their time had come. First one hour passed; then another, and still they waited. Perhaps this was the hardest part of all. At last heavy footsteps could be heard approaching the cell. By the sound of voices it seemed that two men were coming. Then the key turned slowly and both Hal and Nicholas rose to their feet. Even before they could see who stood at the door Hal heard a familiar and well-loved voice booming out his greeting: 'Ho! Ho! Ho! Master Hal! And it's back to work we go! And about time too, I say. The queen is dead. Long live Queen Elizabeth!'

---

3   Isaiah 43:2

'Master Ebenezer!' cried Hal in astonishment, 'What means this?'

'What means this? You are free, my man, you are free! And you too, Master Platt. The Queen Mary died this very morning. All prisoners of conscience may go free by order of our new queen. Long live Queen Elizabeth!'

Snatched from the very jaws of death, Hal at last broke down and wept like a child: tears of joy, tears of relief, but most of all tears of thankfulness that God had given him a second opportunity and out of his weakness had enabled him to triumph over his fear.

The happiness of his reunion with Sarah; the gladness of seeing his children once more; the success of his subsequent career as Sir William Cecil's right-hand man as he served Queen Elizabeth; his devoted care both for his own mother and for Master Ebenezer Squires as they grew old—all lay in the future for Hal, but these are beyond the scope of this story.

Suggestions
for further reading

The Martyrs of Mary Tudor—the burning of Protestants in England's Reign of Terror, Day One, 2005

Cook, Faith. *Lady Jane Grey, Nine-Day Queen of England*, Evangelical Press, 2004

d'Aubigné, J. H. Merle. *The Reformation in England*, Banner of Truth Trust, 1963, 2 vols.

Loane, Sir Marcus. *Masters of the English Reformation*, Banner of Truth Trust, 2006

Ridley, Jasper. *Bloody Mary's Martyrs*, Carroll and Graf Publishers, New York, 2001

Ridley, Jasper. *A Brief History of the Tudor Age*, Robinson, London, 2002

Ryle, J. C. *Five English Reformers*, Banner of Truth Trust, 1960.

Weir, Alison. *Children of England*, Pimlico, 1996

Lightning Source UK Ltd.
Milton Keynes UK
UKHW020611070219
336888UK00006B/805/P